THEOLOGICAL TRANSLATION LIBRARY

VOL XIV.

WHAT IS CHRISTIANITY?

WHAT IS CHRISTIANITY?

*Sixteen Lectures delivered in the University
of Berlin during the Winter-Term
1899-1900*

BY

ADOLF HARNACK

RECTOR OF, AND PROFESSOR OF CHURCH HISTORY IN, THE UNIVERSITY, AND
MEMBER OF THE ROYAL PRUSSIAN ACADEMY, BERLIN

Translated into English

BY

THOMAS BAILEY SAUNDERS

WILLIAMS AND NORGATE
14 HENRIETTA STREET, COVENT GARDEN, LONDON
20 SOUTH FREDERICK STREET, EDINBURGH
AND 7 BROAD STREET, OXFORD
NEW YORK: G. P. PUTNAM'S SONS
1901

Copyright 1901 in U.S.A.

G. P. Putnam's Sons.

AUTHOR'S PREFACE TO THE ENGLISH EDITION

To meet the wishes of my English friends I have assented to the publication of these Lectures in English as well as in German, and, as my esteemed friend Mr. Bailey Saunders was so self-denying and obliging as to undertake the translation of them, I was sure of their being in the best hands. Whether there is as great a need in England as there is in Germany for a short and plain statement of the Gospel and its history, I do not know. But this I know: the theologians of every country only half discharge their duties if they think it enough to treat of the Gospel in the recondite language of learning and bury it in scholarly folios.

A. HARNACK.

BERLIN, October 1900.

TRANSLATOR'S PREFACE

The following Lectures were delivered extempore to a class of some six hundred students drawn from all the Faculties in the University of Berlin. An enthusiastic listener took them down in shorthand, and at the close surprised Professor Harnack with a complete report of what he had said. A few alterations sufficed to transform the Lectures into a book, and German readers everywhere were thus happily enabled to share in some of the privileges of the original audience.

I deem it an honour to have any hand in offering to my fellow-countrymen a similar advantage. Goethe, writing in his last years to Carlyle, described translators, in grandiloquent language, as the agents of intellectual commerce among the nations. The duties of such agency in regard to the contents of this volume I have done my humble best to discharge, convinced as I am that in the traffic in ideas between Germany and the English-speaking peoples all over the world both the matter of Professor Harnack's discourse and the spirit in which he treats it are alike worthy of attention.

T. BAILEY SAUNDERS.

LONDON, *November* 1900.

CONTENTS

WHAT IS CHRISTIANITY?

———•———

LECTURE I.

THE great English philosopher, John Stuart Mill,
has somewhere observed that mankind cannot be too
often reminded that there was once a man of the
name of Socrates. That is true; but still more important is it to remind mankind again and again that
a man of the name of Jesus Christ once stood in their
midst. The fact, of course, has been brought home
to us from our youth up; but unhappily it cannot be
said that public instruction in our time is calculated
to keep the image of Jesus Christ before us in any impressive way, and make it an inalienable possession
after our school-days are over and for our whole life.
And although no one who has once absorbed a ray of
Christ's light can ever again become as though he had
never heard of him; although at the bottom of every
soul that has been once touched an impression remains,
a confused recollection of this kind, which is often only
a " superstitio," is not enough to give strength and
life. But where the demand for further and more

A

trustworthy knowledge about him arises, and a man wants positive information as to who Jesus Christ was, and as to the real purport of his message, he no sooner asks for it than he finds himself, if he consults the literature of the day, surrounded by a clatter of contradictory voices. He hears some people maintaining that primitive Christianity was closely akin to Buddhism, and he is accordingly told that it is in fleeing the world and in pessimism that the sublime character of this religion and its profound meaning are revealed. Others, on the contrary, assure him that Christianity is an optimistic religion, and that it must be thought of simply and solely as a higher phase of Judaism; and these people also suppose that in saying this they have said something very profound. Others, again, maintain the opposite; they assert that the Gospel did away with Judaism, but itself originated under Greek influences of mysterious operation; and that it is to be understood as a blossom on the tree of Hellenism. Religious philosophers come forward and declare that the metaphysical system which, as they say, was developed out of the Gospel is its real kernel and the revelation of its secret; but others reply that the Gospel has nothing to do with philosophy, that it was meant for feeling and suffering humanity, and that philosophy has only been forced upon it. Finally, the latest critics that have come into the field assure us that the whole history of religion, morality, and philosophy, is nothing but wrapping and ornament; that what at all times underlies them, as the only real motive power, is the history of economics; that, accordingly, Christianity, too, was in its origin nothing more than a social movement and Christ a social deliverer, the deliverer of the oppressed lower classes.

There is something touching in the anxiety which everyone shows to rediscover himself, together with his own point of view and his own circle of interest, in this Jesus Christ, or at least to get a share in him. It is the perennial repetition of the spectacle which was seen in the "Gnostic" movement even as early as the second century, and which takes the form of a struggle, on the part of every conceivable tendency of thought, for the possession of Jesus Christ. Why, quite recently, not only, I think, Tolstoi's ideas, but even Nietzsche's, have been exhibited in their special affinity with the Gospel; and there is perhaps more to be said even upon this subject that is worth attention than upon the connexion between a good deal of "theological" and "philosophical" speculation and Christ's teaching.

But nevertheless, when taken together, the impression which these contradictory opinions convey is disheartening: the confusion seems hopeless. How can we take it amiss of anyone, if, after trying to find out how the question stands, he gives it up? Perhaps he goes further, and declares that after all the question does not matter. How are we concerned with events that happened, or with a person who lived, nineteen

hundred years ago? We must look for our ideals
and our strength to the present; to evolve them
laboriously out of old manuscripts is a fantastic proceeding that can lead nowhere. The man who so
speaks is not wrong; but neither is he right. What
we are and what we possess, in any high sense, we
possess from the past and by the past—only so much
of it, of course, as has had results and makes its
influence felt up to the present day. To acquire a
sound knowledge of the past is the business and the
duty not only of the historian but also of every one
who wishes to make the wealth and the strength so
gained his own. But that the Gospel is a part of
this past which nothing else can replace has been
affirmed again and again by the greatest minds.
"Let intellectual and spiritual culture progress, and
the human mind expand, as much as it will; beyond
the grandeur and the moral elevation of Christianity,
as it sparkles and shines in the Gospels, the human
mind will not advance." In these words Goethe,
after making many experiments and labouring inde-
fatigably at himself, summed up the result to which
his moral and historical insight had led him. Even
though we were to feel no desire on our own part, it
would still be worth while, because of this man's testimony, to devote our serious attention to what he came
to regard as so precious; and if, contrary to his declaration, louder and more confident voices are heard
to-day, proclaiming that the Christian religion has
outlived itself, let us accept that as an invitation to

make a closer acquaintance with this religion whose
certificate of death people suppose that they can
already exhibit.

But in truth this religion and the efforts which
it evokes are more active to-day than they used
to be. We may say to the credit of our age that
it takes an eager interest in the problem of the
nature and value of Christianity, and that there
is more search and inquiry in regard to this subject
now than was the case thirty years ago. Even
in the experiments that are made in and about
it, the strange and abstruse replies that are given
to questions, the way in which it is caricatured,
the chaotic confusion which it exhibits, nay even
in the hatred that it excites, a real life and an
earnest endeavour may be traced. Only do not
let us suppose that there is anything exemplary
in this endeavour, and that we are the first who,
after shaking off an authoritative religion, are struggling after one that shall really make us free and
be of independent growth—a struggle which must
of necessity give rise to much confusion and half-
truth. Sixty-two years ago Carlyle wrote:—
"In these distracted times, when the Religious
Principle, driven out of most Churches, either lies
unseen in the hearts of good men, looking and
longing and silently working there towards some
new Revelation; or else wanders homeless over the
world, like a disembodied soul seeking its terrestrial
organisation, — into how many strange shapes, of

Superstition and Fanaticism, does it not tentatively
and errantly cast itself! The higher Enthusiasm of
man's nature is for the while without Exponent; yet
does it continue indestructible, unweariedly active,
and work blindly in the great chaotic deep : thus Sect
after Sect, and Church after Church, bodies itself
forth, and melts again into new metamorphosis."

No one who understands the times in which we
live can deny that these words sound as if they
had been written to-day. But it is not with "the
religious principle" and the ways in which it has
developed that we are going to concern ourselves
in these lectures. We shall try to answer the
more modest but not less pressing question, What
is Christianity? What was it? What has it become?
The answer to this question may, we hope, also
throw light by the way on the more comprehensive
one, What is Religion, and what ought it to be to us?
In dealing with religion, is it not after all with the
Christian religion alone that we have to do? Other
religions no longer stir the depths of our hearts.

What is Christianity? It is solely in its historical
sense that we shall try to answer this question
here; that is to say, we shall employ the methods
of historical science, and the experience of life
gained by studying the actual course of history.
This excludes the view of the question taken by
the apologist and the religious philosopher. On
this point permit me to say a few words.

Apologetics holds a necessary place in religious knowledge, and to demonstrate the validity of the Christian religion and exhibit its importance for the moral and intellectual life is a great and a worthy undertaking. But this undertaking must be kept quite separate from the purely historical question as to the nature of that religion, or else historical research will be brought into complete discredit. Moreover, in the kind of apologetics that is now required no really high standard has yet been attained. Apart from a few steps that have been taken in the direction of improvement, apologetics as a subject of study is in a deplorable state : it is not clear as to the positions to be defended, and it is uncertain as to the means to be employed. It is also not infrequently pursued in an undignified and obtrusive fashion. Apologists imagine that they are doing a great work by crying up religion as though it were a job-lot at a sale, or a universal remedy for all social ills. They are perpetually snatching, too, at all sorts of baubles, so as to deck out religion in fine clothes. In their endeavour to present it as a glorious necessity, they deprive it of its earnest character, and at the best only prove that it is something which may be safely accepted because it can do no harm. Finally, they cannot refrain from slipping in some church programme of yesterday and " demonstrating " its claims as well. The structure of their ideas is so loose that an idea or two more makes no difference. The mischief that has been thereby

done already and is still being done is indescribable.
No! the Christian religion is something simple and
sublime; it means one thing and one thing only:
Eternal life in the midst of time, by the strength and
under the eyes of God.   It is no ethical or social *ar-
canum* for the preservation or improvement of things
generally.   To make what it has done for civilisation
and human progress the main question, and to determine its value by the answer, is to do it violence
at the start.   Goethe once said, "Mankind is always
advancing, and man always remains the same."   It is
to *man* that religion pertains, to man, as one who in
the midst of all change and progress himself never
changes.   Christian apologetics must recognise, then,
that it is with religion in its simple nature and its
simple strength that it has to do.   Religion, truly,
does not exist for itself alone, but lives in an inner
fellowship with all the activities of the mind and
with moral and economical conditions as well.   But
it is emphatically not a mere function or an exponent
of them ; it is a mighty power that sets to work of
itself, hindering or furthering, destroying or making
fruitful.   The main thing is to learn what religion
is and in what its essential character consists ; no
matter what position the individual who examines it
may take up in regard to it, or whether in his own
life he values it or not.

But the point of view of the philosophical theorist,
in the strict sense of the word, will also find no place
in these lectures.   Had they been delivered sixty

years ago, it would have been our endeavour to try to arrive by speculative reasoning at some general conception of religion, and then to define the Christian religion accordingly. But we have rightly become sceptical about the value of this procedure. *Latet dolus in generalibus.* We know to-day that life cannot be spanned by general conceptions, and that there is no general conception of religion to which actual religions are related simply and solely as species to genus. Nay, the question may even be asked whether there is any such generic conception as " religion " at all. Is the common element in it anything more than a vague disposition? Is it only an empty place in our innermost being that the word denotes, which every one fills up in a different fashion and many do not perceive at all? I am not of this opinion; I am convinced, rather, that at bottom we have to do here with something which is common to us all, and which in the course of history has struggled up out of torpor and discord into unity and light. I am convinced that Augustine is right when he says, " Thou, Lord, hast made us for Thyself, and our heart is restless until it finds rest in Thee." But to prove that this is so; to exhibit the nature and the claims of religion by psychological analysis, including the psychology of peoples, is not the task that we shall undertake in what follows. We shall keep to the purely historical theme : What is the Christian religion ?

Where are we to look for our materials? The answer seems to be simple and at the same time exhaustive: Jesus Christ and his Gospel. But however little doubt there may be that this must form not only our point of departure but also the matter with which our investigations will mainly deal, it is equally certain that we must not be content to exhibit the mere image of Jesus Christ and the main features of his Gospel. We must not be content to stop there, because every great and powerful personality reveals a part of what it is only when seen in those whom it influences. Nay, it may be said that the more powerful the personality which a man possesses, and the more he takes hold of the inner life of others, the less can the sum-total of what he is be known only by what he himself says and does. We must look at the reflection and the effects which he produced in those whose leader and master he became. That is why a complete answer to the question, What is Christianity, is impossible so long as we are restricted to Jesus Christ's teaching alone. We must include the first generation of his disciples as well—those who ate and drank with him—and we must listen to what they tell us of the effect which he had upon their lives.

But even this does not exhaust our materials. If Christianity is an example of a great power valid not for one particular epoch alone; if in and through it, not once only, but again and again, great forces have been disengaged, we must include all the later products of its spirit. It is not a question of a "doc-trine" being handed down by uniform repetition or arbitrarily distorted; it is a question of a *life*, again and again kindled afresh, and now burning with a flame of its own. We may also add that Christ himself and the apostles were convinced that the religion which they were planting would in the ages to come have a greater destiny and a deeper meaning than it possessed at the time of its institution; they trusted to its spirit leading from one point of light to another and developing higher forces. Just as we cannot obtain a complete knowledge of a tree without regarding not only its root and its stem but also its bark, its branches, and the way in which it blooms, so we cannot form any right estimate of the Christian religion unless we take our stand upon a compre-hensive induction that shall cover all the facts of its history. It is true that Christianity has had its classical epoch; nay more, it had a founder who himself was what he taught—to steep ourselves in him is still the chief matter; but to restrict ourselves to him means to take a point of view too low for his significance. Individual religious life was what he wanted to kindle and what he did kindle; it is, as we shall see, his peculiar greatness to have led men to God, so that they may thenceforth live their own life with Him. How, then, can we be silent about the history of the Gospel if we wish to know what he was?

It may be objected that put in this way the problem is too difficult, and that its solution threatens to be accompanied by many errors and defects. That is not to be denied; but to state a problem in easier terms, that is to say in this case inaccurately, because of the difficulties surrounding it, would be a very perverse expedient. Moreover, even though the difficulties increase, the work is, on the other hand, facilitated by the problem being stated in a larger manner; for it helps us to grasp what is essential in the phenomena, and to distinguish kernel and husk.

Jesus Christ and his disciples were situated in their day just as we are situated in ours; that is to say, their feelings, their thoughts, their judgments and their efforts were bounded by the horizon and the framework in which their own nation was set and by its condition at the time. Had it been otherwise, they would not have been men of flesh and blood, but spectral beings. For seventeen hundred years, indeed, people thought, and many among us still think, that the "humanity" of Jesus Christ, which is a part of their creed, is sufficiently provided for by the assumption that he had a human body and a human soul. As if it were possible to have that without having any definite character as an individual! To be a man means, in the first place, to possess a certain mental and spiritual disposition, determined in such and such a way, and thereby limited and circumscribed; and, in the second place, it means to be situated, with this disposition, in an historical environment which in its turn is also limited and circumscribed. Outside this

there are no such things as "men." It at once
follows, however, that a man can think, speak, and
do absolutely nothing at all in which his peculiar
disposition and his own age are not coefficients. A
single word may seem to be really classical and valid
for all time, and yet the very language in which it is
spoken gives it very palpable limitations. Much less
is a spiritual personality, as a whole, susceptible of
being represented in a way that will banish the
feeling of its limitations, and with those limitations,
the sense of something strange or conventional; and
this feeling must necessarily be enhanced the farther
in point of time the spectator is removed.

From these circumstances it follows that the
historian, whose business and highest duty it is to
determine what is of permanent value, is of necessity required not to cleave to words but to find out
what is essential. The "whole" Christ, the "whole"
Gospel, if we mean by this motto the external image
taken in all its details and set up for imitation, is
just as bad and deceptive a shibboleth as the "whole"
Luther, and the like. It is bad because it enslaves
us, and it is deceptive because the people who proclaim it do not think of taking it seriously, and
could not do so if they tried. They cannot do so
because they cannot cease to feel, understand and
judge as children of their age.

There are only two possibilities here: either the
Gospel is in all respects identical with its earliest
form, in which case it came with its time and has

departed with it; or else it contains something
which, under differing historical forms, is of permanent validity. The latter is the true view. The
history of the Church shows us in its very commencement that "primitive Christianity" had to disappear
in order that "Christianity" might remain; and in
the same way in later ages one metamorphosis
followed upon another. From the beginning it was
a question of getting rid of formulas, correcting
expectations, altering ways of feeling, and this is a
process to which there is no end. But by the very
fact that our survey embraces the whole course as
well as the inception we enhance our standard of
what is essential and of real value.

We enhance our standard, but we need not
wait to take it from the history of those later ages.
The thing itself reveals it. We shall see that the
Gospel in the Gospel is something so simple,
something that speaks to us with so much power,
that it cannot easily be mistaken. No far-reaching
directions as to method, no general introductions, are necessary to enable us to find the way
to it. No one who possesses a fresh eye for
what is alive, and a true feeling for what is really
great, can fail to see it and distinguish it from its
contemporary integument. And even though there
may be many individual aspects of it where the
task of distinguishing what is permanent from what
is fleeting, what is rudimentary from what is
merely historical, is not quite easy, we must not

- Explain Away -

be like the child who, wanting to get at the kernel of a bulb, went on picking off the leaves until there was nothing left, and then could not help seeing that it was just the leaves that made the bulb. Endeavours of this kind are not unknown in the history of the Christian religion, but they fade before those other endeavours which seek to convince us that there is no such thing as either kernel or husk, growth or decay, but that everything is of equal value and alike permanent.

In these lectures, then, we shall deal first of all with the Gospel of Jesus Christ, and this theme will occupy the greater part of our attention. We shall then show what impression he himself and his Gospel made upon the first generation of his disciples. Finally, we shall follow the leading changes which the Christian idea has undergone in the course of history, and try to recognise its chief types. What is common to all the forms which it has taken, corrected by reference to the Gospel, and, conversely, the chief features of the Gospel, corrected by reference to history, will, we may be allowed to hope, bring us to the kernel of the matter. Within the limits of a short series of lectures it is, of course, only to what is important that attention can be called; but perhaps there will be no disadvantage in fixing our attention, for once, only on the strong lines and prominent points of the relief, and, by putting what is secondary into the background, in looking at the vast material in a concentrated form. We shall even

refrain, and permissibly refrain, from enlarging, by
way of introduction, on Judaism and its external and
internal relations, and on the Græco-Roman world.
We must never, of course, wholly shut our eyes to
them—nay, we must always keep them in mind; but
diffuse explanations in regard to these matters are
unnecessary. Jesus Christ's teaching will at once
bring us by steps which, if few, will be great, to
a height where its connexion with Judaism is seen
to be only a loose one, and most of the threads
leading from it into "contemporary history" become
of no importance at all. This may seem a paradoxical thing to say; for just now we are being
earnestly assured, with an air as though it were some
new discovery that was being imparted to us, that
Jesus Christ's teaching cannot be understood, nay,
cannot be accurately represented, except by having
regard to its connexion with the Jewish doctrines
prevalent at the time, and by first of all setting them
out in full. There is much that is true in this
statement, and yet, as we shall see, it is incorrect.
It becomes absolutely false, however, when worked
up into the dazzling thesis that the Gospel is intelligible only as the religion of a despairing section
of the Jewish nation; that it was the last effort of
a decadent age, driven by distress into a renunciation
of this earth, and then trying to storm heaven
and demanding civic rights there—a religion of
miserabilism! It is rather remarkable that the
really desperate were just those who did not welcome

it, but fought against it ; remarkable that its leaders, so far as we know them, do not, in fact, bear any of the marks of sickly despair ; most remarkable of all, that while indeed renouncing the world and its goods, they establish, in love and holiness, a brotherly union which declares war on the world's misery. The oftener I re-read and consider the Gospels, the more do I find that the contemporary discords, in the midst of which the Gospel stood, and out of which it arose, sink into the background. I enter-tain no doubt that the founder had his eye upon *man* in whatever external situation he might be found—upon *man* who, fundamentally, always re-mains the same, whether he be moving upwards or downwards, whether he be in riches or poverty, whether he be of strong mind or of weak. It is the consciousness of all these oppositions being ultimately beneath it, and of its own place above them, that gives the Gospel its sovereignty ; for in every man it looks to the point that is unaffected by all these differences. This is very clear in Paul's case ; he dominates all earthly things and circumstances like a king, and desires to see them so dominated. The thesis of the decadent age and the religion of the wretched may serve to lead us into the outer court ; it may even correctly point to that which originally gave the Gospel its form ; but if it is offered us as a key for the understanding of this religion in itself, we must reject it. Moreover, this thesis and the pretensions which it makes are only illustrations of a fashion which has become general in the writing of history,

B

and which in that province will naturally have a
longer reign than other fashions, because by its
means much that was obscure has, as a matter of
fact, been cleared up.   But to the heart of the
matter its devotees do not penetrate, as they silently
assume that no such heart exists.

Let me conclude this lecture by touching briefly
on one other important point. In history absolute
judgments are impossible.   This is a truth which in
these days—I say advisedly, in these days—is clear
and incontestable.   History can only show how things
have been ; and even where we can throw light upon
the past, and understand and criticize it, we must not
presume to think that by any process of abstraction
absolute judgments as to the value to be assigned
to past events can be obtained from the results of
a purely historical survey.   Such judgments are the
creation only of feeling and of will; they are a
subjective act.   The false notion that the understanding can produce them is a heritage of that
protracted epoch in which knowing and knowledge
were expected to accomplish everything; in which it
was believed that they could be stretched so as to
be capable of covering and satisfying all the needs
of the mind and the heart.   That they cannot do.
This is a truth which, in many an hour of ardent work,
falls heavily upon our soul, and yet—what a hopeless thing it would be for mankind if the higher peace
to which it aspires, and the clearness, the certainty
and the strength for which it strives, were dependent
on the measure of its learning and its knowledge.

LECTURE II.

OUR first section deals with the main features of the message delivered by Jesus Christ. They include the form in which he delivered what he had to say. We shall see how essential a part of his character is here exhibited, for "he spoke as one having authority and not as the Scribes." But before describing these features I feel it my duty to tell you briefly how matters stand in regard to the sources of our knowledge.

Our authorities for the message which Jesus Christ delivered are—apart from certain important statements made by Paul — the first three Gospels. Everything that we know, independently of these Gospels, about Jesus' history and his teaching, may be easily put on a small sheet of paper, so little does it come to. In particular, the fourth Gospel, which does not emanate or profess to emanate from the apostle John, cannot be taken as an historical authority in the ordinary meaning of the word. The author of it acted with sovereign freedom, transposed events and put them in a strange light, drew up the discourses himself, and illustrated great thoughts

19

by imaginary situations. Although, therefore, his
work is not altogether devoid of a real, if scarcely re-
cognisable, traditional element, it can hardly make
any claim to be considered an authority for Jesus'
history ; only little of what he says can be accepted,
and that little with caution. On the other hand, it is
an authority of the first rank for answering the question, What vivid views of Jesus' person, what kind
of light and warmth, did the Gospel disengage ?

Sixty years ago David Friedrich Strauss thought
that he had almost entirely destroyed the historical
credibility not only of the fourth but also of the
first three Gospels as well. The historical criticism
of two generations has succeeded in restoring that
credibility in its main outlines. These Gospels are
not, it is true, historical works any more than the
fourth ; they were not written with the simple object
of giving the facts as they were ; they are books
composed for the work of evangelisation. Their
purpose is to awaken a belief in Jesus Christ's
person and mission ; and the purpose is served by
the description of his deeds and discourses, as well
as by the references to the Old Testament. Nevertheless they are not altogether useless as sources of
history, more especially as the object with which
they were written is not supplied from without, but
coincides in part with what Jesus intended. But
such other great leading purposes as have been
ascribed to the evangelists have been one and all
shown to lack any foundation, although with each

individual evangelist many secondary purposes may
have come into play. The Gospels are not "party
tracts"; neither are they writings which as yet
bear the radical impress of the Greek spirit. In their
essential substance they belong to the first, the Jewish, epoch of Christianity, that brief epoch which
may be denoted as the palæontological. That we
possess any reports dating from that time, even
though, as is obvious in the first and third Gospel,
the setting and the composition are by another hand,
is one of those historical arrangements for which we
cannot be too thankful. Criticism to-day univers-
ally recognises the unique character of the Gospels.
What especially marks them off from all subsequent
literature is the way in which they state their facts.
This species of literary art, which took shape
partly by analogy with the didactic narratives of the
Jews, and partly from catechetical necessities—this
simple and impressive form of exposition was, even a
few decades later, no longer capable of exact repro-
duction. From the time that the Gospel was transferred to the broad ground of the Græco-Roman world
it appropriated the literary forms of the Greeks, and
the style of the evangelists was then felt to be
something strange but sublime. When all is said,
the Greek language lies upon these writings only like
a diaphanous veil, and it requires hardly any effort to
retranslate their contents into Hebrew or Aramaic.
That the tradition here presented to us is, in the
main, at first hand is obvious.

How fixed this tradition was in regard to its form is proved by the third Gospel. It was composed by a Greek, probably in the time of Domitian; and in the second part of his work, the Acts of the Apostles—besides the preface to the first—he shows us that he was familiar with the literary language of his nation and that he was an excellent master of style. But in the Gospel narrative he did not dare to abandon the traditional type: he tells his story in the same style as Mark and Matthew, with the same connexion of sentences, the same colour, nay, with many of precisely the same details; it is only the ruder words and expressions, which would offend literary taste, that are sparingly corrected. There is another respect, too, in which his Gospel strikes us as remarkable: he assures us at the beginning of it that he has " had perfect understanding of all things from the very first," and has examined many accounts. But if we test him by his authorities, we find that he has kept in the main to Mark's Gospel, and to a source which we also find appearing again in Matthew. These accounts both seemed to him, as a respectable chronicler, to be preferable to the crowd of others. That offers a good guarantee for them. No historian has found that it is possible or necessary to substitute any other tradition for the one which we have here.

Another point: this tradition is, apart from the story of the Passion, almost exclusively Galilean in its character. Had not the history of Jesus' public

activity been really bounded by this geographical
horizon, tradition could not have so described it; for
every historical narrative with an eye to effect would
have represented him as working chiefly in Jerusalem.
That is the account given by the fourth Gospel.
That our first three evangelists almost entirely
refrain from saying anything about Jerusalem arouses
a good prejudice in their favour.

It is true that, measured by the standard of "agreement, inspiration and completeness," these writings
leave a very great deal to be desired, and even when
judged by a more human standard they suffer from
not a few imperfections. Rude additions from a
later age they do not, indeed, exhibit—it will always
remain a noteworthy fact that, conversely, it is only
the fourth Gospel which makes Greeks ask after Jesus
—but still they, too, reflect, here and there, the circumstances in which the primitive Christian community
was placed and the experiences which it afterwards
underwent. People nowadays, however, put such
constructions on the text more readily than is necessary.
Further, the conviction that Old Testament prophecy
was fulfilled in Jesus' history had a disturbing effect
on tradition. Lastly, in some of the narratives the
miraculous element is obviously intensified. On the
other hand, Strauss' contention that the Gospels contain a very great deal that is mythical has not been
borne out, even if the very indefinite and defective
conception of what "mythical" means in Strauss'
application of the word, be allowed to pass. It is

almost exclusively in the account of Jesus' childhood, and there only sparingly, that a mythical touch can be traced. None of these disturbing elements affect the heart of the narrative; not a few of them easily lend themselves to correction, partly by a comparison of the Gospels one with another, partly through the sound judgment that is matured by historical study.

But the miraculous element, all these reports of miracles! Not Strauss only, but many others too, have allowed themselves to be frightened by them into roundly denying the credibility of the Gospels. But, on the other hand, historical science in this last generation has taken a great step in advance by learning to pass a more intelligent and benevolent judgment on those narratives, and accordingly even reports of the marvellous can now be counted amongst the materials of history and turned to good account. I owe it to you and to the subject briefly to specify the position which historical science to-day takes up in regard to these reports.

In the first place, we know that the Gospels come from a time in which the marvellous may be said to have been something of almost daily occurrence. People felt and saw that they were surrounded by wonders, and not by any means only in the religious sphere. Certain spiritualists among us excepted, we are now accustomed to associate the question of miracles exclusively with the question of religion. In those days it was otherwise. The fountains of the marvellous were many. Some sort of divinity was, of course, supposed to be at work in every case; it was a god who accomplished the miracle; but it was not to every god that people stood in a religious relation. Further, in those days, the strict conception which we now attach to the word "miracle" was as yet unknown; it came in only with a knowledge of the laws of nature and their general validity. Before that, no sound insight existed into what was possible and what was impossible, what was rule and what was exception. But where this distinction is not clear, or where, as the case may be, the question has not yet been raised at all in any rigorous form, there are no such things as miracles in the strict sense of the word. No one can feel anything to be an interruption of the order of Nature who does not yet know what the order of Nature is. Miracles, then, could not possess the significance for that age which, if they existed, they would possess for ours. For that age all wonders were only extraordinary events, and, even if they formed a world by themselves, it was certain that there were countless points in which that other world mysteriously encroached upon our own. Nor was it only God's messengers, but magicians and charlatans as well, who were thought to be possessed of some of these miraculous powers. The significance attaching to "miracles" was, therefore, in those days a subject of never-ending controversy; at one moment a high value was set upon them and they were considered to belong to the very essence of religion; at another, they were spoken of with contempt.

In the second place, we now know that it is not after they have been long dead, nor even after the lapse of many years, that miracles have been reported of eminent persons, but at once, often the very next day. The habit of condemning a narrative, or of ascribing it to a later age, only because it includes stories of miracles, is a piece of prejudice.

In the third place, we are firmly convinced that what happens in space and time is subject to the general laws of motion, and that in this sense, as an interruption of the order of Nature, there can be no such things as "miracles." But we also recognise that the religious man—if religion really permeates him and is something more than a belief in the religion of others—is certain that he is not shut up within a blind and brutal course of Nature, but that this course of Nature serves higher ends, or, as it may be, that some inner and divine power can help us so to encounter it as that "everything must necessarily be for the best." This experience, which I might express in one word as the ability to escape from the power and the service of transitory things, is always felt afresh to be a miracle each time that it occurs; it is inseparable from every higher religion, and were it to be surrendered, religion would be at an end. But it is an experience which is equally true of the life of the individual and of the great course of human history. How clearly and logically, then, must a religious man think, if, in spite of this experience, he holds firmly to the inviolable character of what happens in space and time. Who can wonder that even great minds fail to keep the two spheres quite separate? And as we all live, first and foremost, in the domain not of ideas but of perceptions, and in a language of metaphor, how can we avoid conceiving that which is divine and makes us free as a mighty power working upon the order of Nature, and breaking through or arresting it? This notion, though it belong only to the realm of fantasy and metaphor, will, it seems, last as long as religion itself.

In the fourth place, and lastly, although the order of Nature be inviolable, we are not yet by any means acquainted with all the forces working in it and acting reciprocally with other forces. Our acquaintance even with the forces inherent in matter, and with the field of their action, is incomplete; while of psychic forces we know very much less. We see that a strong will and a firm faith exert an influence upon the life of the body, and produce phenomena which strike us as marvellous. Who is there up to now that has set any sure bounds to the province of the possible and the actual? No one. Who can say how far the influence of soul upon soul and of soul upon body reaches? No one. Who can still maintain that any extraordinary phenomenon that may appear in this domain is entirely based on error and delusion?

Miracles, it is true, do not happen; but of the marvellous and the inexplicable there is plenty. In our present state of knowledge we have become more careful, more hesitating in our judgment, in regard to the stories of the miraculous which we have received from antiquity. That the earth in its course stood still; that a she-ass spoke; that a storm was quieted by a word, we do not believe, and we shall never again believe; but that the lame walked, the blind saw, and the deaf heard, will not be so summarily dismissed as an illusion.

From these suggestions you can arrive for yourselves at the right position to take up in regard to the miraculous stories related in the Gospels, and at their net results. In particular cases, that is to say, in the application of general principles to concrete statements, some uncertainty will always remain. So far as I can judge, the stories may be grouped as follows :—(1) Stories which had their origin in an exaggerated view of natural events of an impressive character; (2) stories which had their origin in sayings or parables, or in the projection of inner experiences on to the external world ; (3) stories such as arose in the interests of the fulfilment of Old Testament sayings; (4) stories of surprising cures effected by Jesus' spiritual force; (5) stories of which we cannot fathom the secret. It is very remarkable, however, that Jesus himself did not assign that critical importance to his miraculous deeds which even the evangelist Mark and the others all attributed to them. Did he not exclaim, in tones of complaint and accusation, " Unless ye see signs and wonders, ye will not believe"? He who uttered these words cannot have held that belief in the wonders which he wrought was the right or the only avenue to the recognition of his person and his mission; nay, in all essential points he must have thought of them quite otherwise than his evangelists. And the remarkable fact that these very evangelists, without appreciating its range, hand down the statement that Jesus " did not many mighty works there because of their unbelief," shows us, from another and a different side, with what caution we must receive these miraculous stories, and into what category we must put them.

It follows from all this that we must not try to evade the Gospel by entrenching ourselves behind the miraculous stories related by the evangelists. In spite of those stories, nay, in part even in them, we are presented with a reality which has claims upon our participation. Study it, and do not let yourselves be deterred because this or that miraculous story strikes you as strange or leaves you cold. If there is anything here that you find unintelligible, put it quietly aside. Perhaps you will have to leave it there for ever; perhaps the meaning will dawn upon you later and the story assume a significance of which you never dreamt. Once more, let me say : do not be deterred. The question of miracles is of relative indifference in comparison with everything else which is to be found in the Gospels. It is not miracles that matter; the question on which everything turns is whether we are helplessly yoked to an inexorable necessity, or whether a God exists who rules and governs, and whose power to compel Nature we can move by prayer and make a part of our experience.

Our evangelists, as we know, do not tell us anything about the history of Jesus' early development; they tell us only of his public activity. Two of the Gospels do, it is true, contain an introductory history (the history of Jesus' birth); but we may disregard it; for even if it contained something more trustworthy than it does actually contain, it would be as good as useless for our purpose. That is to say, the evangelists themselves never refer to it, nor make Jesus himself refer to his antecedents. On the contrary, they tell us that Jesus' mother and his brethren were completely surprised at his coming forward, and did not know what to make of it. Paul, too, is silent; so that we can be sure that the oldest tradition knew nothing of any stories of Jesus' birth. We know nothing of Jesus' history for the first thirty years of his life. Is there not a terrible uncertainty here? What is there left us if we have to begin our task by confessing that we are unable to write any life of Jesus? How can we write the history of a man of whose development we know

nothing, and with only a year or two of whose life
we are acquainted? Now, however certain it may be
that our materials are insufficient for a "biography,"
they are very weighty in other respects, and even
their silence on the first thirty years is instructive.
They are weighty because they give us information
upon three important points : *In the first place, they
offer us a plain picture of Jesus' teaching, in
regard both to its main features and to its individual application; in the second place, they tell
us how his life issued in the service of his vocation;
and in the third place, they describe to us the
impression which he made upon his disciples, and
which they transmitted.*

These are, in fact, three important points; nay,
they are the points on which everything turns. It
is because we can get a clear view of them that a
characteristic picture of Jesus is possible; or, to
speak more modestly, that there is some hope for
an attempt to understand what his aims were, what
he was, and what he signifies for us.

As regards the thirty years of silence, we gather
from our evangelists that Jesus did not think it
necessary to give his disciples any information about
them. But much may be said about them negatively. First of all, it is very improbable that he
went through any Rabbinical school; he nowhere
speaks like a man who had assimilated any theological culture of a technical kind, or learned the art
of scholarly exegesis. Compare him in this respect

with the apostle Paul; how clearly it can be seen
from the latter's epistles that he had sat at the feet
of theological teachers. With Jesus we find nothing
of the kind; and hence he caused a stir by appearing in the schools and teaching at all. He lived and
had his being in the sacred writings, but not after
the manner of a professional teacher.

Neither can he have had any relations with the
Essenes, a remarkable order of Jewish monks. Were
that so, he would have belonged to the pupils who
show their dependence on their teachers by proclaiming and doing the opposite of what they have been
taught. The Essenes made a point of the most
extreme purity in the eye of the law, and held
severely aloof not only from the impure but even
from those who were a little lax in their purity. It
is only thus that we can understand their living
strictly apart, their dwelling in particular places, and
their practice of frequent ablutions every day. Jesus
exhibits a complete contrast with this mode of life :
he goes in search of sinners and eats with them. So
fundamental a difference alone makes it certain that
he had nothing to do with the Essenes. His aims
and the means which he employed divide him off
from them. If he appears to coincide with them in
many of his individual injunctions to his disciples,
these are accidental points of contact, as his motives
were quite other than theirs.

Further, unless all appearances are deceptive, no
stormy crisis, no breach with his past, lies behind

the period of Jesus' life that we know. In none of his sayings or discourses, whether he is threatening and punishing or drawing and calling people to him with kindness, whether he is speaking of his relation to the Father or to the world, can we discover the signs of inner revolutions overcome, or the scars of any terrible conflict. Everything seems to pour from him naturally, as though it could not do otherwise, like a spring from the depths of the earth, clear and unchecked in its flow. Where shall we find the man who at the age of thirty can so speak, if he has gone through bitter struggles—struggles of the soul, in which he has ended by burning what he once adored, and by adoring what he burned? Where shall we find the man who has broken with his past, in order to summon others to repentance as well as himself, but who through it all never speaks of his own repentance? This consideration makes it impossible that his life could have been spent in inner conflict, however little it may have been lacking in deep emotion, in temptation and in doubt.

One final point: the picture of Jesus' life and his discourses stand in no relation with the Greek spirit. That is almost a matter for surprise ; for Galilee was full of Greeks, and Greek was then spoken in many of its cities, much as Swedish is nowadays in Finland. There were Greek teachers and philosophers there, and it is scarcely conceivable that Jesus should have been entirely unacquainted with their language. But that he was in any way influenced by them, that he

c

was ever in touch with the thoughts of Plato or the Porch, even though it may have been only in some popular redaction, it is absolutely impossible to maintain. Of course if religious individualism—God and the soul, the soul and its God; if subjectivism; if the full self-responsibility of the individual; if the separation of the religious from the political—if all this is only Greek, then Jesus, too, stands within the sphere of Greek development; then he, too, breathed the pure air of Greece and drank from the Greek spring. But it cannot be proved that it is only on this one line, only in the Hellenic people, that this development took place; nay, it is rather the contrary that can be shown; other nations also advanced to similar states of knowledge and feeling; although they did so, it is true, as a rule, only after Alexander the Great had pulled down the barriers and fences which separated the peoples. For these nations, too, no doubt it was in the majority of cases the Greek element that was the liberating and progressive factor. But I do not believe that the Psalmist who uttered the words, "Whom have I in heaven but thee? and there is none upon earth that I desire beside thee," had ever heard anything of Socrates or of Plato.

Enough: from their silence on the first thirty years of Jesus' life, and from what the evangelists do *not* tell us of the period of his activity, there are important things to be learnt.

He lived in religion, and it was breath to him in

the fear of God; his whole life, all his thoughts and
feelings, were absorbed in the relation to God, and
yet he did not talk like an enthusiast and a fanatic,
who sees only one red-hot spot, and so is blind to
the world and all that it contains. He spoke his
message and looked at the world with a fresh and
clear eye for the life, great and small, that surrounded him. He proclaimed that to gain the
whole world was nothing if the soul were injured,
and yet he remained kind and sympathetic to every
living thing. That is the most astonishing and the
greatest fact about him! His discourses, generally
in the form of parables and sayings, exhibit every
degree of human speech and the whole range of the
emotions. The sternest tones of passionate accusation and indignant reproof, nay, even irony, he
does not despise; but they must have formed the
exception with him. He is possessed of a quiet,
uniform, collected demeanour, with everything
directed to one goal. He never uses any ecstatic
language, and the tone of stirring prophecy is rare.
Entrusted with the greatest of all missions, his eye
and ear are open to every impression of the life
around him—a proof of intense calm and absolute
certainty. " Mourning and weeping, laughing and
dancing, wealth and poverty, hunger and thirst,
health and sickness, children's play and politics,
gathering and scattering, the leaving of home, life
in the inn and the return, marriage and funeral, the
splendid house of the living and the grave of the

dead, the sower and the reaper in the field, the lord
of the vintage among his vines, the idle workman
in the marketplace, the shepherd searching for the
sheep, the dealer in pearls on the sea, and, then
again, the woman at home anxious over the barrel
of meal and the leaven, or the lost piece of money,
the widow's complaint to the surly official, the
earthly food that perishes, the mental relation of
teacher and pupil, on the one side regal glory and
the tyrant's lust of power, on the other childish
innocence and the industry of the servant—all these
pictures enliven his discourse and make it clear
even to those who are children in mind." They do
more than tell us that he spoke in picture and
parable. They exhibit an ʾnner freedom and a
cheerfulness of soul in the midst of the greatest
strain, such as no prophet ever possessed before
him. His eye rests kindly upon the flowers and
the children, on the lily of the field—" Solomon in all
his glory is not clothed like one of them "—on the
birds in the air and the sparrows on the house-top.
The sphere in which he lived, above the earth and
its concerns, did not destroy his interest in it; no !
he brought everything in it into relation with
the God whom he knew, and he saw it as protected
in him : " Your Father in heaven feeds them." The
parable is his most familiar form of speech. Insensibly, however, parable and sympathy pass into
each other. Yet he who had not where to lay his
head does not speak like one who has broken with

everything, or like an heroic penitent, or like an
ecstatic prophet, but like a man who has rest and
peace for his soul, and is able to give life and
strength to others. He strikes the mightiest notes;
he offers men an inexorable alternative; he leaves
them no escape; and yet the strongest emotion
seems to come naturally to him, and he expresses
it as something natural; he clothes it in the
language in which a mother speaks to her child.

LECTURE III.

In the previous lecture we spoke of our evangelists and of their silence on the subject of Jesus' early development. We described in brief the mode and character of his teaching. We saw that he spoke like a prophet and yet not like a prophet. His words breathe peace, joy, and certainty. He urges the necessity of struggle and decision—"where your treasure is, there will your heart be also"—and yet the quiet symmetry of a parable is over all that he says : under God's sun and the dew of heaven everything is to grow and increase until the harvest. He lived in the continual consciousness of God's presence. His food and drink was to do God's will. But—and this seemed to us the greatest thing about him and the seal of his inner freedom—he did not speak like an heroic penitent, or like an ascetic who has turned his back upon the world. His eye rested kindly upon the whole world, and he saw it as it was, in all its varied and changing colours. He ennobled it in his parables; his gaze penetrated the veil of the earthly, and he recognised everywhere the hand of the living God.

When he came forward, another was already at work among the Jewish people : John the Baptist. Within a few months a great movement had arisen on the banks of the Jordan. It differed altogether from those messianic movements which for several generations had by fits and starts kept the nation alive. The Baptist, it is true, also proclaimed that the kingdom of God was at hand; and that meant nothing less than that the day of the Lord, the judgment, the end, was then coming. But the day of judgment which John the Baptist announced was not the day when God was going to take vengeance upon the heathen and raise up his own people; it was the day of judgment for this very people that he prophesied. " Who hath warned you to flee from the wrath to come? Think not to say within yourselves, We have Abraham to our father: for I say unto you that God is able of these stones to raise up children unto Abraham. And now also the axe is laid unto the root of the trees." In that day of judgment it is not being children of Abraham, but doing works of righteousness, which is to turn the scale. And he, the preacher, himself began with repentance and devoted his life to it; he stands before them in raiment of camel's hair, and his meat is locusts and wild honey. But it is not in the levying of a band of ascetics that he sees his work, or at any rate his main work. He appeals to the whole nation, busy with its various trades and callings, and summons it to repentance. They seem

very simple truths that he utters : to the publicans
he says : "Exact no more than that which is
appointed you"; to the soldiers : "Do violence
to no man, neither accuse any falsely, and be
content with your wages"; to the well-to-do :
"He that hath two coats, let him impart to him
that hath none, and he that hath meat, let him
do likewise"; and to all : "Forget not the poor."
This is the practical proof of the repentance to which
he calls, and it embraces the conversion which he
has in view. It is not a question of a single act,
the baptism of repentance, but of a righteous life in
the face of the avenging justice of God. Of ceremonies, sacrifices, and the works of the law, John
did not speak; apparently he thought them un-
important. It was on a right disposition and good
deeds that everything turned. In the day of
judgment it was by this standard that the God of
Abraham would judge.

Let us pause here for a moment. Questions force
themselves upon us at this point which have often
been answered and still are again and again put.
It is clear that John the Baptist proclaimed the
sovereignty of God and his holy moral law. It is
also clear that he proclaimed to his fellow-countrymen that it was by the moral law that they were to
measure, and that on this alone everything was to
turn. He told them that what they were to care
about most was to be in a right state within and
to do good deeds. It is clear, lastly, that there is

nothing over-refined or artificial in his notion of what was good; he means ordinary morality. It is here that the questions arise.

Firstly: if it was only so simple a matter as the eternal claims of what is right and holy, why all this apparatus about the coming of the day of judgment, about the axe being laid to the root of the trees, about the unquenchable fire, and so on?

Secondly: is not this baptism in the wilderness and this proclamation that the day of judgment was at hand simply the reflection or the product of the political and social state of the nation at the time?

Thirdly: what is there that is really new in this proclamation and had not been already expressed in Judaism?

These three questions are very intimately connected with one another.

Firstly, then, as to the whole dramatic eschatological apparatus about the coming of the kingdom of God, the end being at hand, and so on. Well, every time that a man earnestly, and out of the depths of his own personal experience, points others to God and to what is good and holy, whether it be deliverance or judgment that he preaches, it has always, so far as history tells us, taken the form of announcing that the end is at hand. How is that to be explained? The answer is not difficult. Not only is religion a life in and with God; but, just because it is that, it is also the revelation of the meaning and responsibility of life. Every one who has awakened to a sense of religion perceives that, without it, the search for such meaning is in vain, and that the individual, as well as the multitude, wanders aimlessly and falls : " they go astray ; every one turns to his own way." But the prophet who has become conscious of God is filled with terror and agony as he recognises that all mankind is sunk in error and indifference. He feels like a traveller who sees his companions blindly rushing to the edge of a precipice. He wants to call them back at all costs. The time is running out ; he can still warn them ; he can still adjure them to turn back ; in a single hour, perhaps, all will be lost. The time is running out, it is the last moment—this is the cry in which, then, in all nations and at all times, any energetic call to conversion has been voiced whenever a fresh prophet has been granted them. The prophet's gaze penetrates the course of history ; he sees the irrevocable end ; and he is filled with boundless astonishment that the godlessness and blindness, the frivolity and indolence, have not long since brought everything to utter ruin and destruction. That there is still a brief moment left in which conversion is possible seems to him the greatest marvel of all, and to be ascribed only to God's forbearance. But certain it is that the end cannot be very far off. This is the way in which with every great cry for repentance the idea of the approaching end always arises. The individual forms in which it shapes itself depend upon contemporary circumstances and are of subordinate importance. It is only the

religion which has been built up into an intellectual
system that does not make this emphasising of the
end all-important; without such emphasis no actual
religion is conceivable, whether it springs up anew like
a sudden flame or glows in the soul like a secret fire.

I pass now to the second question : whether the
social and political conditions of the time were not
causes of the religious movement. Let us see briefly
where we are. You are aware that at the time of
which we speak the peaceful days of the Jewish
theocracy were long past. For two centuries blow
had followed upon blow; from the terrible days of
Antiochus Epiphanes onwards the nation had never
had any rest. The kingdom of the Maccabees had
been set up, and through inner strife and external
foe had soon disappeared again. The Romans had
invaded the country and had laid their iron hand
upon everything. The tyranny of that Edomite par-
venu, King Herod, had robbed the nation of every
pleasure in life and maimed it in all its members.
So far as human foresight went, it looked as if no
improvement in its position could ever again be
effected; the lie seemed to be given to all the
glorious old prophecies; the end appeared to have
come. How easy it was at such an epoch to despair
of all earthly things, and in this despair to renounce
in utter distress what had once passed as the inseparable accompaniment of the theocracy. How
easy it was now to declare the earthly crown,
political possessions, prestige and wealth, strenuous

effort and struggle, to be one and all worthless, and in place of them to look to heaven for a completely new kingdom, a kingdom for the poor, the oppressed, the weak, and to hope that their virtues of gentleness and patience would receive a crown. And if for hundreds of years the national God of Israel had been undergoing a transformation; if he had broken in pieces the weapons of the mighty, and derided the showy worship of his priests; if he had demanded righteous judgment and mercy— what a temptation there was to proclaim him as the God who wills to see his people in misery that he may then bring them deliverance! We can, in fact, with a few touches construct the religion and its hopes which seemed of necessity to result from the circumstances of the time — a miserabilism which clings to the expectation of a miraculous interference on God's part, and in the meantime, as it were, wallows in wretchedness.

But although the terrible circumstances of the time certainly disengaged and developed many ideas of this kind, and easily account for the wild enterprises of the false Messiahs and the political efforts of fanatical Pharisees, they are very far from being sufficient to explain John the Baptist's message. They do, indeed, explain how it was that deliverance from earthly things was an idea which seized hold of wide circles, and that people were looking to God. Trouble makes men pray. But trouble in itself does not give any moral force, and moral force was the chief element in John the Baptist's message. In appealing to it, in proclaiming that everything must be based on morality and personal responsibility, he took a higher point of view than the feeble piety of the "poor," and drew not from time but from eternity.

It is scarcely a century since Fichte delivered his memorable orations here in Berlin, after the terrible defeat which Germany had suffered. What did he do in these lectures? In the first place, he held up a mirror to the nation, and showed it its sins and their consequences,—frivolity, godlessness, self-complacency, infatuation, weakness. What did he do next? Did he simply call them to arms? Arms were just what they were no longer capable of bearing; they had been struck from their powerless hands. It was to repentance and to inward conversion that he called them; to God, and therefore to the exertion of all their moral force; to truth and to the Spirit, so that by the Spirit everything might be made new. By his powerful personality, and in union with friends of a like mind, he produced an immense impression. He succeeded in opening up once more the choked fountains of our energy, because he knew the strength from which help comes and had drunk of the living water himself. No doubt the necessities of the time taught him and steeled him; but it would be foolish and ridiculous to maintain that Fichte's orations were the product of the general woe. They are the

antithesis of it. Not otherwise must we think of
John the Baptist's message, and—let me say it at
once—of the message which Jesus himself delivered.
That they appealed to those who expected nothing
of the world or of politics—of John the Baptist,
however, this is not directly reported ; that they
would have nothing to do with those popular
leaders who had led the people to ruin ; that they
turned their gaze altogether from earthly things, may
also be accounted for by the circumstances of the
time. But the remedy which they proclaimed was
no product of those circumstances. Nay, was not
calling people to ordinary morality and expecting
everything of it bound to seem a hopeless enterprise ? And whence came the power, the inflexible
power, which compelled others ? This leads us to
the last of the questions which we have raised.

Thirdly, what was there that was new in the
whole movement ? Was it anything new to set up
the sovereignty of God, the sovereignty of the good
and the holy, in opposition to all the other elements
which had forced their way into religion ? Did
John the Baptist, did Christ himself, bring in anything that had not been proclaimed long before ?
Gentlemen, the question as to what is new in
religion is not a question which is raised by those
who live in it. What is there that can have been
" new," seeing that mankind existed so long before
Jesus Christ and had seen so much in the way of
intelligence and knowledge ? Monotheism had long

been introduced, and the few possible types of
monotheistic religious fervour had long made their
appearance here and there, and had taken possession
of whole schools, nay, of a whole nation. Can the
religious individualism of that Psalmist ever be sur-
passed in depth and vigour who confessed : " Lord,
when I have thee, I ask not after heaven and earth " ?
Can we go beyond what Micah said : " He hath
showed thee, O man, what is good ; and what doth
the Lord require of thee but to do justly and to
love mercy, and to walk humbly with thy God " ?
Centuries had passed since these words were spoken.
" What do you want with your Christ," we are
asked, principally by Jewish scholars; " he introduced nothing new." I answer with Wellhausen :
It is quite true that what Jesus proclaimed, what
John the Baptist expressed before him in his exhortations to repentance, was also to be found in the
prophets, and even in the Jewish tradition of their
time. The Pharisees themselves were in possession
of it ; but unfortunately they were in possession
of much else besides. With them it was weighted,
darkened, distorted, rendered ineffective and deprived
of its force, by a thousand things which they also
held to be religious and every whit as important as
mercy and judgment. They reduced everything to
one dead level, wove everything into one fabric ; the
good and holy was only one woof in a broad earthly
warp. You ask again, then : " What was there
that was new ? " The question is out of place in

monotheistic religion. Ask rather : "Had what was here proclaimed any strength and any vigour ? " I answer : Take the people of Israel and search the whole history of their religion ; take history generally, and where will you find any message about God and the good that was ever so pure and so full of strength—for purity and strength go together— as we hear and read of in the Gospels? As regards purity, the spring of holiness had, indeed, long been opened ; but it was choked with sand and dirt, and its water was polluted. For rabbis and theologians to come afterwards and distil this water, even if they were successful, makes no difference. But now the spring burst forth afresh, and broke a new way for itself through the rubbish — through the rubbish which priests and theologians had heaped up so as to smother the true element in religion ; for how often does it happen in history that theology is only the instrument by which religion is discarded ! The other element was that of strength. Pharisaical teachers had proclaimed that everything was contained in the injunction to love God and one's neighbour. They spoke ex- cellently ; the words might have come out of Jesus' mouth. But what was the result of their language? That the nation, that in particular their own pupils, condemned the man who took the words seriously. All that they did was weak and, because weak, harmful. Words effect nothing ; it is the power of the personality that stands behind them. But he

" taught as one having authority and not as the Scribes." Such was the impression of him which his disciples received. His words became to them " the words of life," seeds which sprang up and bore fruit. That was what was new.

Some such message John the Baptist had already begun to deliver. He, too, had undoubtedly placed himself in opposition to the leaders of the people ; for any man who tells people to " reform," and at the same time enjoins nothing more than repentance and good works, always comes into opposition with the official leaders of religion and church. But beyond the lines of the message of repentance John did not go.

Jesus Christ then appeared. He first of all accepted and affirmed the Baptist's message to its full extent, and he acknowledged the Baptist himself ; nay, there was no one of whom he spoke in language of such warm recognition. Did not he say that among them that were born of women there had not arisen a greater than John the Baptist ? Again and again he acknowledged that his cause began with the Baptist and that he was his forerunner. Nay, he had himself been baptised by him, and thereby put himself into the movement which the Baptist began.

But he did not rest there. When he appeared, he, too, it is true, like John proclaimed : " Repent, for the kingdom of God is at hand " ; but his message became one of joy as he delivered it. The traditions about him contain nothing more certain than that his message

D

was an " evangel," and that it was felt to bring blessing
and joy. With good reason, therefore, the evangelist
Luke began his narrative of Jesus' public appearance
with the words of the prophet Isaiah :—" *The
Spirit of the Lord is upon me, because he hath
anointed me to preach the gospel to the poor ; he
hath sent me to heal the broken-hearted, to preach
deliverance to the captives and recovering of sight to
the blind, to set at liberty them that are bruised, to
preach the acceptable year of the Lord.*" Or in
Jesus' own words :—" *Come unto me all ye that
labour and are heavy laden and I will give you rest.
Take my yoke upon you, and learn of me ; for I am
meek and lowly of heart ; and ye shall find rest unto
your souls. For my yoke is easy and my burden is
light.*" These words dominated Jesus' whole work and
message ; they contain the theme of all that he
taught and did. They make it at once obvious
that in this teaching of his he left John the Baptist's
message far behind. The latter, although already in
silent conflict with the priests and the scribes, did
not become a definite signal for contradiction. " The
falling and the rising again," a new humanity opposed
to the old, the God-man—Jesus Christ—was the first
to create. He came into immediate opposition with
the official leaders of the people, and in them with
ordinary human nature in general. They thought
of God as of a despot guarding the ceremonial
observances in His household ; he breathed in the
presence of God. They saw Him only in His law,

which they had converted into a labyrinth of dark
defiles, blind alleys and secret passages; he saw and
felt Him everywhere. They were in possession of a
thousand of His commandments, and thought, therefore, that they knew Him; he had one only, and
knew Him by it. They had made this religion into
an earthly trade, and there was nothing more
detestable; he proclaimed the living God and the
soul's nobility.

If, however, we take a general view of Jesus' teaching, we shall see that it may be grouped under
three heads. They are each of such a nature as to
contain the whole, and hence it can be exhibited in
its entirety under any one of them.

Firstly, the kingdom of God and its coming.

*Secondly, God the Father and the infinite value
of the human soul.*

*Thirdly, the higher righteousness and the com-
mandment of love.*

That Jesus' message is so great and so powerful lies
in the fact that it is so simple and on the other hand
so rich; so simple as to be exhausted in each of the
leading thoughts which he uttered; so rich that every
one of these thoughts seems to be inexhaustible and
the full meaning of the sayings and parables beyond
our reach. But more than that—he himself stands
behind everything that he said. His words speak to
us across the centuries with the freshness of the
present. It is here that that profound saying is truly
verified: "Speak, that I may see thee."

Our course in what follows will be to try to learn what those three heads are, and to classify the thoughts which come under them. They contain the main features of Jesus' message. We shall then try to understand the Gospel in its relations to certain great questions of life.

I. *The kingdom of God and its coming.*

Jesus' message of the kingdom of God runs through all the forms and statements of the prophecy which, taking its colour from the Old Testament, announces the day of judgment and the visible government of God in the future, up to the idea of an inward coming of the kingdom, starting with Jesus' message and then beginning. His message embraces these two poles, with many stages between them that shade off one into another. At the one pole the coming of the kingdom seems to be a purely future event, and the kingdom itself to be the external rule of God ; at the other, it appears as something inward, something which is already present and making its entrance at the moment. You see, therefore, that neither the conception of the kingdom of God, nor the way in which its coming is represented, is free from ambiguity. Jesus took it from the religious traditions of his nation, where it already occupied a foremost place ; he accepted various aspects of it in which the conception was still a living force, and he added new ones.

Eudemonistic expectations of a mundane and political character were all that he discarded.

Jesus, like all those of his own nation who were really in earnest, was profoundly conscious of the great antithesis between the kingdom of God and that kingdom of the world in which he saw the reign of evil and the evil one. This was no mere image or empty idea; it was a truth which he saw and felt most vividly. He was certain, then, that the kingdom of the world must perish and be destroyed. But nothing short of a battle can effect it. With dramatic intensity battle and victory stand like a picture before his soul, drawn in those large firm lines in which the prophets had seen them. At the close of the drama he sees himself seated at the right hand of his Father, and his twelve disciples on thrones judging the twelve tribes of Israel; so objective was this picture to him, so completely in harmony with the ideas of his time. Now we may take the view—and not a few of us take it—that in these dramatic pictures, with their hard colours and contrasts, we have the actual purport of Jesus' message and the fundamental form which it took; and that all his other statements of it must be simply regarded as secondary. We may say that they are all variations of it more or less edifying, variations which were added, perhaps, only by later reporters; but that the only positive factor is the dramatic hope for the future. In this view I cannot concur. It is considered a perverse procedure in similar cases to judge eminent, epoch-making per-

sonalities first and foremost by what they share with
their contemporaries, and on the other hand to put
what is great and characteristic in them into the
background. The tendency as far as possible to
reduce everything to one level, and to efface what
is special and individual, may spring in some minds
from a praiseworthy sense of truth, but it has proved
misleading. More frequently, however, we get the
endeavour, conscious or unconscious, to refuse greatness any recognition at all, and to throw down anything that is exalted. There can be no doubt about
the fact that the idea of the two kingdoms, of God
and of the devil, and their conflicts, and of that last
conflict at some future time when the devil, long
since cast out of heaven, will be also defeated on
earth, was an idea which Jesus simply shared with
his contemporaries. He did not start it, but he grew
up in it and he retained it. The other view, however, that the kingdom of God "cometh not with
observation," that it is already here, was his own.

For us, gentlemen, to-day, it is difficult to reconcile,
nay, it is scarcely possible to bridge over, such an
opposition as is involved, on the one side in a
dramatic picture of God's kingdom existing in the
future, and on the other in the announcement that
"it is in the midst of you," a still and mighty power
in the hearts of men. But to understand why it was
that with other historical traditions and other forms
of culture no opposition was felt to exist between
these views, nay, that both were able to exist side

by side, we must reflect, we must steep ourselves in the history of the past. I imagine that a few hundred years hence there will be found to exist in the intellectual ideas which we shall have left behind us much that is contradictory; people will wonder how we put up with it. They will find much hard and dry husk in what we took for the kernel; they will be unable to understand how we could be so short-sighted, and fail to get a sound grasp of what was essential and separate it from the rest. Some day the knife will be applied and pieces will be cut away where as yet we do not feel the slightest inclination to distinguish. Let us hope that then we may find fair judges, who will measure our ideas not by what we have unwittingly taken over from tradition and are neither able nor called upon to correct, but by what was born of our very own, by the changes and improvements which we have effected in what was handed down to us or was commonly prevalent in our day.

Truly the historian's task of distinguishing between what is traditional and what is peculiar, between kernel and husk, in Jesus' message of the kingdom of God is a difficult and responsible one. How far may we go? We do not want to rob this message of its innate character and colour; we do not want to change it into a pale scheme of ethics. On the other hand, we do not want to lose sight of its peculiar character and strength, as we should do were we to side with those who resolve it into the general ideas

prevailing at the time. The very way in which
Jesus distinguished between the traditional elements
—he left out none in which there was a spark of
moral force, and he accepted none which encouraged
the selfish expectations of his nation—this very
discrimination teaches us that it was from a deeper
knowledge that he spoke and taught. But we possess
testimonies of a much more striking kind. If anyone
wants to know what the kingdom of God and the
coming of it meant in Jesus' message, he must read
and study his parables. He will then see what it
is that is meant. The kingdom of God comes by
coming to the individual, by entering into his soul
and laying hold of it. True, the kingdom of God is
the rule of God; but it is the rule of the holy God in
the hearts of individuals; *it is God himself in his
power*. From this point of view everything that
is dramatic in the external and historical sense has
vanished; and gone, too, are all the external hopes
for the future. Take whatever parable you will, the
parable of the sower, of the pearl of great price, of
the treasure buried in the field—the word of God,
God himself, is the kingdom. It is not a question of
angels and devils, thrones and principalities, but of
God and the soul, the soul and its God.

LECTURE IV.

WE last spoke of Jesus' message in so far as it proclaimed the kingdom of God and its coming. We
saw that it runs through all the forms in which the
prophecy of the day of judgment is expressed in the
Old Testament, up to the idea of an inward coming
of the kingdom then beginning. Finally we tried to
show why the latter idea is to be regarded as the
dominant one. Before examining it more closely,
however, I should like to draw your attention to
two particularly important expressions of it, lying
between the extremes of the "day of judgment"
and the "inner coming."

In the first of them, the coming of the kingdom
of God signifies that the kingdom of the devil is
destroyed and the demons vanquished. Hitherto it
is they who have been ruling; they have taken
possession of men and even of whole nations, and
forced them to their will. Jesus not only declares
that he is come to destroy the works of the devil, but
he actually drives out the demons and releases men
from their power.

Let me here digress a little from our subject.

Nothing in the Gospels strikes us as stranger than
the frequently recurring stories of demons, and the
great importance which the evangelists attach to
them.   For many among us the very fact that these
writings report such absurdities is sufficient reason
for declining to accept them.   Now in this connexion
it is well to know that absolutely similar stories are
to be found in numerous writings of that age, Greek,
Roman, and Jewish.   The notion of people being
" possessed " was current everywhere ; nay, even the
science of the time looked upon a whole section of
morbid phenomena in this light.   But the consequence of these phenomena being explained as
meaning that some evil and invisible power had taken.
possession of a man was that mental affections took
forms which looked as if an alien being had really
entered into the soul.   There is nothing paradoxical
in this.   If modern science were to declare nervous
disease to consist, in great part, of " possession," and
the newspapers were to spread this announcement
amongst the public, the same thing would recur.   We
should soon have numerous cases in which nervous
patients looked as if they were in the grip of an evil
spirit and themselves believed that they were so.
Theory and belief would work by suggestion and
again create a class of " demoniacs " amongst the
insane, just as they created them hundreds, nay
thousands, of years ago.   It is unhistorical and
foolish to attribute any peculiar notion or " theory "
about demons and the demoniac to the Gospels and

the evangelists. They only shared the general notions of their time. The forms of mental disease in question are of rare occurrence nowadays, but nevertheless they are not yet quite extinct. Where they occur the best means of encountering them is to-day, as it was formerly, the influence of a strong personality. It manages to threaten and subdue the "devil" and so heal the patient. In Palestine "demoniacs" must have been particularly numerous. Jesus saw in them the forces of evil and mischief, and by his marvellous power over the souls of those who trusted him he banished the disease. This brings us to the second point.

When John the Baptist in prison was disturbed by doubts as to whether Jesus was "he who was to come," he sent two of his own disciples to him to ask him himself. There is nothing more touching than this question of the Baptist's, nothing more edifying than the Lord's answer. But we will not dwell upon the scene. What was the answer? "Go and shew John again those things which you do hear and see : the blind receive their sight, and the lame walk, the lepers are cleansed, and the deaf hear, the dead are raised up, and the poor have the Gospel preached to them." That is what the "coming of the kingdom" means, or, rather, it is there already in this saving activity. By vanquishing and banishing misery, need and disease, by the actual influence which Jesus was exerting, John was to see that a new day had dawned. The healing of the possessed was only a part of this saving activity; the activity itself, however, was what Jesus denoted as the meaning and the seal of his mission. It was, then, to the wretched, to the sick, and to the poor, that he addressed himself; but not as a moralist and without any trace of weak-minded sentimentality. He makes no division of evils into departments and groups; he spends no time in asking whether the sick one "deserves" to be healed; he is far, too, from having any sympathy for pain and death. He nowhere says that disease is salutary and that evil is a blessing. No! disease he calls disease, and health he calls health. To him all evil, all misery, is something terrible; it is part of the great realm of Satan. But he feels the power of the Saviour within him. He knows that progress is possible only by overcoming weakness and healing disease.

But he goes further. It is by his healing, above all by his forgiving sin, that the kingdom of God comes. This is the first complete transition to the conception of the kingdom of God as the power that works inwardly. As he calls the sick and the poor to him, so he calls sinners also, and it is this call which is all-important. "The Son of Man is come to seek and to save that which was lost." Here for the first time everything that is external and merely future is abandoned : it is the individual, not the nation or the state, which is redeemed; it is new men who are to arise, and the kingdom of God is to be at once their strength and the goal

at which they aim. They search for the treasure
hidden in the field and find it; they sell all that
they have and buy the pearl of great price; they
are converted and become as children; but thereby
they are redeemed and made God's children and
God's champions.

It was in this connexion that Jesus spoke of the
kingdom of God which the violent take by force,
and, again, of the kingdom of God which grows
steadily and silently like a seed and bears fruit. It
is in the nature of spiritual force, a power which
sinks into a man within, and can be understood only
from within. Thus, although the kingdom is also
in heaven; although it will come with the day of
judgment, he can still say of it: "It is not here or
there, it is within you."

At a later period the view of the kingdom, according to which it was already come and still comes in
Jesus' saving activity, was not kept up by his
disciples: nay, they continued to speak of it as of
something that was solely in the future. But the
thing itself retained its force; it was only given
another title. It underwent the same experience as
the conception of the "Messiah." As we shall see
hereafter, there was scarcely anyone in the Church of
the Gentiles who sought to explain Jesus' significance
by regarding him as the "Messiah." But the thing
itself did not perish.

The essential elements in the message of the kingdom
were preserved. The kingdom has a triple meaning.

Firstly, it is something supernatural, a gift from above, not a product of ordinary life. Secondly, it is a purely religious blessing, the inner link with the living God; thirdly, it is the most important experience that a man can have, that on which everything else depends; it permeates and dominates his whole existence, because sin is forgiven and misery banished.

This kingdom, which comes to the humble and makes them new men and joyful, is the key that first unlocks the meaning and the aim of life. This was what Jesus himself found, and what his disciples found. It is a supernatural element alone that ever enables us to get at the meaning of life; for natural existence ends in death. But a life that is bound up with death can have no meaning; it is only sophisms that can blind us to this fact. But here the kingdom of God, the Eternal, entered into time. "Eternal light came in and made the world look new." This is Jesus' message of the kingdom. Everything else that he proclaimed can be brought into connexion with this; his whole "doctrine" can be conceived as a message of the kingdom. But we shall recognise this, and the blessing which he means, still more clearly, if we turn to the second of the sections indicated in the previous lecture, and thereby progressively acquaint ourselves with the fundamental features of Jesus' message.

II. *God the Father and the infinite value of the human soul.*

To our modern way of thinking and feeling, Christ's message appears in the clearest and most direct light when grasped in connexion with the idea of God the Father and the infinite value of the human soul. Here the elements which I would describe as the restful and restgiving in Jesus' message, and which are comprehended in the idea of our being children of God, find expression. I call them *restful* in contrast with the impulsive and stirring elements; although it is just they that are informed with a special strength. But the fact that the whole of Jesus' message may be reduced to these two heads—-God as the Father, and the human soul so ennobled that it can and does unite with him—shows us that the Gospel is in nowise a positive religion like the rest; that it contains no statutory or particularistic elements; *that it is, therefore, religion itself.* It is superior to all antithesis and tension between this world and a world to come, between reason and ecstasy, between work and isolation from the world, between Judaism and Hellenism. It can dominate them all, and there is no factor of earthly life to which it is confined or necessarily tied down. Let us, however, get a clearer idea of what being children of God, in Jesus' sense, means, by briefly considering four groups containing sayings of his, or, as the case may be, a single

saying, viz.:—(1) The Lord's Prayer; (2) that utterance, "Rejoice not that the spirits are subject unto
you; but rather rejoice because your names are
written in heaven"; (3) the saying, "Are not two
sparrows sold for a farthing? and one of them shall
not fall on the ground without your Father. But
the very hairs of your head are all numbered";
(4) the utterance, "What shall it profit a man if he
shall gain the whole world and lose his own soul?"

Let us take the Lord's Prayer first. It was com-
municated by Jesus to his disciples at a particularly
solemn moment. They had asked him to teach them
how to pray, as John the Baptist had taught his
disciples. Thereupon he uttered the Lord's Prayer.
It is by their prayers that the character of the
higher religions is determined. But this prayer was
spoken—as every one must feel who has ever given
it a thought in his soul—by one who has overcome
all inner unrest, or overcomes it the moment that
he goes before God. The very apostrophe of the
prayer, "Our Father," exhibits the steady faith of
the man who knows that he is safe in God, and
it tells us that he is certain of being heard.
Not to hurl violent desires at heaven or to obtain
this or that earthly blessing does he pray, but
to preserve the power which he already possesses
and strengthen the union with God in which
he lives. No one, then, can utter this prayer
unless his heart is in profound peace and his
mind wholly concentrated on the inner relation

of the soul with God. All other prayers are of a lower order, for they contain particularistic elements, or are so framed that in some way or other they stir the imagination in regard to the things of sense as well; whilst this prayer leads us away from everything to the height where the soul is alone with its God. And yet the earthly element is not absent. The whole of the second half of the prayer deals with earthly relations, but they are placed in the light of the Eternal. In vain will you look for any request for particular gifts of grace, or special blessings, even of a spiritual kind. " All else shall be added unto you." The name of God, His will, and His kingdom—these elements of rest and permanence are poured out over the earthly relations as well. Everything that is small and selfish melts away, and only four things are left with regard to which it is worth while to pray—the daily bread, the daily trespass, the daily temptations, and the evil in life. There is nothing in the Gospels that tells us more certainly what the Gospel is, and what sort of disposition and temper it produces, than the Lord's Prayer. With this prayer we ought also to confront all those who disparage the Gospel by representing it as an ascetic or ecstatic or sociological pronouncement. It shows the Gospel to be the Fatherhood of God applied to the whole of life; to be an inner union with God's will and God's kingdom, and a joyous certainty of the possession of eternal blessings and protection from evil.

F

As to the second utterance: when Jesus says "Rejoice not that the spirits are subject unto you, but rejoice rather that your names are written in heaven," it is another way of laying special emphasis on the idea that the all-important element in this religion is the consciousness of being safe in God. The greatest achievements, nay the very works which are done in the strength of this religion, fall below the assurance, at once humble and proud, of resting for time and eternity under the fatherly care of God. Moreover, the genuineness, nay the actual existence, of religious experience is to be measured, not by any transcendency of feeling nor by great deeds that all men can see, but by the joy and the peace which are diffused through the soul that can say "My Father."

How far did Christ carry this idea of the fatherly providence of God? Here we come to the third saying: "Are not two sparrows sold for a farthing? and one of them shall not fall to the ground without your Father. But the very hairs of your head are all numbered." The assurance that God rules is to go as far as our fears go, nay, as far as life itself—life down even to its smallest manifestations in the order of nature. It was to disabuse his disciples of the fear of evil and the terrors of death that he gave them the sayings about the sparrows and the flowers of the field; they are to learn how to see the hand of the living God everywhere in life, and in death too

Finally, in asking—and after what has gone before the question will not sound surprising—" What shall it profit a man if he shall gain the whole world and lose his own soul?" he put a man's value as high as it can be put. The man who can say " My Father " to the Being who rules heaven and earth, is thereby raised above heaven and earth, and himself has a value which is higher than all the fabric of this world. But this great saying took the stern tone of a warning. He offered them a gift and with it set them a task. How different was the Greek doctrine! Plato, it is true, had already sung the great hymn of the mind; he had distinguished it from the whole world of appearance and maintained its eternal origin. But the mind which he meant was the knowing mind; he contrasted it with blind, insensible matter; his message made its appeal to the wise. Jesus Christ calls to every poor soul; he calls to every one who bears a human face: You are children of the living God, and not only better than many sparrows but of more value than the whole world. The value of a truly great man, as I saw it put lately, consists in his increasing the value of all mankind. It is here, truly, that the highest significance of great men lies: to have enhanced, that is, to have progressively given effect to human value, to the value of that race of men which has risen up out of the dull ground of Nature. But Jesus Christ was the first to bring the value of every human soul to light, and what he did no one

can any more undo. We may take up what relation to him we will : in the history of the past no
one can refuse to recognise that it was he who
raised humanity to this level.

This highest estimate of a man's value is based
on a transvaluation of all values. To the man who
boasts of his possessions he says : " Thou fool." He
confronts everyone with the thought : " Whosoever
will lose his life shall save it." He can even say :
" He that hateth his life in this world shall keep it
unto life eternal." This is the transvaluation of
values of which many before him had a dim idea ;
of which they perceived the truth as through a veil ;
the redeeming power of which—that blessed mystery
—they felt in advance. He was the first to give
it calm, simple, and fearless expression, as though it
were a truth which grew on every tree. It was
just this that stamped his peculiar genius, that he
gave perfectly simple expression to profound and all-
important truths, as though they could not be otherwise ; as though he were uttering something that
was self-evident ; as though he were only reminding
men of what they all know already, because it lives
in the innermost part of their souls.

In the combination of these ideas—God the Father,
Providence, the position of men as God's children,
the infinite value of the human soul—the whole
Gospel is expressed. But we must recognise what
a paradox it all is ; nay, that the paradox of religion
here for the first time finds its full expression.

Measured by the experience of the senses and by
exact knowledge, not only are the different religions
a paradox, but so are all religious phenomena.
They introduce an element, and pronounce it to be
the most important of all, which is not cognisable
by the senses and flies in the face of things as
they are actually constituted. But all religions
other than Christianity are in some way or other
so bound up with the things of the world that
they involve an element of earthly advantage, or,
as the case may be, are akin in their substance
to the intellectual and spiritual condition of a
definite epoch. But what can be less obvious than
the statement : the hairs of your head are all
numbered; you have a supernatural value; you
can put yourselves into the hands of a power
which no one has seen? Either that is nonsense,
or else it is the utmost development of which
religion is capable; no longer a mere phenomenon
accompanying the life of the senses, a coefficient,
a transfiguration of certain parts of that life, but
something which sets up a paramount title to be
the first and the only fact that reveals the fundamental basis and meaning of life. Religion sub-
ordinates to itself the whole motley world of phenomena, and defies that world if it claims to be the
only real one. Religion gives us only a single experience, but one which presents the world in a new
light : the Eternal appears; time becomes means to
an end ; man is seen to be on the side of the Eternal.

This was certainly Jesus' meaning, and to take
anything from it is to destroy it.   In applying
the idea of Providence to the whole of humanity
and the world without any exception; in showing
that humanity is rooted in the Eternal; in proclaiming the fact that we are God's children as at once
a gift and a task, he took a firm grip of all fumbling
and stammering attempts at religion and brought
them to their issue.   Once more let it be said: we
may assume what position we will in regard to him
and his message, certain it is that thence onward
the value of our race is enhanced; human lives,
nay, we ourselves, have become dearer to one another.
A man may know it or not, but a real reverence for
humanity follows from the practical recognition of
God as the Father of us all.

III. *The higher righteousness and the command-*
ment of love.

This is the third head, and the whole of the
Gospel is embraced under it.   To represent the
Gospel as an ethical message is no depreciation of its
value.   The ethical system which Jesus found prevailing in his nation was both ample and profound.
To judge the moral ideas of the Pharisees solely by
their childish and casuistical aspects is not fair.   By
being bound up with religious worship and petrified
in ritual observance, the morality of holiness had,
indeed, been transformed into something that was

the clean opposite of it. But all was not yet hard and dead; there was some life still left in the deeper parts of the system. To those who questioned him Jesus could still answer: "You have the law, keep it; you know best yourselves what you have to do; the sum of the law is, as you yourselves say, to love God and your neighbour." Nevertheless, there is a sphere of ethical thought which is peculiarly expressive of Jesus' Gospel. Let us make this clear by citing four points.

Firstly: Jesus severed the connexion existing in his day between ethics and the external forms of religious worship and technical observance. He would have absolutely nothing to do with the purposeful and self-seeking pursuit of "good works" in combination with the ritual of worship. He exhibited an indignant contempt for those who allow their neighbours, nay, even their parents, to starve, and on the other hand send gifts to the temple. He will have no compromise in the matter. Love and mercy are ends in themselves; they lose all value and are put to shame by having to be anything else than the service of one's neighbour.

Secondly: in all questions of morality he goes straight to the root, that is, to the disposition and the intention. It is only thus that what he calls the "higher righteousness" can be understood. The "higher righteousness" is the righteousness that will stand when the depths of the heart are probed. Here, again, we have something that is seemingly very

simple and self-evident. Yet the truth, as he uttered
it, took the severe form: "It was said of old . . .
but I say unto you." After all, then, the truth was
something new; he was aware that it had never yet
been expressed in such a consistent form and with
such claims to supremacy. A large portion of the
so-called Sermon on the Mount is occupied with what
he says when he goes in detail through the several
departments of human relationships and human fail-
ings so as to bring the disposition and intention
to light in each case, to judge a man's works by
them, and on them to hang heaven and hell.

Thirdly: what he freed from its connexion with
self-seeking and ritual elements, and recognised as
the moral principle, he reduces to *one* root and to *one*
motive—love. He knows of no other, and love itself,
whether it takes the form of love of one's neighbour
or of one's enemy, or the love of the Samaritan, is of
one kind only. It must completely fill the soul; it
is what remains when the soul dies to itself. In this
sense love is the new life already begun. But it is
always the love which *serves*, and only in this function
does it exist and live.

Fourthly: we saw that Jesus freed the moral
element from all alien connexions, even from its
alliance with the public religion. Therefore to say
that the Gospel is a matter of ordinary morality is
not to misunderstand him. And yet there is one
all-important point where he combines religion and
morality. It is a point which must be felt; it is

not easy to define. In view of the Beatitudes it may, perhaps, best be described as *humility*. Jesus made love and humility one. Humility is not a virtue by itself; but it is pure receptivity, the expression of inner need, the prayer for God's grace and forgiveness, in a word, the opening up of the heart to God. In Jesus' view, this humility, which is the love of God of which we are capable—take, for instance, the parable of the Pharisee and the publican — is an abiding disposition towards the good, and that out of which everything that is good springs and grows. "Forgive us our trespasses even as we forgive them that trespass against us" is the prayer at once of humility and of love. This, then, is the source and origin of the love of one's neighbour; the poor in spirit and those who hunger and thirst after righteousness are also the peace-makers and the merciful.

It was in this sense that Jesus combined religion and morality, and in this sense religion may be called the soul of morality, and morality the body of religion. We can thus understand how it was that Jesus could place the love of God and the love of one's neighbour side by side; the love of one's neighbour is the only practical proof on earth of that love of God which is strong in humility.

In thus expressing his message of the higher right-eousness and the new commandment of love in these four leading thoughts, Jesus defined the sphere of the ethical in a way in which no one before him had ever defined it. But should we be threatened with doubts as to what he meant, we must steep ourselves again and again in the Beatitudes of the Sermon on the Mount. They contain his ethics and his religion, united at the root, and freed from all external and particularistic elements.

LECTURE V.

At the close of the last lecture I referred to the Beatitudes, and mentioned that they exhibit Jesus' religion in a particularly impressive way. I desire to remind you of another passage which shows that Jesus recognised the practical proof of religion to consist in the exercise of neighbourly love and mercy. In one of his last discourses he spoke of the Judgment, bringing it before his hearers' eyes in the parable of the shepherd separating the sheep from the goats. The sole principle of separation is the question of mercy. The question is raised by asking whether men gave food and drink to Jesus himself, and visited him; that is to say, it is put as a *religious* question. The paradox is then resolved in the sentence: "Inasmuch as ye have done it unto one of the least of these my brethren, ye have done it unto me." We can have no clearer illustration of the fact that in Jesus' view mercy was the quality on which everything turned, and that the temper in which it is exercised is the guarantee that a man's *religious* position is the right one. How so? Because in exercising this

virtue men are imitating God : "Be merciful, even
as your Father in heaven is merciful." He who
exercises mercy exercises God's prerogative; for
God's justice is not accomplished by keeping to
the rule, "an eye for an eye and a tooth for a
tooth," but is subject to the power of His mercy.

Let us pause here for a moment. The history of
religion marked an enormous advance, religion itself
was established afresh, when through poets and
thinkers in Greece on the one hand, and through
the prophets in Palestine on the other, the idea of
righteousness and a righteous God became a living
force and transformed tradition. The gods were
raised to a higher level and civilised; the warlike and capricious Jehovah became a holy Being
in whose court of judgment a man might trust,
albeit in fear and trembling. The two great provinces
of religion and morality, hitherto separated, were now
brought into close relation; for " the Godhead is holy
and just." It is *our* history that was then developed;
for without that all-important transformation there
would be no such thing as "mankind," no such thing
as a "history of the world" in the higher sense. The
most immediate result of this development may be
summed up in the maxim : "What ye would not
that men should do unto you, do ye also not unto
them." Insufficient and prosaic as the rule may
seem, yet, if extended so as to cover all human relationships and really observed, it contains a civilising
force of enormous strength.

But it does not contain the ultimate step. Not until justice was compelled to give way to mercy, and the idea of brotherhood and self-sacrifice in the service of one's neighbour became paramount—another re-establishment of religion—was the last advance accomplished that it was possible and necessary to make. Its maxim, "What ye would that men should do unto you, do ye also unto them," also seems prosaic; and yet rightly understood it leads to the summit and comprises a new method of apprehension, and a new way of judging one's own life. The thought that "he who loses his life shall save it," runs side by side with this maxim and effects a transvaluation of values, in the certainty that a man's true life is not tied to this span of time and is not rooted in material existence.

I hope that I have thus shown, although briefly, that in the sphere of thought which is indicated by "the higher righteousness" and "the new commandment of love" Jesus' teaching is also contained in its entirety. As a matter of fact, the three spheres which we have distinguished—the kingdom of God, God as the Father and the infinite value of the human soul, and the higher righteousness showing itself in love—coalesce; for ultimately the kingdom is nothing but the treasure which the soul possesses in the eternal and merciful God. It needs only a few touches to develop this thought into everything that, taking Jesus' sayings as its groundwork, Christendom has known and strives to maintain as hope, faith, and love.

To proceed : Now that we have established the fundamental characteristics of Jesus' message, let us try, in the second place, to treat of the main bearings of the Gospel as applied to individual problems. There are six points or questions which call for special attention, as being the most important in themselves, and consequently felt and regarded as such in all ages. And although, in the course of the Church's history, one or other of these questions may have passed into the background for a decade or two, it has always reappeared afresh, and with redoubled force :—

(1) The Gospel and the world, or the question of asceticism ;

(2) The Gospel and the poor, or the social question ;

(3) The Gospel and law, or the question of public order ;

(4) The Gospel and work, or the question of civilisation ;

(5) The Gospel and the Son of God, or the Christological question ;

(6) The Gospel and doctrine, or the question of creed.

By these six questions—the first four hang together, and the last two stand by themselves—I hope to be able to exhibit, of course only in outline, the most important bearings of Jesus' message.

(1) *The Gospel and the world, or the question of asceticism.*

There is a widespread opinion—it is dominant in the Catholic churches and many Protestants share it nowadays—that, in the last resort and in the most important things which it enjoins, the Gospel is a strictly world-shunning and ascetic creed. Some people proclaim this piece of intelligence with sympathy and admiration; nay, they magnify it into the contention that the whole value and meaning of genuine Christianity, as of Buddhism, lies in its world-denying character. Others emphasise the world-shunning doctrines of the Gospel in order thereby to expose its incompatibility with modern ethical principles, and to prove its uselessness as a religion. The Catholic churches have found a curious way out of the difficulty and one which is, in reality, a product of despair. They recognise, as I have said, the world-denying character of the Gospel, and they teach, accordingly, that it is only in the form of monasticism—that is, in the " vita religiosa "—that true Christian life finds its expression. But they admit a "lower" kind of Christianity without asceticism, as "sufficient." We will say nothing about this strange concession now; the Catholic doctrine is that it is only monks who can follow Christ fully. With this doctrine a great philosopher, and a still greater writer, of the nineteenth century, has made common cause. Schopenhauer extols Christianity because, and in so far as, it has produced great ascetics like St. Anthony or St. Francis; but, beyond that, everything in the Christian message seems to him to be useless and a stumbling-block. With a much deeper insight than Schopenhauer, and with a strength of feeling and power of language that carry us away, Tolstoi has emphasised the ascetic and world-shunning features of the Gospel, and erected them into a rule of observance. That the ascetic ideal which he derives from the Gospel is endowed with warmth and strength, and includes the service of one's neighbour, is a fact which we cannot deny; but to him, too, the shunning of the world is the leading characteristic of Christianity. There are thousands of our "educated" readers who find his stories suggestive and exciting, but who at the bottom of their hearts are pleased and relieved to know that Christianity means the denial of the world; for then they know very well that it does not concern them. They are certain, and rightly certain, that this world is given them to be made the best of, within the bounds of its own blessings and its own regulations; and that if Christianity makes any other claim, it thereby shows that it is unnatural. If Christianity has no goal to set before this life; if it transfers everything to a Beyond; if it declares all earthly blessings to be valueless, and points exclusively to a world-shunning and contemplative life, it is an offence to all energetic, nay, ultimately, to all true natures; for such natures

are certain that our faculties are given us to be
employed, and that the earth is assigned to us to be
cultivated and subdued.

But is not the Gospel really a world-denying
creed? Certain very well-known passages are appealed to which do not seem to admit of any other
interpretation : " If thy right eye offend thee, pluck
it out and cast it from thee"; "If thy right hand
offend thee, cut it off"; or the answer to the rich
young man : " Go and sell that thou hast, and give
to the poor, and thou shalt have treasure in
heaven "; or the saying about those who have made
themselves eunuchs for the kingdom of heaven's sake ;
or the utterance : " If any man come to me, and hate
not his father, and mother, and wife, and children,
and brethren and sisters, yea, and his own life also,
he cannot be my disciple." These and other passages
seem to settle the matter, and to prove that the
Gospel is altogether world-shunning and ascetic in its
character. But to this thesis I oppose three considerations which point in another direction. The
first is derived from the way in which Jesus came
forward, and from his manner and course of life ;
the second is based upon the impression which he
made upon his disciples and was reflected in their
own lives ; the third springs from what we said about
the fundamental features of Jesus' message.

1. We find in our Gospels a remarkable utterance
by Jesus, as follows : " John came neither eating
nor drinking, and they say, He hath a devil. The

F

Son of Man came eating and drinking, and they say, Behold a man gluttonous and a wine-bibber." A glutton, then, and a wine-bibber was he called in addition to the other abusive names which were given him. From this it clearly follows that in his whole demeanour and manner of life he made an impression quite different from that of the preacher of repentance on the banks of the Jordan. Towards the various fields in which asceticism had been traditionally practised, he must have taken up an attitude of indifference. We see him in the houses of the rich and of the poor, at meals, with women and amongst children ; according to tradition, even at a wedding. He allows his feet to be washed and his head to be anointed. Further, he is glad to lodge with Mary and Martha ; he does not ask them to leave their home. When he finds, to his joy, people with a firm faith, he leaves them in the calling and the position in which they were. We do not hear of his telling them to sell all and follow him. Apparently he thinks it possible, nay, fitting, that they should live unto their belief in the position in which God has placed them. His circle of disciples is not exhausted by the few whom he summoned directly to follow him. He finds God's children everywhere ; to discover them in their obscurity and to be allowed to speak to them some word of strength is his highest pleasure. But he did not organise his disciples into a band of monks, and he gave them no directions as to what they were to do and leave undone in the life of the day. No one who reads the Gospels with an unprejudiced mind, and does not pick his words, can fail to acknowledge that this free and active spirit does not appear to be bent under the yoke of asceticism, and that such words, therefore, as point in this direction must not be taken in a rigid sense and generalised, but must be regarded in a wider connexion and from a higher point of view.

2. It is certain that the disciples did not understand their master to be a world-shunning ascetic. We shall see later what sacrifices they made for the Gospel and in what sense they renounced the world. But it is evident they did not give ascetic practices the chief place ; they maintained the rule that the labourer is worthy of his hire ; they did not send away their wives. We are incidentally told of Peter that his wife accompanied him on his missionary journeys. Apart from what we are told of an attempt to institute a kind of communism in the congregation at Jerusalem—and we may put it aside, as it is not trustworthy and, moreover, bore no ascetic character—we find nothing in the apostolic age which suggests a community of men who were ascetics on principle ; on the contrary, we find the conviction prevailing everywhere that it is within the given circumstances, in the calling and position in which he finds himself, that a man is to be a Christian. How differently things developed in Buddhism from the very start !

3. The all-important consideration is the third.

Let me remind you of what we said in regard to
Jesus' leading thoughts. In the sphere indicated
by trust in God, humanity, the forgiveness of sins
and the love of one's neighbour, there is no room
for the introduction of any other maxim, least of
all for one of a legal character. At the same time
Jesus makes it clear in what sense the kingdom of
God is the antithesis of the world. The man who
associates any ascetic practice with the words "Take
no thought," "Be merciful even as your Father in
heaven is merciful," and so on, and puts it upon the
same level as those words, does not understand the
sublime character of these sayings, and has either
lost or has never attained the feeling that there
is a union with God in which all such questions
as shunning the world and asceticism are left far
behind.

For these reasons we must decline to regard the
Gospel as a message of world-denial.

On the other hand, Jesus speaks of three enemies,
and the watchword which he gives in dealing with
them is not that we are to flee them ; rather, he com-
mands us to annihilate them. These three enemies
are mammon, care, and selfishness. Observe that here
there is no question of flight or denial, but of a battle
which is to be fought until the enemy is annihilated ;
the forces of darkness are to be overthrown. By
mammon he understands money and worldly goods
in the widest sense of the word, worldly goods which
try to gain the mastery over us, and make us tyrants

over others; for money is "compressed force."
Jesus speaks of this enemy as if it were a person,
as if it were a knight in armour, or a king; nay,
as if it were the devil himself. It is at this enemy
that the saying, "Ye cannot serve two masters,"
is aimed. Wherever anything belonging to the
domain of mammon is of such value to a man that
he sets his heart upon it, that he trembles at the
thought of losing it, that he is no longer willing
to give it up, such a man is already in bondage.
Hence, when the Christian feels that this danger
confronts him, he is not to treat with the enemy,
but to fight, and not fight only but also destroy
the mammon. Were Christ to preach among us
to-day, he would certainly not talk in general terms,
and say to everyone, "give away everything you
have"; but there are thousands among us to whom
he would so speak, and that there is scarcely anyone
who feels compelled to apply these sayings of the
Gospel to himself is a fact that ought to make us
suspicious.

The second enemy is care. At first sight it may
surprise us that Jesus should describe care as so
terrible a foe. He ranks it with "heathenism."
It is true that in the Lord's Prayer he also taught
men to pray, "Give us this day our daily bread";
but a confident request of this kind he does not
call care. The care which he means is that which
makes us timorous slaves of the day and of material
things; the care through which bit by bit we fall

a prey to the world. Care is to him an outrage
on God, who preserves the very sparrows on the
housetop; it destroys the fundamental relation with
the Father in heaven, the childlike trust, and thus
ruins our inmost soul. This is also a point in
regard to which, as in respect to mammon, we
must confess that we do not feel deeply and strongly
enough to recognise the full truth of Jesus' message.
But the question is, Who is right—he with the
inexorable "Take no thought," or we with our
debilitating fears? We, too, in a measure feel that
a man is not really free, strong, and invincible,
until he has put aside all his cares and cast them
upon God. How much we could accomplish and
how strong we should be, if we did not fret.

And then, thirdly: selfishness. It is self-denial,
not asceticism, which Jesus requires; self-denial to
the point of self-renunciation. "If thy right eye
offend thee, pluck it out; if thy right hand offend
thee, cut it off." Wherever some desire of the
senses gains the upper hand of you, so that you
become coarse and vulgar, or in your selfishness a
new master arises in you, you must destroy it; not
because God has any pleasure in mutilation, but
because you cannot otherwise preserve your better
part. It is a hard demand. But it is not met by
any act of general renunciation, such as monks
perform—the act may leave things just as they
were before—but only by a struggle and a resolute
renunciation at the critical point.

With all these enemies, mammon, care, and selfishness, what we have to exercise is *self-denial*, and therewith the relation of Christianity to asceticism is determined. Asceticism maintains the theory that all worldly blessings are in themselves of no value. This is not the theory to which we should be led if we were to go by the Gospel; "for the earth is the Lord's, and the fulness thereof." But according to the Gospel a man is to ask: Can and ought I to regard property and honour, friends and relations as blessings, or must I put them away? If certain of Jesus' sayings to this effect have been handed down to us in a general form and were, no doubt, so uttered, still they must be limited by the whole tenour of his discourses. What the Gospel asks of us is solemnly to examine ourselves, to maintain an earnest watch, and to destroy the enemy. There can be no doubt, however, that Jesus demanded self-denial and self-renunciation to a much greater extent than we like to think.

To sum up: Ascetic in the primary meaning of the word the Gospel is not; for it is a message of trust in God, of humility, of forgiveness of sin, and of mercy. This is a height which nothing else can approach, and into this sphere nothing else can force its way. Further, worldly blessings are not of the devil but of God—"Your heavenly Father knoweth that ye have need of all these things; he arrays the lilies of the field and feeds the fowls of the air." Asceticism has no place in the Gospel at all; what it asks is that we should struggle against mammon, against care, against selfishness; what it demands and disengages is *love*; the love that serves and is self-sacrificing. This struggle and this love are the kind of asceticism which the Gospel means, and whoever encumbers Jesus' message with any other kind fails to understand it. He fails to understand its grandeur and its importance; for there is something still more important than "giving one's body to be burned and bestowing all one's goods to feed the poor," namely, self-denial and love.

(2) *The Gospel and the poor, or the social question.*

The bearings of the Gospel in regard to the social question form the second point which we proposed to consider. It is closely akin to the first. Here also we encounter different views prevalent at the present moment, or, to be more exact, two views, which are mutually opposed. We are told, on the one hand, that the Gospel was in the main a great social message to the poor, and that everything else in it is of secondary importance—mere contemporary wrapping, ancient tradition, or new forms supplied by the first generations of Christians. Jesus, they say, was a great social reformer, who aimed at relieving the lower classes from the wretched condition in which they were languishing; he set up a social programme which embraced the equality of all men,

relief from economical distress, and deliverance from
misery and oppression. It is only so, they add, that
he can be understood, and therefore so he was; or
perhaps—so he was, because it is only so that we can
understand him. For years books and pamphlets
have been written dealing with the Gospel in this
sense; well-meant performances which aim at thus
providing Jesus with a defence and a recommendation.
But amongst those who take the Gospel to be an
essentially social message there are also some who
draw the opposite conclusion. By trying to prove
that Jesus' message was wholly directed to bringing
about an economical reform, they declare the Gospel
to be an entirely Utopian and useless programme;
the view, they say, which Jesus took of the world
was gentle, but also weak; coming himself from the
lower and oppressed classes, he shared the suspicion
entertained by small people of the great and the
rich; he abhorred all profitable trade and business;
he failed to understand the necessity of acquiring
wealth; and accordingly he shaped his programme so
as to disseminate pauperism in the " world "—to him
the world was Palestine—and then, by way of contrast
with the misery on earth, to build up a kingdom
in heaven; a programme unrealisable in itself, and
offensive to men of energy. This, or something like
this, is the view held by another section of those
who identify the Gospel with a social message.

Opposed to this group of persons, united in the
way in which they look at the Gospel but divided

in their opinions in regard to it, there is another group upon whom it makes quite a different impression. They assert that as for any direct interest on Jesus' part in the economical and social conditions of his age; nay, further, as for any rudimentary interest in economical questions in general, it is only read into the Gospel, and that with economical questions the Gospel has absolutely nothing to do. Jesus, they say, certainly borrowed illustrations and examples from the domain of economics, and took a personal interest in the poor, the sick, and the miserable, but his purely religious teaching and his saving activity were in no way directed to any improvement in their earthly position : to say that his objects and intentions were of a social character is to secularize them. Nay, there are not a few among us who think him, like themselves, a "Conservative," who respected all these existing social differences and ordinances as " divinely ordained."

The voices which make themselves heard here are, as you will observe, very different, and the different points of view are defended with zeal and pertinacity. Now, if we are to try to find the position which corresponds to the facts, there is, first of all, a brief remark to be made on the age in which Jesus lived. Our knowledge of the social conditions in Palestine in his age and for some considerable time previously does not go very far; but there are certain leading features of it which we can establish, and two things more particularly which we can assert.

The governing classes, to which, above all, the Pharisees, and also the priests, belonged—the latter partly in alliance with the temporal rulers—had little feeling for the needs of the people. The condition of those classes may not have been much worse than it generally is at all times and in all nations, but it was bad. Moreover, there was here the additional circumstance that mercy and sympathy with the poor had been put into the background by devotion to public worship and to the cult of "righteousness." Oppression and tyranny on the part of the rich had long become a standing and inexhaustible theme with the Psalmists and with all men of any warm feelings. Jesus, too, could not have spoken of the rich as he did speak, unless they had grossly neglected their duties.

In the poor and oppressed classes, in the huge mass of want and evil, amongst the multitude of people for whom the word "misery" is often only another expression for the word "life," nay, is life itself—in this multitude there were groups of people at that time, as we can surely see, who, with fervent and steadfast hope, were hanging upon the promises and consoling words of their God, waiting in humility and patience for the day when their deliverance was to come. Often too poor to pay even for the barest advantages and privileges of public worship, oppressed, thrust aside, and unjustly treated, they could not raise their eyes to the temple; but they looked to the God of Israel, and fervent prayers went

up to him : " Watchman, what of the night ? " Thus
their hearts were opened to God and ready to receive
him, and in many of the Psalms, and in the later
Jewish literature which was akin to them, the word
" poor " directly denotes those who have their hearts
open and are waiting for the consolation of Israel.
Jesus found this usage of speech in existence and
adopted it. Therefore when we come across the
expression " the poor " in the Gospels we must not
think, without further ceremony, of the poor in the
economic sense. As a matter of fact, poverty in the
economic sense coincided to a large extent in those
days with religious humility and an openness of the
heart towards God, in contrast with the elevated
" practice of virtue " of the Pharisees and its routine
observance in " righteousness." But if this were the
prevailing condition of affairs, then it is clear that
our modern categories of " poor " and " rich " cannot
be unreservedly transferred to that age. Yet we
must not forget that in those days the economical
sense was also, as a rule, included in the word " poor."
We shall, therefore, have to examine in our next
lecture the direction in which a distinction can be
made, or perhaps to ask, whether it is possible to fix
the inner sense of Jesus' words in spite of the peculiar
difficulty attaching to the conception of " poverty."
We can have some confidence, however, that we shall
not have to remain in obscurity on this point ; for in
its fundamental features the Gospel also throws a
bright light upon the field covered by this question.

LECTURE VI.

At the close of the last lecture I referred to the problem presented by " the poor " in the Gospel. As a rule, the poor of whom Jesus was thinking were also those whose hearts are open towards God, and hence what is said of them cannot be applied without further ceremony to the poor generally. In considering the social question we must, therefore, put aside all those sayings of Jesus which obviously refer to the poor in the spiritual sense. These include, for instance, the first Beatitude, whether we accept it in the form in which it appears in Luke or in Matthew. The Beatitudes associated with it make it clear that Jesus was thinking of the poor whose hearts were inwardly open towards God. But, as we have no time to go through all the sayings separately, we must content ourselves with some leading considerations in order to establish the most important points.

Jesus regarded the possession of worldly goods as a grave danger for the soul, as hardening the heart, entangling us in earthly cares, and seducing us into a vulgar life of pleasure. "A rich man shall hardly enter the kingdom of heaven."

The contention that Jesus desired, so to speak, to bring about a general condition of poverty and distress, in order that he might afterwards make it the basis of his kingdom of heaven—a contention which we encounter in different forms—is erroneous. The very opposite is the case. Want he called want, and evil he called evil. Far from showing them any favour, he made the greatest and strongest efforts to combat and destroy them. In this sense, too, his whole activity was a saving activity, that is to say, a struggle against evil and against want. Nay, we might almost think that he over-estimated the depressing load of poverty and affliction; that he occupied himself too much with it; and that, taking the moral bearings of life as a whole, he attributed too great an importance to those forces of sympathy and mercy which are expected to counteract this state of things. But neither, of course, would this view be correct. He knows of a power which he thinks still worse than want and misery, namely, sin; and he knows of a force still more emancipating than mercy, namely, forgiveness. His discourses and actions leave no doubt upon this point. It is certain, therefore, that Jesus never and nowhere wished to keep up poverty and misery, but, on the contrary, he combated them himself and bid others combat them. The Christians who in the course of the Church's history were for countenancing mendicancy and recommending universal pauperisation, or sentimentally coquetted with misery and distress, cannot with any show of reason appeal to him. Upon those, however, who were anxious to devote their whole lives to the preaching of the Gospel and the ministry of the Word—he did not ask this of everyone, but regarded it as a special calling from God and a special gift—upon them he enjoined the renunciation of all that they had, that is to say, all worldly goods. Yet that does not mean that he relegated them to a life of beggary. On the contrary, they were to be certain that they would find their bread and their means of livelihood. What he meant by that we learn from a saying of his which was accidentally omitted from the Gospels, but has been handed down to us by the apostle Paul. In the ninth chapter of his first epistle to the Corinthians he writes: "The Lord hath ordained that they which preach the gospel should live of the gospel." An absence of worldly possessions he required of the ministers of the Word, that is, of the missionaries, in order that they might live entirely for their calling. But he did not mean that they were to beg. This is a Franciscan misconception which is perhaps suggested by Jesus' words but carries us away from his meaning.

In this connexion allow me to digress for a moment from our subject. Those members of the Christian churches who have become professional evangelists or ministers of the Word in their parishes have not, as a rule, found it necessary to follow the Lord's injunction to dispossess themselves of their worldly goods. So far as priests or pastors, as the case may be, and not missionaries, are concerned, it may be said with some justice that the injunction does not refer to them; for it presupposes that a man has undertaken the office of *propagating* the Gospel. It may be said, further, that the Lord's injunctions, over and above those relating to the commandment of love, must not be made into inviolable laws, as otherwise Christian liberty will be impaired, and the high privilege of the Christian religion to adapt its shape to the course of history, free from all constraint, will be prejudiced. But still it may be asked whether it would not have been an extraordinary gain to Christianity if those who are called to be its ministers,—the missionaries and pastors, had followed the Lord's rules. At the very least, it ought to be a strict principle with them to concern themselves with property and worldly goods only so far as will prevent them being a burden to others, and beyond that to renounce them. I entertain no doubt that the time will come when the world will tolerate a life of luxury among those who are charged with the cure of souls as little as it tolerates priestly government. Our feelings in this respect are becoming finer, and that is an advantage. It will no longer be thought fitting, in the higher sense of the word, for anyone to preach resignation and contentment to the poor, who is well off himself, and zealously concerned for the increase of his property. A healthy man may well offer consolation to the sick; but how shall a man of property convince those who have none that worldly goods are of no value? The Lord's injunction that the minister of the Word is to divest himself of worldly possessions will still come to be honoured in the history of his communion.

Jesus laid down no social programme for the suppression of poverty and distress, if by programme we mean a set of definitely prescribed regulations. With economical conditions and contemporary circumstances he did not interfere. Had he become entangled in them; had he given laws which were ever so salutary for Palestine, what would have been gained by it? They would have served the needs of a day, and to-morrow would have been antiquated; to the Gospel they would have been a burden and a source of confusion. We must be careful not to exceed the limits set to such injunctions as " Give to him that asketh thee " and others of a similar kind. They must be understood in connexion with the time and the situation. They refer to the immediate wants of the applicant, which were satisfied with a piece of bread, a drink of water, an article of clothing to cover his nakedness. We must remember that in the Gospel we are in the East, and in circumstances which from an economical point of view are somewhat undeveloped. Jesus was no social

G

reformer. He could say on occasion, "The poor ye have always with you," and thereby, it seems, indicate that the conditions would undergo no essential change. He refused to be a judge between contending heirs, and a thousand problems of economics and social life he would have just as resolutely put aside as the unreasonable demand that he would settle a question of inheritance. Yet again and again people have ventured to deduce some concrete social programme from the Gospel. Even evangelical theologians have made the attempt, and are still making it—an endeavour hopeless in itself and full of danger, but absolutely bewildering and intolerable when people try to "fill up the gaps"—and they are many—to be found in the Gospel with regulations and programmes drawn from the Old Testament.

No religion, not even Buddhism, ever went to work with such an energetic social message, and so strongly identified itself with that message as we see to be the case in the Gospel. How so? Because the words "Love thy neighbour as thyself" were spoken in deep earnest; because with these words Jesus turned a light upon all the concrete relations of life, upon the world of hunger, poverty and misery; because, lastly, he uttered them as a religious, nay, as *the* religious maxim. Let me remind you once more of the parable of the Last Judgment, where the whole question of a man's worth and destiny is made dependent on whether he has practised the love of his neighbour; let me remind you of the other parable of the rich man and poor Lazarus. I should like to cite another story, too, which is little known, because it occurs in this wording not in our four Gospels but in the Gospel of the Hebrews. The story of the rich young man is there handed down as follows :—"A rich man said to the Lord : Master, what good must I do that I may have life ? He answered him : Man, keep the law and the prophets. The other answered : That have I done. He said to him : Go, sell all thy possessions and distribute them to the poor, and come and follow me. Then the rich man began to scratch his head, and the speech did not please him. And the Lord said to him : How canst thou say : I have kept the law and the prophets, as it is written in the law, Love thy neighbour as thyself ? Behold, many of thy brethren, sons of Abraham, lie in dirty rags and die of hunger, and thy house is full of many goods, and nothing comes out of it to them." You observe how Jesus felt the material wants of the poor, and how he deduced a remedy for such distress from the commandment : " Love thy neighbour as thyself." People ought not to speak of loving their neighbours if they can allow men beside them to starve and die in misery. It is not only that the Gospel preaches solidarity and the helping of others ; it is in this message that its real import consists. In this sense it is profoundly socialistic, just as it is also profoundly individualistic, because it establishes the infinite and independent

value of every human soul. Its tendency to union
and brotherliness is not so much an accidental phenomenon in its history as the essential feature of its
character. The Gospel aims at founding a community among men as wide as human life itself and
as deep as human need. As has been truly said, its
object is to transform the socialism which rests on
the basis of conflicting interests into the socialism
which rests on the consciousness of a spiritual unity.
In this sense its social message can never be outbid.
In the course of the ages people's opinions as to
what constitutes "an existence worthy of a man"
have, thank God, become much changed and improved. But Jesus, too, knew of this way of
measuring things. Did he not once refer, almost
bitterly, to his own position : " The foxes have holes,
and the birds of the air have nests : but the Son of
Man hath not where to lay his head " ? A dwelling,
sufficient daily bread, cleanliness—all these needs
he touched upon, and their satisfaction he held to be
necessary, and a condition of earthly life. If a man
cannot procure them for himself, others are to step
in and do it for him. There can be no doubt, therefore, that if Jesus were with us to-day he would side
with those who are making great efforts to relieve
the hard lot of the poor and procure them better
conditions of life. The fallacious principle of the free
play of forces, of the " live and let live " principle—
a better name for it would be the " live and let die "—
is entirely opposed to the Gospel. And it is not as our

servants, but as our brothers, that we are to help the poor.

Lastly, our riches do not belong to us alone. The Gospel has prescribed no regulations as to how we are to use them, but it leaves us in no doubt that we are to regard ourselves not as owners but as admin- istrators in the service of our neighbour. Nay, it almost looks as if Jesus contemplated the possibility of a union among men in which wealth, as private property in the strict sense of the word, was non- existent. Here, however, we touch upon a question which is not easy to decide, and which, perhaps, ought not to be raised at all, because Jesus' eschato- logical ideas and his particular horizon enter into it. Nor is it a question that we need raise. It is the disposition which Jesus kindled in his disciples to- wards poverty and want that is all-important.

The Gospel is a social message, solemn and over- powering in its force ; it is the proclamation of solidarity and brotherliness, in favour of the poor. But the message is bound up with the recognition of the infinite value of the human soul, and is contained in what Jesus said about the kingdom of God. We may also assert that it is an essential part of what he there said. But laws or ordinances or injunctions bidding us forcibly alter the conditions of the age in which we may happen to be living are not to be found in the Gospel.

(3) *The Gospel and the law, or the question of public order.*

The problem dealing with the relation of the Gospel to law embraces two leading questions: (1) the relation of the Gospel to constituted authority; (2) the relation of the Gospel to legal ordinances generally, in so far as they possess a wider range than is covered by the conception "constituted authority." It is not easy to mistake the answer to the first question, but the second is more complicated and beset with greater difficulties; and very diverse opinions are entertained in regard to it.

As to Jesus' relation to the constituted authorities of his day, I need scarcely remind you again in express terms that he was no political revolutionary, and that he laid down no political programme. Although he is sure that his Father would send him twelve legions of angels were he to ask Him, he did not ask Him. When they wanted to make him a king, he disappeared. Ultimately, indeed, when he thought well to reveal himself to the whole nation as the Messiah—how he came to the decision and carried it out are points in which we are left in the dark—he made his entry into Jerusalem as a king; but of the modes of presenting himself which prophecy suggested, he chose that which was most remote from a political manifestation. The way in which he understood his Messianic duty is shown by his driving the buyers and sellers from the temple. In this cleansing of the temple it was not the constituted authorities whom he attacked, but those who had assumed to themselves rights of authority over the soul. In every nation, side by side with the constituted authorities, an unconstituted authority is established, or rather two unconstituted authorities. They are the political church and the political parties. What the political church wants, in the widest sense of the word and under very various guises, is to rule; to get hold of men's souls and bodies, consciences and worldly goods. What political parties want is the same; and when the heads of these parties set themselves up as popular leaders, a terrorism is developed which is often worse than the fear of royal despots. It was not otherwise in Palestine in Jesus' day. The priests and the Pharisees held the nation in bondage and murdered its soul. For this unconstituted "authority" Jesus showed a really emancipating and refreshing disrespect. He was never tired of attacking it—nay, in his struggle with it he roused himself to a state of holy indignation—of exposing its wolfish nature and hypocrisy, and of declaring that its day of judgment was at hand. In whatever domain it had any warrant to act, he accepted it: "Go and show yourselves unto the priests." So far as they really

proclaimed God's law he recognised them : "Whatever they tell you to do, that do." But these
were the people to whom he read the terrible
lecture given in Matthew xxiii.: "Woe unto you,
scribes and Pharisees, hypocrites! for ye are like
unto whited sepulchres, which indeed appear beautiful outward, but are within full of dead men's
bones and of all uncleanness." Towards these
spiritual "authorities," then, he filled his disciples
with a holy want of respect, and even of "King"
Herod he spoke with bitter irony: "Go ye and
tell that fox." On the other hand, so far as we
can judge from the scanty evidence before us, his
attitude towards the real authorities, those who
wielded the sword, was different. He recognised
that they had an actual right to be obeyed, and
he never withdrew his own person from their juris-
diction. Nor are we to understand the commandment against swearing as including an oath taken
before a magistrate. No one with a grain of salt,
as Wellhausen has rightly said, can miss the inner
meaning of this commandment. On the other
hand, we must be careful not to rate Jesus' position in regard to constituted authority too high.
People usually appeal to the often quoted saying:
"Render unto Cæsar the things which are Cæsar's
and unto God the things that are God's." But
this saying is often misunderstood. Wherever it
is explained as meaning that Jesus recognised God
and Cæsar as the two powers which in some way

or other exist side by side, or are even in secret
alliance, it is taken in a wrong sense. Jesus had no
such thought; on the contrary, he spoke of the
two powers as separate and divorced from each
other. God and Cæsar are the lords of two quite
different provinces. Jesus settled the question that
was in dispute by pointing out this difference,
which is so great that no conflict between the
powers can arise. The penny is an earthly coin
and bears Cæsar's image; let it be given, then,
to Cæsar, but—this we may take as the comple-
ment—the soul and all its powers have nothing
to do with Cæsar; they belong to God. In a
word, the all-important matter, in Jesus' view, is
not to mix up the two provinces. When we are
once quite clear about this, then we may go
on to remark on the significance of the fact that
Jesus enjoined compliance with the demand for
payment of the imperial taxes. No doubt it is
important to note that he himself respected the
constituted authorities, and wished to see them
respected; but in regard to the estimate which
he formed of them, what he said is, at the least,
of a neutral character.

On the other hand, we possess another saying of
Jesus in regard to constituted authority which is much
less often quoted, and nevertheless affords us a deeper
insight into the Lord's thoughts than the one which we
have just discussed. Let us consider it for a moment.
The fact that it forms a point of transition to the

consideration of the attitude which Jesus took up in
regard to legal regulations in general also makes it
worth our attention.   In Mark x. 42, we read:
"Jesus called them (*i.e.* his disciples) to him and
saith unto them, Ye know that they which are
accounted to rule over the Gentiles exercise lordship
over them : and their great ones exercise authority
upon them.   But so shall it not be among you :
but whosoever shall be great among you shall be your
minister : and whosoever of you will be the chiefest
shall be servant of all."   Observe here, first of all, the
" transvaluation of values."   Jesus simply reverses the
usual process: to be great and to occupy the foremost
position means, in his view, to serve ; his disciples are
to aim, not at ruling, but at each being all other men's
servant.   Next observe the opinion which he has
of authority as it was then constituted.   Their
functions are based on *force,* and this is the very
reason which, in Jesus' view, puts them outside
the moral sphere ; nay, there is a fundamental
opposition between it and them : " Thus do the
earthly rulers."   Jesus tells his disciples to act
differently.   Law and legal ordinance, as resting
on force only, on actual power and its exercise,
have no moral value.   Nevertheless Jesus did not
command men not to subject themselves to these
authorities ; they were to rate them according to
their value, that is, according to their non-value,
and they were to arrange their own lives on other
principles, namely, on the opposite ; they were not

to use force, but to serve. Here we have already
passed to the general ground of legal ordinance, for
it seems to be an essential feature of all law to secure
observance by force when called in question.

When we approach the second point, the relation
of the Gospel to legal ordinance generally, we again
encounter two different views. One of them—
in modern times more particularly maintained, in
his treatise on Canon Law, by Prof. Sohm of Leipzig,
who presents points of contact with Tolstoi—lays
down that in their respective natures law and the
world of spiritual things are diametrically opposed;
and that it is in contradiction with the character
of the Gospel and the community founded thereon
that the Church has developed any legal ordinances
at all. In his survey of the earliest development
of the Church Prof. Sohm has gone so far as to
see in the moment when Christendom gave a
place in its midst to legal ordinances a second Fall.
Nevertheless he is unwilling to impugn the law
in its own province. But Tolstoi refuses, in the
name of the Gospel, to allow the law any rights
at all. He maintains that the leading principle
of the Gospel is that a man is never to insist upon
his rights, and that not even constituted authority
is to offer any external resistance to evil. Authority
and law are simply to cease. Opposed to Tolstoi
there are others who more or less positively contend
that the Gospel takes law and legal relations under
its protection; that it sanctifies them and thereby

raises them into a divine sphere. These are, briefly, the two leading points of view which are here in conflict.

As regards the latter, there is little that need be said. It is a mockery of the Gospel to say that it protects and sanctifies everything that presents itself as law and legal relation at a given moment. Leaving a thing alone and bearing with it are not the same as sanctioning and preserving it. Nay, it is a serious question whether even bearing with it is not too much to say, and whether Tolstoi is not right. The difficulty of the matter makes it necessary that I should take you back a little way in Jewish history.

For hundreds of years the poor and oppressed in the people of Israel had been crying out for justice. It was a cry which still affects us to-day as we hear it in the words of the prophets and out of the prayers of the Psalmists; but time after time it passed unheeded. None of the legal regulations in force was free from the power of tyrannical authorities, to be distorted and exploited by them just as they saw fit. In speaking of legal regulations and their exercise, and in examining Jesus' attitude towards them, we must not straightway think of our own legal relations, which have grown up partly on the basis of Christianity. Jesus was of a nation the greater part of which had for generations been in vain asking for their rights, and which was familiar with law only in the form

of force. The necessary consequence was that in
such a nation a feeling of despair arose in regard
to the law; despair, as much of the possibility of
ever getting justice on earth as, conversely, of the
moral claim of law to have any validity at all.
We can see something of this temper even in the
Gospel. But there is a second consideration which
is a standing corrective to this temper. Jesus, like
all truly religious minds, was firmly convinced that
in the end God will do justice. If He does not do
it here, He will do it in the Beyond, and that is
the main point. In this connexion there was,
in Jesus' view, nothing objectionable in the idea
of law in the sense of a just recompense; it was a
lofty, nay, a dominating idea. Just recompense is
the function of God's majesty; to what extent it
is modified by His mercy is a question which we
need not here consider. The contention that Jesus
took a depreciatory view of law as such, and of the
exercise of law, cannot be sustained for a moment.
On the contrary, everyone is to get his rights;
nay more, his disciples are one day to share in
administering God's justice and themselves judge.
It was only the justice which was exercised with
violence and therefore unjustly, the justice which
lay upon the nation like a tyrannical and bloody
decree, that he set aside. He believed in true
justice, and he was certain, too, that it would
prevail; so certain, that he did not think it necessary for justice to use force in order to remain justice.

This brings us to the last point. We possess
a number of Jesus' sayings in which he directs
his disciples to renounce all their lawful demands,
and so forego their just rights. You all know
those sayings. Let me remind you of one only :
"But I say unto you, That ye resist not evil, but
whosoever shall smite thee on thy right cheek,
turn to him the other also. And if any man will
sue thee at the law, and take away thy coat, let
him have thy cloak also." The demand here made
seems to proscribe law and disorganise all the
legal relations of life. Again and again these
words have been appealed to with the object of
showing either that Christianity is incompatible
with life as it actually is, or that Christendom has
fallen away from the principles of its Master. By
way of reply to this argument the following
observations may be made :—(i.) Jesus was, as
we have seen, steeped in the conviction that God
does justice ; in the end, therefore, the oppressor
will not prevail, but the oppressed will get his
rights. (ii.) Earthly rights are in themselves of
little account, and it does not much matter if we
lose them. (iii.) The world is in such an unhappy
state, injustice has got so much the upper hand in
it, that the victim of oppression is incapable of
making good his rights even if he tries. (iv.) As
God—and this is the main point—mingles His
justice with mercy, and lets His sun shine on the
just and on the unjust, so Jesus' disciple is to show

love to his enemies and disarm them by gentleness.
Such are the thoughts which underlie those lofty
sayings and at the same time set them their due
limits. And is the demand which they contain
really so supramundane, so impossible? Do we
not in the circle of our family and friends advise
those who belong to us to act in the same way,
and not to return evil for evil and abuse for abuse?
What family, what society, could continue to exist,
if every member of it were anxious only to pursue
his own rights, and did not learn to renounce them
even when attacked? Jesus regards his disciples
as a circle of friends, and he looks out beyond this
circle to a league of brothers which will take shape
in the future and extend. But, we are asked, are
we in all cases to renounce the pursuit of our rights
in the face of our enemies? are we to use no weapons
but those of gentleness? To speak with Tolstoi, are
the magistrates not to inflict punishment, and thereby to be effaced? are nations not to fight for house
and home when they are wantonly attacked? I
venture to maintain that, when Jesus spoke the
words which I have quoted, he was not thinking
of such cases, and that to interpret them in this
direction involves a clumsy and dangerous misconception of their meaning. Jesus never had anyone
but the individual in mind, and the abiding disposition of the heart in love. To say that this
disposition cannot coexist with the pursuit of
one's own rights, with the conscientious administra-

tion of justice, and with the stern punishment of crime, is a piece of prejudice, in support of which we may appeal in vain to the letter of those sayings, which did not aim at being laws or, therefore, at prescribing regulations. This much, however, must be added, in order that the loftiness of the demand which the Gospel makes may be in no way abated: Jesus' disciple ought to be able to renounce the pursuit of his rights, and ought to co-operate in forming a nation of brothers, in which justice is done, no longer by the aid of force, but by free obedience to the good, and which is united not by legal regulations but by the ministry of love.

LECTURE VII.

WE were occupied in the last lecture with the relation of the Gospel to law and legal ordinance. We saw that Jesus was convinced that God does, and will do, justice. We saw, further, that he demanded of his disciples that they should be able to renounce their rights. In giving expression to this demand, far from having all the circumstances of his own time in mind, still less the more complex conditions of a later age, he has one and one only present to his soul, namely, the relation of every man to the kingdom of God. Because a man is to sell all that he has in order to buy the pearl of great price, so he must also be able to abandon his earthly rights and subordinate everything to that highest relation. But in connexion with this message of his, Jesus opens up to us the prospect of a union among men, which is held together not by any legal ordinance, but by the rule of love, and where a man conquers his enemy by gentleness. It is a high and glorious ideal, and we have received it from the very foundation of our religion. It ought to float before our eyes as the goal and guiding star of our historical development.

113   H

Whether mankind will ever attain to it, who can say?
but we can and ought to approximate to it, and in
these days—otherwise than two or three hundred
years ago—we feel a moral obligation in this
direction. Those of us who possess more delicate
and therefore more prophetic perceptions no longer
regard the kingdom of love and peace as a mere
Utopia.

But for this very reason there are many among
us to-day upon whom a very serious and difficult
question presses with redoubled force. We see a
whole class struggling for its rights; or, rather, we
see it struggling to extend and increase its rights.
Is that compatible with the Christian temper? Does
not the Gospel forbid such a struggle? Have we not
been told that we are to renounce the rights we have,
to say nothing of trying to get more? Must we,
then, as Christians, recall the labouring classes from
the struggle for their rights, and exhort them only
to patience and submission?

The problem with which we have here to do is also
stated more or less in the form of an accusation against
Christianity. Earnest men in political circles of a
socialistic tendency, who would gladly be guided by
Jesus Christ, complain that in this matter the Gospel
leaves them in the lurch. They say that it imposes
restraint upon aspirations which with a clear conscience they feel to be justified; that in requiring
absolute meekness and submission it disarms everyone who wants to fight; that it narcotises, as it were,

all real energy. Some say this with pain and regret, others with satisfaction. The latter assert that they always knew that the Gospel was not for the healthy and the strong, but for the broken-down ; that it knows, and wants to know, nothing of the fact that life, and especially modern life, is a struggle, a struggle for one's own rights. What answer are we to give them ?

My own opinion is that these statements and complaints are made by people who have never yet clearly realised with what it is that the Gospel has to do, and who rashly and improperly connect it with earthly things. The Gospel makes its appeal to the inner man, who, whether he is well or wounded, in a happy position or a miserable, obliged to spend his earthly life fighting or quietly maintaining what he has won, always remains the same. " My kingdom is not of this world "; it is no earthly kingdom that the Gospel establishes. These words not only exclude such a political theocracy as the Pope aims at setting up and all worldly dominion ; they have a much wider range. Negatively they forbid all direct and formal interference of religion in worldly affairs. Positively what the Gospel says is this : Whoever you may be, and whatever your position, whether bondman or free, whether fighting or at rest—your real task in life is always the same. There is only *one* relation and *one* idea which you must not violate, and in the face of which all others are only transient wrappings and vain show : to be a child of God and a citizen of His kingdom, and to exercise love. How you are to maintain yourself in this life on earth, and in what way you are to serve your neighbour, is left to you and your own liberty of action. This is what the apostle Paul understood by the Gospel, and I do not believe that he misunderstood it. Then let us fight, let us struggle, let us get justice for the oppressed, let us order the circumstances of the world as we with a clear conscience can, and as we may think best for our neighbour; but do not let us expect the Gospel to afford us any direct help; let us make no selfish demands for ourselves; and let us not forget that the world passes away, not only with the lusts thereof, but also with its regulations and its goods! Once more be it said: the Gospel knows only one goal, one idea; and it demands of a man that he shall never put them aside. If the exhortation to renounce takes, in a harsh and onesided way, a foremost place in Jesus' words, we must be careful to keep before our eyes the paramount and exclusive claims of the relation to God and the idea of love. The Gospel is above all questions of mundane development; it is concerned not with material things but with the souls of men.

With this we have already passed to the next question which was to occupy our attention, and we have half answered it.

(4) *The Gospel and work, or the question of civilisation.*

The points which we shall have to consider here are essentially the same as those which we emphasized in regard to the question just discussed; and we shall therefore be able to proceed more concisely.

Jesus' teaching has been felt again and again, but above all in our own day, to exhibit no interest in any systematic work or calling, and no appreciation of those ideal possessions which go by the name of Art and Science. Nowhere, people say, does Jesus summon men to labour and to put their hands to the work of progress; in vain shall we look in his words for any expression of pleasure in vigorous activity; these ideal possessions lay far beyond his field of vision. In that last, unhappy book of his, *The Old Faith and the New*, David Friedrich Strauss gave particularly harsh expression to this feeling. He speaks of a fundamental defect in the Gospel, which he considers antiquated and useless because out of sympathy with the progress of civilisation. But long before Strauss the Pietistic movement exhibited the same sort of feeling. The Pietists tried to evade the difficulty in a way of their own. They started from the position that Jesus must be able to serve as a direct example for all men, whatever their calling; that he must have proved himself in all the situations in which a man can be placed. They admitted that

a cursory examination of Jesus' life disclosed the fact
that this requirement was not fulfilled; but they
were of opinion that on a closer inspection it would
be found that he was really the best bricklayer, the
best tailor, the best judge, the best scholar, and so
on, and that he had the best knowledge and understanding for everything. They turned and twisted
what Jesus said and did until it was made to express
and corroborate what they wanted. Although it was
a childish attempt which they made, the problem of
which they were sensible was nevertheless of some
moment. They felt that their consciences and their
callings bound them to a definite activity and a
definite business; they were clear that they ought
not to become monks; and yet they were anxious to
practise the imitation of Christ in the full sense.
They felt, then, that he must have stood in the same
situation as they themselves, and that his horizon
must have been the same as theirs.

Here we have the same case as we dealt with in
the last section, only covering a wider field. It is
the ancient and constantly recurring error, that the
Gospel has to do with the affairs of the world, and
that it is its business to prescribe how they are to
be carried on. Here, too, the old and almost in-
eradicable tendency of mankind to rid itself of its
freedom and responsibility in higher things and
subject itself to a law, comes into play. It is much
easier, in fact, to resign oneself to any, even the
sternest, kind of authority, than to live in the liberty

of the good. But apart from this, the question
remains : Is it not a real defect in the Gospel that
it betrays so little sympathy with the business of
life, and is out of touch with the *humaniora* in the
sense of science, art, and civilisation generally ?

I answer, in the first place : What would have
been gained if it had not possessed this "defect"?
Suppose that it had taken an active interest in all
those efforts, would it not have become entangled
in them, or, at any rate, have incurred the risk
of appearing to be so entangled ?   Labour, art,
science, the progress of civilisation—these are not
things which exist in the abstract ; they exist in
the particular phase of an age. The Gospel, then,
would have had to ally itself with them.   But phases
change.   In the Roman Church of to-day we see
how heavily religion is burdened by being connected with a particular epoch of civilisation.
In the Middle Ages this Church, anxious to parti-
cipate to the full in all questions of progress and
civilisation, gave them form and shape, and laid
down their laws. Insensibly, however, the Church
identified its sacred inheritance and its peculiar
mission with the knowledge, the maxims, and the
interests which it then acquired ; so that it is now,
as it were, firmly pinned down to the philosophy,
the political economy, in short, to the whole
civilisation, of the Middle Ages. On the other
hand, what a service the Gospel has rendered to
mankind by having sounded the notes of re-

ligion in mighty chords and banished every other
melody!

In the second place, labour and the progress of
civilisation are, no doubt, very precious, and summon
us to strenuous exertion. But they do not comprise
the highest ideal. They are incapable of filling
the soul with real satisfaction. Although work
may give pleasure, that is only one aspect of the
matter. I have always found that the people who
talk loudest about the pleasure which work affords
make no very great efforts themselves; whilst those
who are uninterruptedly engaged in heavy labour
are hesitating in its praises. As a matter of fact,
there is a great deal of hypocritical twaddle talked
about work. Three-fourths of it and more is nothing
but stupefying toil, and the man who really works
hard shares the poet's aspirations as he looks forward to evening :

Head, hands and feet rejoice: the work is done.

And, then, think of the results of all this labour!
When a man has done a piece of work, he would
like to do it over again, and the knowledge of its
defects falls heavily on soul and conscience. No!
it is not in so far as we work that we live, but in
so far as we rejoice in the love of others, and ourselves exercise love. Faust is right : Labour which
is labour and nothing else becomes an aversion.
We long for the streams of living water, and for the
spring itself from which those waters flow :

Man sehnt sich nach des Lebens Bächen,
Ach! nach des Lebens Quelle hin.

Labour is a valuable safety-valve and useful in keeping off greater ills, but it is not in itself an absolute good, and we cannot include it amongst our ideals. The same may be said of the progress of civilisation. It is of course to be welcomed ; but the piece of progress in which we delight to-day becomes something mechanical by to-morrow, and leaves us cold. The man of any deep feeling will thankfully receive anything that the development of progress may bring him ; but he knows very well that his situation inwardly — the problems that agitate him and the fundamental position in which he stands—is not essentially, nay is scarcely even unessentially, altered by it all. It is only for a moment that it seems as if something new were coming, and a man were being really relieved of his burden. Gentlemen, when a man grows older and sees more deeply into life, he does not find, if he possesses any inner world at all, that he is advanced by the external march of things, by " the progress of civilisation." Nay, he feels himself, rather, where he was before, and forced to seek the sources of strength which his forefathers also sought. He is forced to make himself a native of the kingdom of God, the kingdom of the Eternal, the kingdom of Love ; and he comes to understand that it was only of this kingdom that Jesus Christ desired to speak and to testify, and he is grateful to him for it.

But, in the third place, Jesus had a strong and positive conviction of the aggressive and forward character of his message. " I am come to send fire on the earth, and "—he added—" what will I if it be already kindled ? " The fire of the judgment and the forces of love were what he wanted to summon up, so as to create a new humanity. If he spoke of these forces of love in the simple manner corresponding to the conditions nearest at hand—the feeding of the hungry, the clothing of the naked, the visiting of the sick and those in prison—it is nevertheless clear that a great inward transformation of the humanity which he saw in the mirror of the little nation in Palestine hovered before his eyes : " One is your master, and all ye are brethren." The last hour is come ; but in the last hour from a small seed a tree is to grow up which shall spread its branches far and wide. Further, he was revealing the knowledge of God, and he was certain that it would ripen the young, strengthen the weak, and make them God's champions. Knowledge of God is the spring that is to fructify the barren field, and pour forth streams of living water. In this sense he spoke of it as the highest and the only necessary good, as the condition of all edification, and, we may also say, of all true growth and progress. Lastly, he saw on his horizon not only the judgment, but also a kingdom of justice, of love, and of peace, which, though it came from heaven, was nevertheless for this earth. When it is to come, he himself knows not—the hour is known to the Father only; but he knows how and by what means it will spread ; and side by side with the highly-coloured, dramatic pictures which pass through his soul there are quiet perceptions which are fixed and steady. He sees the vineyard of God on this earth and God calling His labourers into it—happy the man who receives a call! They labour in the vineyard, stand no longer idle in the market-place, and at last receive their reward. Or take the parable of the talents distributed in order to be employed, and therefore not to be buried in a napkin. A day's work, labour, increase, progress—he sees it all, but placed at the service of God and neighbour, encircled by the light of the Eternal, and removed from the service of transient things.

To sum up what we have here tried to indicate : Is the complaint from which we started at the beginning of this section justified ? Ought we really to desire that the Gospel had adapted itself to "the progress of civilisation" ? Here too, I think, we have to learn from the Gospel and not to find fault with it. It tells us of the real work which humanity has to accomplish, and we ought not to meet its message by entrenching ourselves behind our miserable "work of civilisation." "The image of Christ," as a modern historian justly says, "remains the sole basis of all moral culture, and in the measure in which it succeeds in making its light penetrate is the moral culture of the nations increased or diminished."

(5) *The Gospel and the Son of God, or the Christological question.*

We now pass from the sphere of questions of which we have been treating hitherto. The four previous questions are all intimately connected with one another. Failure to answer them rightly always proceeds from not rating the Gospel high enough; from somehow or other dragging it down to the level of mundane questions and entangling it in them. Or, to put the matter differently: The forces of the Gospel appeal to the deepest foundations of human existence and to them only; it is there alone that their leverage is applied. If a man is unable, then, to go down to the root of humanity, and has no feeling for it and no knowledge of it, he will fail to understand the Gospel, and will then try to profane it or else complain that it is of no use.

We now, however, approach quite a different problem : What position did Jesus himself take up towards the Gospel while he was proclaiming it, and how did he wish himself to be accepted? We are not yet dealing with the way in which his disciples accepted him, or the place which they gave him in their hearts, and the opinion which they formed of him; we are now speaking only of his own testimony of himself. But the question is one which lands us in the great sphere of controverted questions which cover the history of the Church

from the first century up to our own time. In
the course of this controversy men put an end to
brotherly fellowship for the sake of a *nuance*; and
thousands were cast out, condemned, loaded with
chains and done to death. It is a gruesome story.
On the question of "Christology" men beat their
religious doctrines into terrible weapons, and spread
fear and intimidation everywhere. This attitude
still continues : Christology is treated as though the
Gospel had no other problem to offer, and the accompanying fanaticism is still rampant in our own
day. Who can wonder at the difficulty of the
problem, weighed down as it is with such a burden
of history and made the sport of parties? Yet anyone who will look at our Gospels with unprejudiced
eyes will not find that the question of Jesus' own
testimony is insoluble. So much of it, however, as
remains obscure and mysterious to our minds ought
to remain so ; as Jesus meant it to be, and as in
the very nature of the problem it is. It is only in
pictures that we can give it expression. "There
are phenomena which cannot, without the aid of
symbols, be brought within the range of the understanding."

Before we examine Jesus' own testimony about
himself, two leading points must be established.
In the first place, he desired no other belief in his
person and no other attachment to it than is contained in the keeping of his commandments. Even
in the fourth Gospel, in which Jesus' person often

seems to be raised above the contents of the Gospel, the idea is still clearly formulated : " If ye love me, keep my commandments." He must himself have found, during his labours, that some people honoured, nay, even trusted him, without troubling themselves about the contents of his message. It was to them that he addressed the reprimand : " Not everyone that saith unto me Lord, Lord, shall enter into the kingdom of Heaven ; but he that doeth the will of my Father." To lay down any " doctrine " about his person and his dignity independently of the Gospel was, then, quite outside his sphere of ideas. In the second place, he described the Lord of heaven and earth as his God and his Father ; as the Greater, and as Him who is alone good. He is certain that everything which he has and everything which he is to accomplish comes from this Father. He prays to Him ; he subjects himself to His will ; he struggles hard to find out what it is and to fulfil it. Aim, strength, understanding, the issue, and the hard *must*, all come from the Father. This is what the Gospels say, and it cannot be turned and twisted. This feeling, praying, working, struggling and suffering individual is a man who in the face of his God also associates himself with other men.

These two facts mark out, as it were, the boundaries of the ground covered by Jesus' testimony of himself. They do not, it is true, give us any positive information as to what he said ; but we shall understand what he really meant by his

testimony if we look closely at the two descriptions
which he gave of himself: the *Son of God* and the
Messiah (the Son of David, the Son of Man).

The description of himself as the Son of God,
Messianic though it may have been in its original
conception, lies very much nearer to our modern
way of thinking than the other, for Jesus himself
gave a meaning to this conception which almost
takes it out of the class of messianic ideas, or at all
events does not make its inclusion in that class
necessary to a proper understanding of it. On the
other hand, if we do not desire to be put off with
a lifeless word, the description of himself as the
Messiah is at first blush one that is quite foreign
to our ideas. Without some explanation we cannot understand, nay, unless we are Jews, we cannot
understand at all, what this post of honour means
and what rank and character it possesses. It is
only when we have ascertained its meaning by
historical research that we can ask whether the
word has a significance which in any way survives
the destruction of the husk in which it took shape
in Jewish political life.

Let us first of all consider the designation, "Son
of God." Jesus in one of his discourses made it
specially clear why and in what sense he gave
himself this name. The saying is to be found in
Matthew, and not, as might perhaps have been
expected, in John : "No man knoweth the Son
but the Father; neither knoweth any man the

Father, save the Son, and he to whomsoever the
Son will reveal him." It is " knowledge of God "
that makes the sphere of the Divine Sonship. It
is in this knowledge that he came to know the
sacred Being who rules heaven and earth as Father,
as *his* Father. The consciousness which he possessed of being *the Son of God* is, therefore, nothing but the practical consequence of knowing God
as the Father and as his Father. Rightly understood, the name of Son means nothing but the
knowledge of God. Here, however, two observations
are to be made : Jesus is convinced that he knows
God in a way in which no one ever knew Him
before, and he knows that it is his vocation to
communicate this knowledge of God to others by
word and by deed—and with it the knowledge
that men are God's children. In this consciousness he knows himself to be the Son called and
instituted of God, to be *the* Son of God, and hence
he can say : *My* God and *my* Father, and into
this invocation he puts something which belongs
to no one but himself. How he came to this consciousness of the unique character of his relation to
God as a Son ; how he came to the consciousness
of his power, and to the consciousness of the
obligation and the mission which this power carries
with it, is his secret, and no psychology will
ever fathom it. The confidence with which John
makes him address the Father : " Thou lovedst
me before the foundation of the world " is un-

doubtedly the direct reflection of the certainty
with which Jesus himself spoke. Here all research
must stop. We are not even able to say when
it was that he first knew himself as the Son, and
whether he at once completely identified himself
with this idea and let his individuality be absorbed
in it, or whether it formed an inner problem which
kept him in constant suspense. No one could
fathom this mystery who had not had a parallel
experience. A prophet may, if he chooses, try
to raise the veil, but, for our part, we must be
content with the fact that this Jesus who preached
humility and knowledge of self, nevertheless named
himself and himself alone as *the Son of God*. He
is certain that he knows the Father, that he is
to bring this knowledge to all men, and that
thereby he is doing the work of God. Among
all the works of God this is the greatest ; it is
the aim and end of all creation. The work is given
to him to do, and in God's strength he will accomplish it. It was out of this feeling· of power
and in the prospect of victory that he uttered the
words : "The Father hath committed all things
unto me." Again and again in the history of
mankind men of God have come forward in the
sure consciousness of possessing a divine message,
and of being compelled, whether they will or not,
to deliver it. But the message has always happened to be imperfect ; in this spot or that, defective ;
bound up with political or particularistic elements ;

I

designed to meet the circumstances of the moment ;
and very often the prophet did not stand the test
of being himself an example of his message. But
in this case the message brought was of the profoundest and most comprehensive character ; it went
to the very root of mankind and, although set in
the framework of the Jewish nation, it addressed
itself to the whole of humanity — the message
from God the Father. Defective it is not, and its
real kernel may be readily freed from the inevitable husk of contemporary form. Antiquated it
is not, and in life and strength it still triumphs
to-day over all the past. He who delivered it has
as yet yielded his place to no man, and to human
life he still to-day gives a meaning and an aim—
he *the Son of God.*

This already brings us to the other designation
which Jesus gave of himself : *the Messiah.* Before
I attempt briefly to explain it, I ought to mention
that some scholars of note — and among them,
Wellhausen—have expressed a doubt whether Jesus
described himself as the Messiah. In that doubt
I cannot concur ; nay, I think that it is only by
wrenching what the evangelists tell us off its
hinges that the opinion can be maintained. The
very expression " Son of Man "—that Jesus used it
is beyond question—seems to me to be intelligible
only in a Messianic sense. To say nothing of anything else, such a story as that of Christ's entry
into Jerusalem would have to be simply expunged,

if the theory is to be maintained that he did not consider himself the promised Messiah and also desire to be accepted as such. Moreover, the forms in which Jesus expressed what he felt about his own consciousness and his vocation become quite incomprehensible unless they are taken as the outcome of the Messianic idea. Finally, the positive arguments which are advanced in support of the theory are either so very weak, or else so highly questionable, that we may remain quite sure that Jesus called himself the Messiah.

The idea of a Messiah and the Messianic notions generally, as they existed in Jesus' day, had been developed on two combined lines, on the line of the kings and on that of the prophets. Alien influences had also been at work, and the whole idea was transfigured by the ancient expectation that God Himself in visible form would take up the government of His people. The leading features of the Messianic idea were taken from the Israelitish kingdom in the ideal splendour in which it was invested after the kingdom itself had disappeared. Memories of Moses and of the great prophets also played a part in it. In the following lecture we shall briefly show what shapes the Messianic hopes had assumed up to Jesus' time, and in what way he took them up and transformed them.

LECTURE VIII.

ALTHOUGH the Messianic doctrines prevalent in the Jewish nation in Jesus' day were not a positive "dogma," and had no connexion with the legal precepts which were so rigidly cultivated, they formed an essential element of the hopes, religious and political, which the nation entertained for the future. They were of no very definite character, except in certain fundamental features; beyond these the greatest differences prevailed. The old prophets had looked forth to a glorious future in which God would Himself come down, destroy the enemies of Israel, and work justice, peace, and joy. At the same time, however, they had also promised that a wise and mighty king of the house of David would appear and bring this glorious state of things to pass. They had ended by indicating the people of Israel itself as the Son of God, chosen from amongst the nations of the world. These three views exercised a determining influence in the subsequent elaboration of the Messianic ideas. The hope of a glorious future for the people of Israel remained the frame into which all expectations

were fitted, but in the two centuries before Christ
the following factors were added : (i.) The extension
of their historical horizon strengthened the interest
of the Jews in the nations of the world, introduced
the notion of "mankind" as a whole and brought
it within the sphere of the expected end, including,
therefore, the operations of the Messiah. The day
of judgment is regarded as extending to the whole
world, and the Messiah not only as judging the
world but as ruling it as well. (ii.) In early times,
although the moral purification of the people had
been thought of in connexion with the glorious
future, the destruction of Israel's enemies seemed to
be the main consideration ; but now the feeling of
moral responsibility and the knowledge of God as
the Holy one became more active ; the view pre-
vails that the Messianic age demands a holy people,
and that the judgment to come must of necessity
also be a judgment upon a part of Israel itself.
(iii.) As individualism became a stronger force,
so the relation of God to the individual was
prominently emphasized. The individual Israelite
comes to feel that he is in the midst of his people,
and he begins to look upon it as a sum of individuals ;
the individual belief in Providence appears side by
side with the political belief, and combines with
the feeling of personal worth and responsibility ;
and in connexion with the expectation of the end,
we get the first dawn of the hope of an eternal
life and the fear of eternal punishment. The pro-

ducts of this inner development are an interest
in personal salvation, and a belief in the resurrection, and the roused conscience is no longer able
to hope for a glorious future for all in view of
the open profanity of the people and the power
of sin; only a remnant will be saved. (iv.) The
expectations for the future become more and more
transcendent; they are increasingly shifted to the
realm of the supernatural and the supramundane;
something quite new comes down from heaven to
earth, and the new course on which the world enters
severs it from the old; nay, this earth, transfigured
as it will be, is no longer the final goal; the idea
of an absolute bliss arises, whose abode can only
be heaven itself. (v.) The personality of the long-
expected Messiah is sharply distinguished, as well
from the idea of an earthly king, as from the idea
of the people as a whole, and from the idea of
God. Although he appears as a man amongst men,
the Messiah retains scarcely any Messianic traits.
He is represented as with God from the first
beginnings of time; he comes down from heaven,
and accomplishes his work by superhuman means;
the moral traits in the picture formed of him come
into prominence; he is the perfectly just man who
fulfils all the commandments. Nay, the idea that
others benefit by his merits forces its way in.
The notion, however, of a suffering Messiah, which
might seem to be suggested by Isaiah liii., is not
reached.

But none of these speculations succeeded in displacing the older and simpler conceptions, or in banishing that original, patriotic, and political interpretation of them with which the great majority of the people were familiar. God Himself assuming the sceptre, destroying His enemies, founding the Israelitish kingdom of the world, and availing Himself of a kingly champion for the purpose ; every man sitting under his own fig-tree, in his own vineyard, enjoying the fruits of peace, with his foot upon the neck of his enemies—that was, after all, still the most popular conception of the coming of the Messiah, and it was fixed in the minds even of those who were at the same time attracted to higher views. But a portion of the people had undoubtedly awakened to the feeling that the kingdom of God presupposes a moral condition of a corresponding character, and that it could come only to a righteous people. Some looked to acquiring this righteousness by means of a punctilious observance of the law, and no zeal that they could show for it was enough ; others, under the influences of a deeper self-knowledge, began to have a dim idea that the righteousness which they so ardently desired could itself come only from the hand of God, and that in order to shake off the burden of sin—for they had begun to be tortured by an inner sense of it—divine assistance, and divine grace and mercy, were needful.

Thus in Christ's time there was a surging chaos of disparate feeling, as well as of contradictory theory, in regard to this one matter. At no other time, perhaps, in the history of religion, and in no other people, were the most extreme antitheses so closely associated under the binding influence of religion. At one moment the horizon seems as narrow as the circle of the hills which surround Jerusalem; at another it embraces all mankind. Here everything is put upon a high plane and regarded from the spiritual and moral point of view; and there, at but a stone's throw, the whole drama seems as though it must close with a political victory for the nation. In one group all the forces of divine trust and confidence are disengaged, and the upright man struggles through to a solemn "Nevertheless"; in another, every religious impulse is stifled by a morally obtuse, patriotic fanaticism.

The idea which was formed of the Messiah must have been as contradictory as the hopes to which it was meant to respond. Not only were people's formal notions about him continually changing— questions were being raised, for instance, as to the sort of bodily nature which he would have; above all, his inmost character and the work to which he was to be called appeared in diverse lights. But wherever the moral and really religious elements had begun to get the upper hand, people were forced to abandon the image of the political and warlike ruler, and let that of *the prophet*, which had always to some extent helped to form the general notions about the Messiah, take its place. That he would bring God near; that somehow or other he would do justice; that he would deliver from the burden of torment within—this was what was hoped of him. The story of John the Baptist as related in our Gospels makes it clear that there were devout men in the Jewish nation at that time who were expecting a Messiah in this form, or at least did not absolutely reject the idea. We learn from that story that some were disposed to take John for the Messiah. What elasticity the Messianic ideas must have possessed, and how far, in certain circles, they must have travelled from the form which they originally assumed, when this very unkinglike preacher of repentance, clad in a garment of camel's hair, and with no message but that the nation had degenerated and its day of judgment was at hand, could be taken for the Messiah himself. And when the Gospels go on to tell us that not a few among the people took Jesus for the Messiah only because he taught as one with authority, and worked miraculous cures, how fundamentally the idea of the Messiah seems to be changed! They regarded this saving activity, it is true, only as the beginning of his mission; they expected that the wonder-worker would presently throw off his disguise and "set up the kingdom"; but all that we are concerned with here is that they were capable of welcoming as the promised one a man whose origin and previous life they knew, and who had as yet done nothing but preach repentance and proclaim that the kingdom of heaven was at

hand. We shall never fathom the inward development by which Jesus passed from the assurance that
he was the Son of God to the other assurance that
he was the promised Messiah. But when we see
that the idea which others as well had formed of
the Messiah at that time had, by a slow process of
change, developed entirely new features, and had
passed from a political and religious idea into a
spiritual and religious one—when we see this, the
problem no longer wears a character of complete
isolation. That John the Baptist and the twelve
disciples acknowledged Jesus to be the Messiah;
that the positive estimate which they formed of his
person did not lead them to reject the shape in which
he appeared, but, on the contrary, was fixed in this
very shape, is a proof of the flexible character of the
Messianic idea at the time, and also explains how it
was that Jesus could himself adopt it. "Strength is
made perfect in weakness." That there is a divine
strength and glory which stands in no need of
earthly power and earthly splendour, nay, excludes
them; that there is a majesty of holiness and love
which saves and blesses those upon whom it lays
hold, was what he knew who in spite of his lowliness
called himself the Messiah, and the same must have
been felt by those who recognised him as the king of
Israel anointed of God.

How Jesus arrived at the consciousness of being
the Messiah we cannot explain, but still there are
some points connected with the question which can

be established. An inner event which Jesus experienced at his baptism was in the view of the oldest tradition the foundation of his Messianic consciousness. It is not an experience which is subject to any criticism; still less are we in a position to contradict it. On the contrary, there is a strong probability that when he made his public appearance he had already settled accounts with himself. The evangelists preface their account of his public activity with a curious story of a temptation. This story assumes that he was already conscious of being the Son of God and the one who was intrusted with the all-important work for God's people, and that he had overcome the temptations which this consciousness brought with it. When John sent to him from prison to ask:—"Art thou he that should come, or do we look for another?" the answer which he sent necessarily led his questioner to understand that he was the Messiah, but at the same time showed him how Jesus conceived the Messianic office. Then came the day at Cæsarea Philippi, when Peter acknowledged him as the expected Messiah, and Jesus joyfully confirmed what he said. This was followed by the question to the Pharisees "What think ye of Christ, whose son is he?"—the scene which ended with the fresh question: "If David then call him Lord, how is he his son?" Lastly, there was the entry into Jerusalem before the whole people, together with the cleansing of the temple; actions which were equivalent to a public declaration that he was the Messiah. But his first unequivocal Messianic action was also his last. It was followed by the crown of thorns and the cross.

I have said that it is probable that when Jesus made his public appearance he had already settled accounts with himself, and was therefore clear about his mission as well. By this, however, I do not mean that, so far as he himself was concerned, he had nothing more to learn in the course of it. Not only had he to learn to suffer, and to look forward to the cross with confidence in God, but the consciousness of his Sonship was now for the first time to be brought to the test. The knowledge of the "work" which the Father had intrusted to him could not be developed except by labour and by victory over all opposition. What a moment it must have been for him when he recognised that he was the one of whom the prophets had spoken; when he saw the whole history of his nation from Abraham and Moses downwards in the light of his own mission; when he could no longer avoid the conviction that he was the promised Messiah! No longer avoid it; for how can we refuse to believe that at first he must have felt this knowledge to be a terrible burden? Yet in saying this we have gone too far; and there is nothing more that we can say. But in this connexion we can understand that the evangelist John was right in making Jesus testify over and over again : "I have not spoken of myself; but the Father which sent me ; he gave me a commandment, what I should say, and what I should speak." And again : " For I am not alone, but I and the Father that sent me."

But however we may conceive the " Messiah," it was an assumption that was simply necessary if the man who felt the inward call was to gain an absolute recognition within the lines of Jewish religious history—the profoundest and maturest history that any nation ever possessed, nay, as the future was to show, the true religious history for all mankind. The idea of the Messiah became the means—in the first instance for the devout of his own nation—of effectively setting the man who knew that he was the Son of God, and was doing the work of God, on the throne of history. But when it had accomplished this, its mission was exhausted. Jesus was the " Messiah," and was not the Messiah ; and he was not the Messiah, because he left the idea far behind him ; because he put a meaning into it which was too much for it to bear. Although the idea may strike us as strange we can still feel some of its meaning ; an idea which captivated a whole nation for centuries, and in which it deposited all its ideals, cannot be quite unintelligible. In the prospect of a Messianic period we see once more the old hope of a golden age ; the hope which, when moralised, must necessarily be the goal of every vigorous movement in human life and forms an inalienable element in the religious view of history; in the expectation of a personal Messiah we see an expression of the fact that it is *persons* who form the saving element in history, and that if a union of mankind is ever to come about by their deepest forces and highest aims being brought into accord, this same mankind must agree to acknowledge *one* lord and master. But beyond this there is no other meaning and no other value to be attached to the Messianic idea; Jesus himself deprived it of them.

With the recognition of Jesus as the Messiah the closest possible connexion was established, for every devout Jew, between Jesus' message and his person; for it is in the Messiah's activity that God Himself comes to His people, and the Messiah who does God's work and sits at the right hand of God in the clouds of heaven has a right to be worshipped. But what attitude did Jesus himself take up towards his Gospel? Does he assume a position in it? To this question there are two answers; one negative and one positive.

In those leading features of it which we described in the earlier lectures the whole of the Gospel is contained, and we must keep it free from the intrusion of any alien element: God and the soul, the soul and its God. There was no doubt in Jesus' mind that God could be found, and had been found, in the law and the prophets. "He hath showed thee, O Man, what is good ; and what doth the Lord require of thee, but to do justly, and to love mercy, and to walk humbly with thy God." He takes the publican in the temple, the widow and her mite, the lost son, as his examples ; none of them know anything about "Christology," and yet by his humility the publican was justified. These are facts which cannot be turned and twisted without doing violence to the grandeur and simplicity of Jesus' message in one of its most important aspects. To contend that Jesus meant his whole message to be taken provisionally, and everything in it to receive a different interpretation after his death and resurrection, nay, parts of it to be put aside as of no account, is a desperate supposition. No ! his message is simpler than the churches would like to think it ; simpler, but for that very reason sterner and endowed with a greater claim to universality. A man cannot evade it by the subterfuge of saying that as he can make nothing of this "Christology" the message is not for him. Jesus directed men's attention to great questions ; he promised them God's grace and mercy ; he required them to decide whether they would have God or Mammon, an eternal or an earthly life, the soul or the body, humility or self-righteousness, love or selfishness, the truth or a lie. The sphere which these questions occupy is all-embracing ; the individual is called upon to listen to the glad message of mercy and the Fatherhood of God, and to make

up his mind whether he will be on God's side and
the Eternal's, or on the side of the world and of
time. *The Gospel, as Jesus proclaimed it, has to
do with the Father only and not with the Son.*
This is no paradox, nor, on the other hand, is it
"rationalism," but the simple expression of the
actual fact as the evangelists give it.

But no one had ever yet known the Father in the
way in which Jesus knew Him, and to this knowledge
of Him he draws other men's attention, and thereby
does "the many" an incomparable service. He leads
them to God, not only by what he says, but still
more by what he is and does, and ultimately by
what he suffers. It was in this sense that he spoke
the words, "Come unto me all ye that labour and
are heavy laden, and I will give you rest"; as also,
"The Son of Man came not to be ministered unto,
but to minister and to give his life a ransom for
many." He knows that through him a new epoch
is beginning, in which, by their knowledge of God,
the "least" shall be greater than the greatest of the
ages before ; he knows that in him thousands—the
very individuals who are weary and heavy laden—
will find the Father and gain life ; he knows that
he is the sower who is scattering good seed; his is
the field, his the seed, his the fruit. These things
involve no dogmatic doctrines ; still less any transformation of the Gospel itself, or any oppressive
demands upon our faith. They are the expression
of an actual fact which he perceives to be already

happening, and which, with prophetic assurance, he beholds in advance. When, under the terrible burden of his calling and in the midst of the struggle, he comes to see that it is through him that the blind see, the lame walk, the deaf hear, the poor have the Gospel preached to them, he begins to comprehend the glory which the Father has given him. And he sees that what he now suffers in his person will, through his life crowned in death, remain a fact efficacious and of critical importance for all time : *He is the way to the Father, and as he is the appointed of the Father, so he is the judge as well.*

Was he mistaken ? Neither his immediate posterity, nor the course of subsequent history, has decided against him. It is not as a mere factor that he is connected with the Gospel ; *he was its personal realization and its strength, and this he is felt to be still.* Fire is kindled only by fire ; personal life only by personal forces. Let us rid ourselves of all dogmatic sophistry, and leave others to pass verdicts of exclusion. The Gospel nowhere says that God's mercy is limited to Jesus' mission. But history shows us that he is the one who brings the weary and heavy laden to God ; and, again, that he it was who raised mankind to the new level ; and his teaching is still the touchstone, in that it brings men to bliss and brings them to judgment.

The sentence " I am the Son of God " was not inserted in the Gospel by Jesus himself, and to put that sentence there side by side with the others is

K

to make an addition to the Gospel. But no one
who accepts the Gospel, and tries to understand him
who gave it to us, can fail to affirm that here the
divine appeared in as pure a form as it can appear
on earth, and to feel that for those who followed
him Jesus was himself the strength of the Gospel.
What they experienced, however, and came to know
in and through him, they have told the world ; and
their message is still a living force.

(6) *The Gospel and doctrine, or the question of creed.*

We need not dwell long on this question, as on
the essential points—everything that it is necessary to say has already been said in the course of
our previous observations.

The Gospel is no theoretical system of doctrine
or philosophy of the universe ; it is doctrine only
in so far as it proclaims the reality of God the
Father. It is a glad message assuring us of life
eternal, and telling us what the things and
the forces with which we have to do are worth.
By treating of life eternal it teaches us how
to lead our lives aright. It tells us of the
value of the human soul, of humility, of mercy,
of purity, of the cross, and the worthlessness of
worldly goods and anxiety for the things of which
earthly life consists. And it gives the assurance
that in spite of every struggle, peace, certainty,

and something within that can never be destroyed,
will be the crown of a life rightly led. What
else can " the confession of a creed " mean under
these conditions but to do the will of God, in the
certainty that He is the Father and the one who
will recompense? Jesus never spoke of any other
kind of " creed." Even when he says :—" Whosoever shall confess me before men, him will I confess also before my Father which is in Heaven,"
he is thinking of people doing as he did ; he means
the confession which shows itself in feeling and
action. How great a departure from what he thought
and enjoined is involved in putting a " Christological " creed in the forefront of the Gospel, and
in teaching that before a man can approach it he
must learn to think rightly about Christ. That is
putting the cart before the horse. A man can
think and teach rightly about Christ only if, and
in so far as, he has already begun to live according to Christ's Gospel. There is no forecourt to
his message through which a man must pass ; no
yoke which he must first of all take upon himself.
The thoughts and assurances which the Gospel
provides are the first thing and the last thing,
and every soul is directly arraigned before them.

Still less, however, does the Gospel presuppose
any definite knowledge of nature, or stand in any
connexion with such knowledge ; not even in a
negative sense can this contention be maintained.
It is religion and the moral element that are con-

cerned. The Gospel puts the living God before
us. Here, too, the confession of Him in belief
in Him and in the fulfilment of His will is the
sole thing to be confessed; this is what Jesus
Christ meant. So far as the knowledge is concerned—and it is vast—which may be based upon
this belief, it always varies with the measure of
a man's inner development and subjective intelligence. But to possess the Lord of heaven and
earth as a Father is an experience to which nothing else approaches; and it is an experience which
the poorest soul can have, and to the reality of
which he can bear testimony.

An experience—it is only the religion which a man
has himself experienced that is to be confessed;
every other creed or confession is in Jesus' view
hypocritical and fatal. If there is no broad "theory
of religion" to be found in the Gospel, still less
is there any direction that a man is to begin by
accepting and confessing any ready-made theory.
Faith and creed are to proceed and grow up out of
the all-important act of turning from the world
and to God, and creed is to be nothing but faith
reduced to practice. "All men have not faith," says
the apostle Paul, but all men ought to be veracious
and be on their guard in religion against lip-ser-
vice and light-hearted assent to creeds. "A certain
man had two sons; and he came to the first and
said, Son, go work to-day in my vineyard. He
answered and said, I will not; but afterward he

repented and went. And he came to the second, and said likewise. And he answered and said, I go, Sir ; and went not."

I might stop here, but I am impelled to answer one more objection. The Gospel, it is said, is a great and sublime thing, and it has certainly been a saving power in history, but it is indissolubly connected with an antiquated view of the world and history ; and, therefore, although it be painful to say so, and we have nothing better to put in its place, it has lost its validity and can have no further significance for us. In view of this objection there are two things which I should like to say :—

Firstly, no doubt it is true that the view of the world and history with which the Gospel is connected is quite different from ours, and that view we cannot recall to life, and would not if we could ; but "indissoluble" the connexion is not. I have tried to show what the essential elements in the Gospel are, and these elements are "timeless." Not only are they so ; but the man to whom the Gospel addresses itself is also "timeless," that is to say, it is the man who, in spite of all progress and development, never changes in his inmost constitution and in his fundamental relations with the external world. Since that is so, this Gospel remains in force, then, for us too.

Secondly, the Gospel is based—and this is the all-important element in the view which it takes of

the world and history—upon the antithesis between
Spirit and flesh, God and the world, good and evil.
Now, in spite of ardent efforts, thinkers have not
yet succeeded in elaborating on a monistic basis any
theory of ethics that is satisfactory and answers
to the deepest needs of man. Nor will they succeed. In the end, then, it is essentially a matter
of indifference what name we give to the opposition with which every man of ethical feeling
is concerned : God and the world, the Here and
the Beyond, the visible and the invisible, matter
and spirit, the life of impulse and the life of
freedom, physics and ethics. That there is a unity
underlying this opposition is a conviction which
can be gained by experience; the one realm can
be subordinated to the other; but it is only by a
struggle that this unity can be attained, and when
it is attained it takes the form of a problem that is
infinite and only approximately soluble. It cannot
be attained by any refinement of a mechanical process. It is by self-conquest that a man is freed
from the tyranny of matter—

> *Von der Gewalt die alle Wesen bindet*
> *Befreit der Mensch sich der sich überwindet.*

This saying of Goethe's excellently expresses the
truth that is here in question. It is a truth which
holds good for all time, and it forms the essential
element in the dramatic pictures of contemporary
life in which the Gospel exhibits the antithesis that

is to be overcome. I do not know how our increased knowledge of nature is to hinder us from bearing witness to the truth of the creed that " The world passeth away, and the lust thereof, but he that doeth the will of God abideth for ever." We have to do with a dualism which arose we know not how; but as moral beings we are convinced that, as it has been given us in order that we may overcome it in ourselves and bring it to a unity, so also it goes back to an original unity, and will at last find its reconciliation in the great far-off event, the realised dominion of the Good.

Dreams, it may be said; for what we see before our eyes is something very different. No! not dreams—after all it is here that our true life has its root—but patchwork certainly, for we are unable to bring our knowledge in space and time, together with the contents of our inner life, into the unity of a philosophic theory of the world. It is only in the peace of God which passeth all understanding that this unity dawns upon us.

But we have already passed beyond the limits of our immediate task. We proposed to acquaint ourselves with the Gospel in its fundamental features and in its most important bearings. I have tried to respond to this task; but the last point which we touched takes us beyond it. We now return to it, in order to follow, in the second part of these lectures, the course of the Christian religion through history.

LECTURE IX.

THE task before us in the second half of these lectures is to exhibit the history of the Christian religion in its leading phases, and to examine its development in the apostolic age, in Catholicism, and in Protestantism.

THE CHRISTIAN RELIGION IN THE APOSTOLIC AGE.

The inner circle of the disciples, the band of twelve whom Jesus had gathered around him, formed itself into a community. He himself founded no community in the sense of an organised union for divine worship—he was only the teacher and the disciples were the pupils ; but the fact that the band of pupils at once underwent this transformation became the ground upon which all subsequent developments rested. What were the characteristic features of this society ? Unless I am mistaken there were three factors at work in it : (i.) The recognition of Jesus as the living *Lord* ; (ii.) the fact that in every individual member of the new community—including the very slaves—religion was *an actual experience,* and involved the consciousness of a living union with God; (iii.) the leading of *a holy life* in purity and brotherly fellowship, and the expectation of the *Christ's return in the near future.*

By keeping these three factors in view we can grasp the distinctive character of the new community. Let us look at them more closely.

1. *Jesus Christ the Lord :* in thus confessing their belief in him his disciples took the first step in continuing their recognition of him as the authoritative teacher, of his word as their permanent standard of life, of their desire to keep "everything that he commanded them." But this does not express the full meaning attaching to the words "the Lord"; nay, it is far from touching their peculiar significance. The primitive community called Jesus its Lord because he had sacrificed his life for it, and because its members were convinced that he had been raised from the dead and was then sitting on the right hand of God. There is no historical fact more certain than that the apostle Paul was not, as we might perhaps expect, the first to emphasize so prominently the significance of Christ's death and resurrection, but that in recognising their meaning he stood exactly on the same ground as the primitive community. "I delivered unto you first of all," he wrote to the Corinthians, "that which I also received, how that Christ died for our sins according to the Scriptures, and that he was buried, and that he rose again the third day." Paul did, it is true,

make Christ's death and resurrection the subject of a particular speculative idea, and, so to speak, reduced the whole of the Gospel to these events; but they were already accepted as fundamental facts by the circle of Jesus' personal disciples and by the primitive community. In these two facts it may be said that the permanent recognition of Jesus Christ, and the reverence and adoration which he received, obtained their first hold. They formed the ground on which the whole Christological theory rested. But within two generations from his death Jesus Christ was already put upon the highest plane upon which men can put him. As men were conscious of him as the living Lord, he was glorified as the one who had been raised to the right hand of God and had vanquished death, as the Prince of Life, as the strength of a new existence, as the way, the truth, and the life. The Messianic ideas permitted of his being placed upon God's throne, without endangering monotheism. But, above all, he was felt to be the active principle of individual life: "It is not I that live, but Christ that liveth in me"; he is "my" life, and to press onwards to him through death is great gain. Where can we find in the history of mankind any similar instance of men eating and drinking with their master, seeing him in the characteristic aspects of his humanity, and then proclaiming him not only as the great prophet and revealer of God, but as the divine disposer of history, as the "beginning" of God's

creation, and as the inner strength of a new life!
It was not thus that Mahommed's disciples spoke
of their prophet. Neither is it sufficient to assert
that the Messianic predicates were simply transferred
to Jesus, and that everything may be explained
by Jesus' expected return in glory throwing its
radiance backwards. True, in the certain hope of
Jesus' return, his "coming in lowliness" was over-
looked; but that it was possible to conceive this
certain hope and hold it fast; that in spite of
suffering and death it was possible to see in him
the promised Messiah; and that in and side by side
with the vulgar Messianic image of him, men felt
and opened their hearts to him as the present Lord
and Saviour, that is what is so astonishing! It
was just the death "for our sins," and the resurrection, which confirmed the impression given by
his person, and provided faith with a sure hold:
he died as a sacrifice for us and he now lives.

There are many to-day who have come to regard
both these positions as very strange; and their attitude towards them is one of indifference—towards
the death, on the ground that no such significance
can be attributed to a single event of this kind; towards the resurrection, because what is here affirmed
to have happened is incredible.

It is not our business to defend either the view
which was taken of the death, or the idea that he
had risen again; but it is certainly the historian's
duty to make himself so fully acquainted with both

positions as to be sensible of the significance which
they possessed and still possess.   That these positions
were of capital importance for the primitive community has never been doubted ; even Strauss did
not dispute it ; and the great critic, Ferdinand
Christian Baur, acknowledged that it was on the
belief in them that the earliest Christian communion
was built up.   It must be possible, then, for us in
our turn to get a feeling and an understanding for
what they were ; nay, perhaps we may do more ; if
we probe the history of religion to the bottom, we
shall find the truth and justice of ideas which on the
surface seem so paradoxical and incredible lying at
the very roots of the faith.

Let us first consider the idea that Jesus' death
on the cross was one of expiation.   Now, if we were
to consider the conception attaching to the words
" expiatory death " in the alien realm of formal
speculation, we should, it is true, soon find ourselves in a blind alley, and every chance of our
understanding the idea would vanish.   We should be
absolutely at the end of our tether if we were to
indulge in speculations as to the necessity which can
have compelled God to require such a sacrificial
death.   Let us, in the first place, bear in mind a fact
in the history of religion which is quite universal.
Those who looked upon this death as a sacrifice soon
ceased to offer God any blood-sacrifice at all.   The
value attaching to such sacrifices had, it is true,

been in doubt for generations, and had been steadily diminishing; but it was only now that the sacrifices disappeared altogether. They did not disappear immediately or at one stroke—this is a point with which we need not concern ourselves here—but their disappearance took place within a very brief period and was not delayed until after the destruction of the temple. Further, wherever the Christian message subsequently penetrated, the sacrificial altars were deserted and dealers in sacrificial beasts found no more purchasers. If there is one thing that is certain in the history of religion, it is that the death of Christ put an end to all blood-sacrifices. But that they are based on a deep religious idea is proved by the extent to which they existed among so many nations, and they are not to be judged from the point of view of cold and blind rationalism, but from that of vivid emotion. If it is obvious that they respond to a religious need; if, further, it is certain that the instinct which led to them found its satisfaction and therefore its goal in Christ's death; if, lastly, there was the express declaration, as we read in the Epistle to the Hebrews, that "by one offering he hath perfected for ever them that are sanctified," we can no longer feel this idea of Christ's sacrifice to be so very strange; for history has decided in its favour, and we are beginning to get in touch with it. His death had the value of an expiatory sacrifice, for otherwise it would not have had strength to penetrate into that inner world in

which the blood-sacrifices originated; but it was not
a sacrifice in the same sense as the others, or else it
could not have put an end to them; it suppressed
them by settling accounts with them. Nay, we may
go further; the validity of all material sacrifices was
destroyed by Christ's death. Wherever individual
Christians or whole Churches have returned to them,
it has been a relapse: the earliest Christians knew
that the whole sacrificial system was thenceforth
abolished, and if they asked for a reason, they
pointed to Christ's death.

In the second place: any one who will look into
history will find that the sufferings of the pure and
the just are its saving element; that is to say, that
it is not words, but deeds, and not deeds only but
self-sacrificing deeds, and not only self-sacrificing
deeds, but the surrender of life itself, that forms the
turning point in every great advance in history. In
this sense I believe that, however far we may stand
from any *theories* about vicarious sacrifice, there are
few of us after all who will mistake the truth and
inner justice of such a description as we read in
Isaiah liii. : "Surely he hath borne our griefs and
carried our sorrows." "Greater love hath no man
than this, that a man lay down his life for his
friends"—it is in this light that Jesus' death was
regarded from the beginning. Wherever any great
deed has been accomplished in history, the finer a
man's moral feelings are, the more sensible will he be
of vicarious suffering; the more he will bring that

suffering into relation to himself. Did Luther in the monastery strive only for himself?—was it not for us all that he inwardly bled when he fought with the religion that was handed down to him? But it was by the cross of Jesus Christ that mankind gained such an experience of the power of purity and love true to death that they can never forget it, and that it signifies a new epoch in their history.

Finally, in the third place : no reflection of the "reason," no deliberation of the "intelligence," will ever be able to expunge from the moral ideas of mankind the conviction that injustice and sin deserve to be punished, and that everywhere that the just man suffers, an atonement is made which puts us to shame and purifies us. It is a conviction which is inpenetrable, for it comes out of those depths in which we feel ourselves to be a unity, and out of the world which lies behind the world of phenomena. Mocked and denied as though it had long perished, this truth is indestructibly preserved in the moral experience of mankind. These are the ideas which from the beginning onwards have been roused by Christ's death, and have, as it were, played around it. Other ideas have been disengaged—ideas of less importance but, nevertheless, very efficacious at times—but these are the most powerful. They have taken shape in the firm conviction that by his death in suffering he did a definitive work ; that he did it "for us." Were we to attempt to measure and register what he did, as was soon attempted, we

should fall into dreadful paradoxes; but we can in
our turn feel it for ourselves with the same freedom
with which it was originally felt.   If we also consider
that Jesus himself described his death as a service
which he was rendering to many, and that by a
solemn act he instituted a lasting remembrance
of it—I see no reason to doubt the fact—we can
understand how this death and the shame of the
cross were bound to take the central place.

Jesus, however, was proclaimed as "the Lord"
not only because he had died for sinners but
because he was the risen and the living one.   If
the resurrection meant nothing but that a deceased
body of flesh and blood came to life again, we
should make short work of this tradition.   But it
is not so.   The New Testament itself distinguishes
between the Easter message of the empty grave
and the appearances of Jesus on the one side, and
the Easter faith on the other.   Although the
greatest value is attached to that message, we
are to hold the Easter faith even in its absence.
The story of Thomas is told for the exclusive
purpose of impressing upon us that we must hold
the Easter faith even without the Easter message :
"Blessed are they that have not seen and yet
have believed."   The disciples on the road to
Emmaus were blamed for not believing in the
resurrection even though the Easter message had
not yet reached them.   The Lord is a Spirit,

says Paul; and this carries with it the certainty
of his resurrection. The Easter *message* tells us
of that wonderful event in Joseph of Arimathæa's
garden, which, however, no eye saw; it tells us
of the empty grave into which a few women and
disciples looked; of the appearance of the Lord
in a transfigured form—so glorified that his own
could not immediately recognise him; it soon begins
to tell us, too, of what the risen one said and
did. The reports became more and more complete,
and more and more confident. But the Easter
faith is the conviction that the crucified one
gained a victory over death; that God is just
and powerful; that he who is the firstborn among
many brethren still lives. Paul based his Easter
faith upon the certainty that "the second Adam"
was from heaven, and upon his experience, on the
way to Damascus, of God revealing His Son to
him as still alive. God, he said, revealed him
" in me"; but this inner revelation was coupled
with "a vision" overwhelming as vision never
was afterwards. Did the apostle know of the
message about the empty grave? While there
are theologians of note who doubt it, I think it
probable; but we cannot be quite certain about
it. Certain it is that what he and the disciples
regarded as all-important was not the state in
which the grave was found but Christ's appearances.
But who of us can maintain that a clear account
of these appearances can be constructed out of

L

the stories told by Paul and the evangelists ; and
if that be impossible, and there is no tradition of
single events which is quite trustworthy, how is
the Easter faith to be based on them ? Either we
must decide to rest our belief on a foundation un-
stable and always exposed to fresh doubts, or else we
must abandon this foundation altogether, and with it
the miraculous appeal to our senses. But here, too,
the images of the faith have their roots in truth
and reality. Whatever may have happened at the
grave and in the matter of the appearances, one
thing is certain : *This grave was the birthplace of
the indestructible belief that death is vanquished,
that there is a life eternal.* It is useless to cite
Plato ; it is useless to point to the Persian religion,
and the ideas and the literature of later Judaism.
All that would have perished and has perished ;
but the certainty of the resurrection and of a life
eternal which is bound up with the grave in
Joseph's garden has not perished, and on the
conviction that *Jesus lives* we still base those
hopes of citizenship in an Eternal City which make
our earthly life worth living and tolerable. " He
delivered them who through fear of death were
all their lifetime subject to bondage," as the writer
of the epistle to the Hebrews confesses. That is
the point. And although there be exceptions to
its sway, wherever, despite all the weight of
nature, there is a strong faith in the infinite value
of the soul ; wherever death has lost its terrors ;

wherever the sufferings of the present are measured against a future of glory, this feeling of life is bound up with the conviction that Jesus Christ has passed through death, that God has awakened him and raised him to life and glory. What else can we believe but that the earliest disciples also found the ultimate foundation of their faith in the living Lord to be the strength which had gone out from him? It was a life never to be destroyed which they felt to be going out from him; only for a brief span of time could his death stagger them; the strength of the Lord prevailed over everything; God did not give him over to death; he lives as the first-fruits of those who have fallen asleep. It is not by any speculative ideas of philosophy but by the vision of Jesus' life and death and by the feeling of his imperishable union with God that mankind, so far as it believes in these things, has attained to that certainty of eternal life for which it was meant, and which it dimly discerns—eternal life in time and beyond time. This feeling first established faith in the value of personal life. But of every attempt to demonstrate the certainty of "immortality" by logical process, we may say in the words of the poet:

> *Believe and venture : as for pledges,*
> *The Gods give none.*

Belief in the living Lord and in a life eternal is the *act* of the freedom which is born of God.

As the crucified and risen one Jesus was the Lord. While this confession of belief in him expressed a man's whole relation to him, it also afforded endless matter for thought and speculation. This conception of the "Lord" came to embrace the many-sided image of the Messiah and all the Old Testament prophecies of a similar kind. But as yet no ecclesiastical "doctrines" about him had been elaborated; everyone who acknowledged him as the Lord belonged to the community.

2. *Religion as an actual experience.* — The second characteristic feature of the primitive community is that every individual in it, even the very slaves, possess a living experience of God. This is sufficiently remarkable; for at first sight we might think that all this devotion to Christ, and this unconditional reverence for him, must necessarily have resulted in all religion becoming a punctilious subjection to his words, and so a kind of voluntary servitude. But the Pauline epistles and the Acts of the Apostles give us quite a different picture. While they do, indeed, attest the fact that Jesus' words were held in unqualified reverence, this fact is not the most prominent feature in the picture of earliest Christendom. What is much more characteristic is that individual Christians, moved by the Spirit of God, are placed in a living and entirely personal relation to God Himself. Dr. Weinel has lately presented us

with a fine work on the "Workings of the Spirit
and the Spirits in the post-apostolic age." It contains many passages which take us back to the
apostolic age and treat in greater detail of the
matters which Professor Gunkel has so impressively placed before us in his treatise on "The
Holy Ghost." The neglected problems of the
extent to which, and the forms in which, the
Spirit exercised an influence on the life of the
early Christians, and of the view to be taken of
the phenomena connected with this influence,
are admirably discussed by Dr. Weinel. In
substance, his conclusion is that the expressions
"receiving" and "acting by" the Holy Ghost
signify such an independence and immediacy of
religious life and feeling, and such an inner union
with God, perceived to be the mightiest reality, as
could not have been expected from strict subjection
to Jesus' authority. To be the child of God and
to be gifted with the Spirit are simply the same
as being a disciple of Christ. That a man is not
truly a disciple unless he is pervaded by God's
Spirit is a point which the "Acts of the Apostles"
fully recognises. The pouring out of the Holy
Spirit is placed in the forefront of the narrative.
The author is conscious that the Christian religion
would not be the highest and the ultimate religion,
unless it brought every individual into an immediate and living connexion with God. This
mutual union of a full obedient subjection to the

Lord with freedom in the Spirit is the most important feature in the distinctive character of this religion and the seal of its greatness. The workings of the Spirit were shown everywhere, in the entire domain of the five senses, in the sphere of will and action, in profound philosophical speculation, and in the most delicate appreciation of the facts of the moral life. The elementary forces of the religious temperament, long held in check by systems of doctrine and the ceremonies of public worship, were again set free. They showed themselves in ecstatic phenomena, in signs and wonders, in an enhancement of all the functions of life, down to conditions of a pathological and suspicious character. The fact, however, was not forgotten—and where it threatened to be obscured it was strongly impressed on people's attention—that those strange and violent phenomena were individual, but that side by side with them there are workings of the Spirit which are bestowed upon every one and with which no one can dispense. But "The fruit of the Spirit," as the apostle Paul writes, "is love, joy, peace, longsuffering, gentleness, goodness, faith, meekness, temperance." The other feature in the distinctive character and greatness of this religion is that it does not overestimate the elementary strength which gave it birth; that it makes its spiritual purport and its discipline triumph over all states of ecstasy; and that it holds immoveable to its conviction that the Spirit of God, however it may reveal itself, is a Spirit of holiness and of love. But here we have already passed to the third feature which characterises early Christendom.

3. The third feature is the leading of a *holy life* in purity and brotherly fellowship and in the expectation of Christ's speedy return. The course which the history of the Church followed resulted in the dogmatic details in the New Testament being selected for investigation, rather than those parts of it which depicted the life of the first Christians and exhorted men to morality. And yet not only are the New Testament epistles largely taken up with these moral exhortations, but not a few of the so-called dogmatic portions were also written solely for moral admonition. Jesus directed his disciples to give these exhortations the first place, and the earliest Christians were well aware that the first business of life was to do the will of God and present themselves as a holy community. Upon this their whole existence and their mission in the world were based. There were two points which, in accordance with Jesus' teaching, they put first and foremost, and they were points which at bottom embraced the whole range of moral action : *purity* and *brotherly fellowship.* They took purity in the deepest and most comprehensive sense of the word, as the horror of everything that is unholy, and as the inner plea- sure in everything that is upright and true, lovely and of good report. They also meant purity in regard

to the body : "Know ye not that your body is the
temple of the Holy Ghost which is in you ? therefore
glorify God in your body." In this sublime consciousness the earliest Christians took up the struggle
against the sins of impurity, which in the heathen
world were not accounted sins at all. As sons
of God, "blameless and harmless in the midst of a
crooked and perverse nation," they were to "shine as
lights in the world." It was thus that they were
to show of what they were made, and it was thus
that they showed it : to be holy as God was holy,
to be pure as disciples of Christ. Here too, we get
the measure of the renunciation of the world which
this community imposed upon itself. "To keep oneself unspotted from the world" was the asceticism
which it practised itself and required of its adherents. The other point is *brotherly fellowship*. In
joining the love of God with the love of neighbour
in his sayings, Jesus himself had a new union
of men with one another in view. The earliest
Christians understood him. From the very first
they constituted themselves into a brotherly union,
not in word only but in deed—a living realisation
of what he meant. In calling themselves " brothers,"
they felt all the obligations which the name imposes
and tried to come up to them, not by legal regulations but by voluntary service, each according to the
measure of his own powers and gifts. The Acts of
the Apostles tell us that in Jerusalem they went so
far as to have a voluntary community of goods. Paul

says nothing about it; and if we are to accept this obscure report as really trustworthy, then neither Paul nor the Christian communities among the Gentiles took pattern by the enterprise. They seem not to have been required, nor to have thought it desirable, to order their lives afresh *in externals*. The brotherly fellowship which "the holy" were to cultivate, and did cultivate, was distinguished by two principles: "Whether one member suffer, all the members suffer with it," and "Bear ye one another's burdens and so fulfil the law of Christ."

LECTURE X.

It was as their Lord that the primitive community of Christians believed in Jesus. They thus expressed their absolute devotion to, and confidence in, him as the Prince of Life. As every individual Christian stood in an immediate relation to God through the Spirit, priests and mediations were no longer wanted. Finally, these "holy" people were drawn together into societies, which bound themselves to a strictly moral life in purity and brotherly fellowship. On the last point let me add a few words.

It is a proof of the inwardness and moral power of the new message that, in spite of the enthusiasm arising from personal experience of religion, there were relatively seldom any extravagant outbursts and violent movements to be combated. Such movements may have been more frequent than the direct declarations of our authorities allow us to suppose, but they did not form the rule; and when they arose Paul was certainly not the only one who was concerned to put them down. He had certainly no wish to quench the "Spirit," but

THE COMMUNITY OF BROTHERS 171

when enthusiasm threatened to lead to a repugnance to work, as in Thessalonica, or when, as in Corinth, there was a superabundance of ecstatic talk, he uttered some sober warnings: "If any would not work, neither should he eat," and "I had rather speak five words with my understanding, that by my voice I might teach others also, than ten thousand words in an unknown tongue." Still more plainly are the concentrated repose and power of the leaders shown in the moral admonitions, such as we get not only in the Pauline Epistles but also, for example, in the first epistle of Peter and in the general epistle of James. Christian character is to show itself in the essential circumstances of human life, and that life is to be invigorated, supported and illumined by the Spirit. In the relation of husband to wife and of wife to husband, of parents to children, of masters to servants; further, in the individual's relation to constituted authority, to the surrounding heathen world, and, again, to the widow and the orphan, is "the service of God" to be proved and tested. Where have we another example in history of a religion intervening with such a robust supernatural consciousness, and at the same time laying the moral foundations of the earthly life of the community so firmly as this message? If a man fails to be inwardly affected by the faith proclaimed by the New Testament writers, he must certainly be stirred to the depths by the purity, the wealth,

the power, and the delicacy of the moral knowledge
which invests their exhortations with such incomparable value.

There is another feature of the life of the earliest
Christians which also deserves notice in this connexion. They lived in the expectation of Christ's
near return. This hope supplied them with an
extraordinarily strong motive for disregarding
earthly things, and the joys and sufferings of this
world. That they were mistaken in their expectations we must freely grant; but nevertheless it was a highly efficacious lever for raising
them above the world, and teaching them to make
little of small things and much of great things, and
to distinguish between what is of time and what is
of eternity. For a new and powerful religious
impulse, which effects its own influence, to be
associated with a co-efficient which enhances and
strengthens that influence, is what we see constantly
happening in the history of religion. With every
renewal of the religious experience of sin and grace
since Augustine's day, what a lever has been supplied
by the *idea of predestination*, and yet it is an idea
which is in no way derived from that experience
itself. How much enthusiasm was inspired in Crom-
well's troops, and how greatly were the Puritans
on both sides of the ocean strengthened by *the
consciousness of adoption*, although this consciousness, too, was only a co-efficient. When the religious
experiences of St. Francis developed in the Middle

Ages into a new form of devotion, how much assistance it received from the *doctrine of poverty*, and
yet this doctrine was an independent force. The
conviction which obtained in the apostolic age that
the Lord had really appeared after his death on the
cross may also be regarded as a co-efficient. These
co-efficients teach us that the most inward of all
possessions, namely, religion, does not struggle up
into life free and isolated, but grows, so to speak, in
coverings of bark and cannot grow without them.
In studying the apostolic age, however, it is important to observe that, not only in spite of the religious
enthusiasm but even in spite of the intense eschatological hopes which prevailed, the task of making
earthly life holy was not neglected.

The three principles which we have emphasised
as contributing most to the characteristic features
of primitive Christianity could also, if necessary, have
been brought to bear within the framework of
Judaism and in connexion with the synagogue.
There, too, Jesus could have been acknowledged as
the Lord, the new experience united with the
ancestral religion, and the society of brothers developed in the form of a Jewish conventicle. In
Palestine, as a matter of fact, this was the form
which the earliest communities took. But the new
principles displayed great vigour and pointed far
beyond Judaism : Jesus Christ the Lord is not only
Israel's Lord, but the Lord of history, the Lord of

all men. The new experience of a direct union with
God makes the old worship with its priests and
mediations unnecessary. The society of brothers
towers over all other associations and deprives them
of any value. The inner development which the
new tendency virtually comprised began at once.
Paul was not the first to start it; before and side
by side with him there were obscure and nameless
Christians in the dispersion who took up Gentiles
into the new society. They did away with the
particularistic and statutory regulations of the law
by declaring that they were to be understood in a
purely spiritual sense and to be interpreted as
symbols. There was a branch of the Jewish world
outside Palestine where this declaration had long
taken actual effect—it is true, on other grounds—
and where the Jewish religion was being freed from
its limitations by a process of philosophical interpretation which was bringing it to the level of a
spiritual religion for the whole world. This development may be regarded in the light of a preliminary stage in the history of Christianity and
was in many respects really so. It was the stage
on which those nameless Christians entered. It was
the path upon which a deliverance from historical
Judaism and its outworn religious ordinances was
capable of gradual attainment. But one thing is
certain; it was not the goal of the movement. So
long as the words " the former religion is done away
with " remained unspoken, there was always a fear

that in the next generation the old precepts would be brought forward again in their literal meaning. How often and often in the history of religion has there been a tendency to do away with some traditional form of doctrine or ritual which has ceased to satisfy inwardly, but to do away with it by giving it a new interpretation. The endeavour seems to be succeeding; the temper and the knowledge prevailing at the moment are favourable to it —when, lo and behold! the old meaning suddenly comes back again. The actual words of the ritual, of the liturgy, of the official doctrine, prove stronger than anything else. If a new religious idea cannot manage to make a radical breach with the past *at the critical point*—the rest may remain as it is—and procure itself a new "body," it cannot last; it disappears again. There is no tougher or more conservative fabric than a properly constituted religion; it can only yield to a higher phase by being abolished. No permanent effect, then, could be expected in the apostolic age from the twisting and turning of the law so as to make room for the new faith side by side with it, or so as to approximate the old religion to that faith. Someone had to stand up and say "The old is done away with"; he had to brand any further pursuit of it as a *sin*; he had to show that all things were become new. The man who did that was the apostle Paul, and it is in having done it that his greatness in the history of the world consists.

Paul is the most luminous personality in the history of primitive Christianity, and yet opinions differ widely as to his true significance. Only a few years ago we had a leading Protestant theologian asserting that Paul's rabbinical theology led him to corrupt the Christian religion. Others, conversely, have called him the real founder of that religion. But in the opinion of the great majority of those who have studied him the true view is that he was the one who understood the master and continued his work. This opinion is borne out by the facts. Those who blame him for corrupting the Christian religion have never felt a single breath of his spirit, and judge him only by mere externals, such as clothes and book-learning; those who extol or criticise him as a founder of religion are forced to make him bear witness against himself on the main point, and acknowledge that the consciousness which bore him up and steeled him for his work was illusory and self-deceptive. As we cannot want to be wiser than history, which knows him only as Christ's missionary, and as his own words clearly attest what his aims were and what he was, we regard him as Christ's disciple, as the apostle who not only worked harder but also accomplished more than all the rest put together.

It was Paul who delivered the Christian religion from Judaism. We shall see how he did that if we consider the following points :—

It was Paul who definitely conceived the Gospel as the message of the redemption already effected and of salvation now present. He preached the crucified and risen Christ, who gave us access to God and therewith righteousness and peace.

It was he who confidently regarded the Gospel as a new force abolishing the religion of the law.

It was he who perceived that religion in its new phase pertains to the individual and therefore to all individuals ; and in this conviction, and with a full consciousness of what he was doing, he carried the Gospel to the nations of the world and transferred it from Judaism to the ground occupied by Greece and Rome. Not only are Greeks and Jews to unite on the basis of the Gospel, but the Jewish dispensation itself is now at an end. That the Gospel was transplanted from the East, where in subsequent ages it was never able to thrive properly, to the West, is a fact which we owe to Paul.

It was he who placed the Gospel in the great scheme of spirit and flesh, inner and outer existence, death and life ; he, born a Jew and educated a Pharisee, gave it a *language*, so that it became intelligible, not only to the Greeks but to all *men* generally, and united with the whole of the intellectual capital which had been amassed in previous ages.

These are the factors that go to make the Apostle's greatness in the history of religion. On their inner connexion I cannot here enter in any detail. But, in regard to the first of them, I may remind you of the words of the most important historian

M

of religion in our day. Wellhausen declares that
"Paul's especial work was to transform the Gospel
of the kingdom into the Gospel of Jesus Christ, so
that the Gospel is no longer the prophecy of the
coming of the kingdom, but its actual fulfilment
by Jesus Christ. In his view, accordingly, redemption from something in the future has become
something which has already happened and is now
present. He lays far more emphasis on faith than
on hope; he anticipates the sense of future bliss
in the present feeling of being God's son; he
vanquishes death and already leads the new life on
earth. He extols the strength which is made perfect
in weakness; the grace of God is sufficient for him,
and he knows that no power, present or future, can
take him from His love, and that all things work
together for good to them that love God." What
knowledge, what confidence, what strength, was
necessary to tear the new religion from its mother
earth and plant it in an entirely new one! Islam,
originating in Arabia, has remained the Arabian
religion, no matter where it may have penetrated.
Buddhism has at all times been at its purest in India.
But this religion, born in Palestine, and confined by
its founder to Jewish ground, in only a few years
after his death was severed from that connexion.
Paul put it in competition with the Israelitish
religion : "Christ is the end of the law." Not
only did it bear being thus rooted up and transplanted, but it showed that it was meant to be thus

transplanted. It gave stay and support to the Roman empire and the whole world of western civilisation. If, as Renan justly observes, anyone had told the Roman Emperor in the first century that the little Jew who had come from Antioch as a missionary was his best collaborator, and would put the empire upon a stable basis, he would have been regarded as a madman, and yet he would have spoken nothing but the truth. Paul brought new forces to the Roman empire, and laid the foundations of western and Christian civilisation. Alexander the Great's work has perished; Paul's has remained. But if we praise the man who, without being able to appeal to a single word of his master's, ventured upon the boldest enterprise, by the help of the spirit and with the letter against him, we must none the less pay the meed of honour to those personal disciples of Jesus who after a bitter internal struggle ultimately associated themselves with Paul's principles. That Peter did so we know for certain; of others we hear that they at least acknowledged their validity. It was, indeed, no insignificant circumstance that men in whose ears every word of their master's was still ringing, and in whose recollection the concrete features of his personality were still a vivid memory—that these faithful disciples should recognise a pronouncement to be true which in important points seemed to depart from the original message and portended the downfall of the religion of Israel. What was kernel here, and what was husk, history has itself showed with unmistakeable plainness, and by the shortest process.   Husk were the whole of the Jewish limitations attaching to Jesus' message ; husk were also such definite statements as "I am not sent but unto the lost sheep of the house of Israel." In the strength of Christ's spirit the disciples broke through these barriers.   It was his personal disciples —not, as we might expect, the second or third generation, when the immediate memory of the Lord had already paled—who stood the great test.   That is the most remarkable fact of the apostolic age.

Without doing violence to the inner and essential features of the Gospel—unconditional trust in God as the Father of Jesus Christ, confidence in the Lord, forgiveness of sins, certainty of eternal life, purity and brotherly fellowship—Paul transformed it into the universal religion, and laid the ground for the great Church.   But whilst the original limitations fell away, new ones of necessity made their appearance ; and they modified the simplicity and the power of a movement which was from within.   Before concluding our survey of the apostolic age, we must direct attention to these modifications.

In the first place : the breach with the Synagogue and the founding of entirely independent religious communities had well-marked results.   Whilst the idea was firmly maintained that the community of Christ, the "Church," was something suprasensible and heavenly, because it came from within, there was also a conviction that the Church took visible

shape in every separate community. As a complete
breach had taken place, or no connexion been
established, with the ancient communion, the formation of entirely new societies was logically invested
with a special significance, and excited the liveliest
interest. In his sayings and parables Jesus, careless
of all externals, could devote himself solely to the all-
important point; but *how and in what forms* the seed
would grow was not a question which occupied his
mind; he had the people of Israel with their historical
ordinances before him and was not thinking of
external changes. But the connexion with this people
was now severed, and no religious movement can
remain in a *bodiless* condition. It must elaborate
forms for common life and common public worship.
Such forms, however, cannot be improvised; some of
them take shape slowly out of concrete necessities;
others are derived from the environment and from
existing circumstances. It was in this way that
the "Gentile" communities procured themselves an
organism, a body. The forms which they developed
were in part independent and gradual, and in part
based upon the facts with which they had to deal.

But a special measure of value always attaches
to forms. By being the means by which the
community is kept together, *the value of that to
which they minister is insensibly transferred to
them*; or, at least, there is always a danger of this
happening. One reason for this is that the observance of the forms can always be controlled or

enforced, as the case may be; whilst for the inner life there is no control that cannot be evaded.

When the breach with the Jewish national communion had once taken place, there could be no doubt about the necessity for setting up a new community in opposition to it. The self-consciousness and strength of the Christian movement was displayed in the creation of a Church which knew itself to be the true Israel. But the founding of churches and "the Church" on earth brought an entirely new interest into the field; what came from within was joined by something that came from without; law, discipline, regulations for ritual and doctrine, were developed, and began to assert a position by a logic of their own The measure of value applicable to religion itself no longer remained the only measure, and with a hundred invisible threads religion was insensibly worked into the net of history.

In the second place: we have already referred to the fact that it was above all in his Christology that Paul's significance as a teacher consisted. In his view—we see this as well by the way in which he illuminated the death on the cross and the resurrection, as by his equation, "the Lord is a Spirit"—the Redemption is already accomplished and salvation a present power. "God hath reconciled us to himself through Jesus Christ"; "If any man be in Christ, he is a new creature"; "Who shall separate us from the love of God?"

The absolute character of the Christian religion is thus made clear. But it may also be observed in this connexion that every attempt to formulate a theory has a logic of its own and dangers of its own. There was one danger which the apostle himself had to combat, that of men claiming to be redeemed without giving practical proof of the new life. In the case of Jesus' sayings no such danger could arise, but Paul's formulas were not similarly protected. That men are not to rely upon "redemption," forgiveness of sin, and justification, if the hatred of sin and the imitation of Christ be lacking, inevitably became in subsequent ages a standing theme with all earnest teachers. Who can fail to recognise that the doctrines of "objective redemption" have been the occasion of grievous temptations in the history of the Church, and for whole generations concealed the true meaning of religion? The conception of "redemption," which cannot be inserted in Jesus' teaching in this free and easy way at all, became a snare. No doubt it is true that Christianity is the religion of redemption; but the conception is a delicate one, and must never be taken out of the sphere of personal experience and inner reformation.

But here we are met by a second danger closely connected with the first. If redemption is to be traced to Christ's person and work, everything would seem to depend upon a right understanding of this person together with what he accomplished.

The formation of a correct theory of and about Christ threatens to assume the position of chief importance, and to pervert the majesty and simplicity of the Gospel. Here, again, the danger is of a kind such as cannot arise with Jesus' sayings. Even in John we read :—" If ye love me, keep my commandments." But with the way in which Paul defined the theory of religion, the danger can certainly arise and did arise. No long period elapsed before it was taught in the Church that the all-important thing is to know how the person of Jesus was constituted, what sort of physical nature he had, and so on. Paul himself is far removed from this position—" Whoso calleth Christ Lord speaketh by the Holy Ghost "—but the way in which he ordered his religious conceptions, as the outcome of his speculative ideas, unmistakeably exercised an influence in a wrong direction. That, however great the attraction which his way of ordering them may possess for the understanding, it is a perverse proceeding to make Christology the fundamental substance of the Gospel, is shown by Christ's teaching, which is everywhere directed to the all-important point, and summarily confronts every man with his God. This does not affect Paul's right to epitomise the Gospel in the message of Christ crucified, thus exhibiting God's power and God's wisdom, and in the love of Christ kindling the love of God. There are thousands to-day in whom the Christian faith is still propagated

in the same manner, namely, through Christ. But
to demand assent to a series of propositions about
Christ's person is a different thing altogether.

There is, however, another point to be considered
here. Under the influence of the Messianic dogmas,
and led by the impression which Christ made, Paul
became the author of the speculative idea that not
only was God in Christ, but that Christ himself
was possessed of a peculiar nature of a heavenly
kind. With the Jews, this was not a notion that
necessarily shattered the framework of the Messianic
idea; but with the Greeks it inevitably set an
entirely new theory in motion. Christ's *appearance* in itself, the entrance of a divine being into
the world, came of necessity to rank as the chief
fact, as itself *the real redemption.* Paul did not,
indeed, himself look upon it in this light; for
him the crucial facts are the death on the cross
and the resurrection, and he regards Christ's entrance into the world from an ethical point of
view and as an example for us to follow: "For
our sakes he became poor"; he humbled himself
and renounced the world. But this state of things
could not last. The fact of redemption could
not permanently occupy the second place; it was
too large. But when moved into the first place
it threatened the very existence of the Gospel,
by drawing away men's thoughts and interests in
another direction. When we look at the history of
dogma, who can deny that that was what hap-

pened? To what extent it happened we shall
see in the following lectures.

In the third place : the new church possessed a
sacred book, the Old Testament. Paul, although he
taught that the law had become of no avail, found
a means of preserving the whole of the Old Testament. What a blessing to the church this book has
proved ! As a book of edification, of consolation, of
wisdom, of counsel, as a book of history, what an
incomparable importance it has had for Christian
life and apologetics ! Which of the religions that
Christianity encountered on Greek or Roman ground
could boast of a similar book ? Yet the possession of this book has not been an unqualified advantage to the church. To begin with, there are
many of its pages which exhibit a religion and a
morality other than Christian. No matter how resolutely people tried to spiritualize it and give it an
inner meaning by construing it in some special way,
their efforts did not avail to get rid of the original
sense in its entirety. There was always a danger
of an inferior and obsolete principle forcing its way
into Christianity through the Old Testament. This,
indeed, was what actually occurred. Nor was it
only in individual aspects that it occurred ; the whole
aim was changed. Moreover, on the new ground
religion was intimately connected with a political
power, namely, with nationality. How if people
were seduced into again seeking such a connexion,
not, indeed, with Judaism, but with a new nation,

and not with ancient national laws, but with something of an analogous character? And when even a Paul here and there declared Old Testament laws to be still authoritative in spite of their having undergone an allegorical transformation, how could anyone restrain his successors from also proclaiming other laws, remodelled to suit the circumstances of the time, as valid ordinances of God? This brings us to the second point. Although whatever was drawn from the Old Testament by way of authoritative precept may have been inoffensive in substance, it was a menace to Christian freedom of both kinds. It threatened the freedom which comes from within, and also the freedom to form church communities and to arrange for public worship and discipline.

I have tried to show that the limitations which surrounded the Gospel did not cease with the severance of the tie binding it to Judaism, but that, on the contrary, new limits made their appearance. They arose, however, just at the very points upon which the necessary progress of things depended, or, as the case might be, where an inalienable possession like the Old Testament was in question. Here, again, then, we are reminded of the fact that, so far as history is concerned, as soon as we leave the sphere of pure inwardness, there is no progress, no achievement, no advantage of any sort, that has not its dark side, and does not bring its disadvantages with it. The apostle Paul complained that "we know in part." To a much greater degree is the same thing true of our actions and of everything connected with them. We have always to "pay the penalty" of acting, and not only take the evil consequences but also knowingly and with open eyes resolutely neglect one thing in order to gain another. Our purest and most sacred possessions, when they leave the inward realm and pass into the world of form and circumstance, are no exception to the rule that the very shape which they take in action also proves to be their limitation.

When the great apostle ended his life under Nero's axe in the year 64, he could say of himself what a short time before he had written to a faithful comrade : " I have finished my course; I have kept the faith." What missionary is there, what preacher, what man entrusted with the cure of souls, who can be compared with him, whether in the greatness of the task which he accomplished, or in the holy energy with which he carried it out? He worked with the most living of all messages, and kindled a fire ; he cared for his people like a father and strove for the souls of others with all the forces of his own ; at the same time he discharged the duties of the teacher, the schoolmaster, the organiser. When he sealed his work by his death, the Roman empire from Antioch as far as Rome, nay, as far as Spain, was planted with Christian communities. There were to be found in them few that were " mighty after the flesh" or of noble degree, and yet they were as "lights in the world," and on them the progress of the world's history rested. They had little "illumination," but they had acquired the faith in the living God and in a life eternal; they knew that the value of the human soul is infinite, and that its value is determined by relation to the invisible; they led a life of purity and brotherly fellowship, or at least strove after such a life. Bound together into a new people in Jesus Christ, their head, they were filled with the high consciousness that Jews and Greeks, Greeks and barbarians, would through them become one, and that the last and highest stage in the history of humanity had then been reached.

LECTURE XI.

THE apostolic age now lies behind us. We have seen that in the course of it the Gospel was detached from the mother-soil of Judaism and placed upon the broad field of the Græco-Roman empire. The apostle Paul was the chief agent in accomplishing this work, and in thereby giving Christianity its place in the history of the world. The new connexion which it thus received did not in itself denote any restricted activity; on the contrary, the Christian religion was intended to be realised in mankind, and mankind at that time meant the *orbis Romanus*. But the new connexion involved the development of new forms, and new forms also meant limitation and encumbrance. We shall see more closely how this was effected if we consider

THE CHRISTIAN RELIGION IN ITS DEVELOPMENT INTO CATHOLICISM.

The Gospel did not come into the world as a statutory religion, and therefore none of the forms in which it assumed intellectual and social expression

—not even the earliest—can be regarded as possessing a classical and permanent character. The historian must always keep this guiding idea before him when he undertakes to trace the course of the Christian religion through the centuries from the apostolic age downwards. As Christianity rises above all antitheses of the Here and the Beyond, life and death, work and the shunning of the world, reason and ecstasy, Hebraism and Hellenism, it can also exist under the most diverse conditions; just as it was originally amid the wreck of the Jewish religion that it developed its power. Not only can it so exist—it must do so, if it is to be the religion of the living and is itself to live. As a Gospel it has only *one* aim—the finding of the living God, the finding of Him by every individual as *his* God, and as the source of strength and joy and peace. How this aim is progressively realised through the centuries—whether with the co-efficients of Hebraism or Hellenism, of the shunning of the world or of civilisation, of Gnosticism or of Agnosticism, of ecclesiastical institution or of perfectly free union, or by whatever other kinds of bark the core may be protected, the sap allowed to rise— is a matter that is of secondary moment, that is exposed to change, that belongs to the centuries, that comes with them and with them perishes.

Now the greatest transformation which the new religion ever experienced—almost greater even than that which gave rise to the Gentile Church and

thrust the Palestinian communities into the background—falls in the second century of our era, and
therefore in the period which we shall consider in
the present lecture.

If we place ourselves at about the year 200, about
a hundred or a hundred and twenty years after the
apostolic age—not more than three or four generations
had gone by since that age came to an end—what
kind of spectacle does the Christian religion offer?

We see a great ecclesiastical and political community, and side by side with it numerous " sects "
calling themselves Christian, but denied the name
and bitterly opposed. That great ecclesiastical and
political community presents itself as a league of
individual communities spanning the Empire from
end to end. Although independent they are all
constituted essentially alike, and interconnected by
one and the same law of doctrine, and by fixed rules
for the purposes of intercommunion. The law of
doctrine seems at first sight to be of small scope,
but all its tenets are of the widest significance; and
together they embrace a profusion of metaphysical,
cosmological, and historical problems, give them
definite answers, and supply particulars of mankind's
development from the creation up to its future form
of existence. Jesus' injunctions for the conduct of
life are not included in this law of doctrine; as the
" rule of discipline " they were sharply distinguished
from the " rule of faith." Each church, however, also
presents itself as an institution for public worship,

where God is honoured in conformity with a solemn ritual. The distinction between priests and laymen is already a well-marked characteristic of this institution; certain acts of divine worship can be performed only by the priest; his mediation is an absolute necessity. It is only by mediation that a man can approach God at all, by the mediation of right doctrine, right ordinance, and a sacred book. The living faith seems to be transformed into a creed to be believed; devotion to Christ, into Christology; the ardent hope for the coming of "the kingdom," into a doctrine of immortality and deification; prophecy, into technical exegesis and theological learning; the ministers of the Spirit, into clerics; the brothers, into laymen in a state of tutelage; miracles and miraculous cures disappear altogether, or else are priestly devices; fervent prayers become solemn hymns and litanies; the "Spirit" becomes law and compulsion. At the same time individual Christians are in full touch with the life of the world, and the burning question is, "In how much of this life may I take part without losing my position as a Christian?" This enormous transformation took place within a hundred and twenty years. The first thing which we have to determine is, How did that happen? next, Did the Gospel succeed in holding its own amid this change, and how did it do so?

Before, however, we try to answer these two questions, we must call to mind a piece of advice

N

which no historian ought ever to neglect. Anyone who wants to determine the real value and significance of any great phenomenon or mighty product of history must first and foremost inquire into the work which it accomplished, or, as the case may be, into the problem which it solved. As every individual has a right to be judged, not by this or that virtue or defect, not by his talents or by his frailties, but by what he has done, so the great edifices of history, the States and the Churches, must be estimated first and foremost, we may perhaps say, exclusively, by what they have achieved. It is *the work done* that forms the decisive test. With any other test we are involved in judgments of the vaguest kind, now optimistic, now pessimistic, and mere historical twaddle. So here, too, in considering the church as developed into Catholicism, we must first of all ask, In what did its work consist? What problem did it solve? What did it achieve? I will answer the last question first. It achieved two things: it waged war with nature-worship, polytheism, and political religion, and beat them back with great energy; and it exploded the dualistic philosophy of religion. Had the Church at the beginning of the third century been asked in tones of reproach, "How could you recede so far from where you began? to what have you come?" it might have answered: "Yes, it is to this that I have come; I have been obliged to discard much and admit much; I have had to fight—my body

is full of scars, and my clothes are covered with dust;
but I have won my battles and built my house;
I have beaten back polytheism; I have disabled
and almost annihilated that monstrous abortion,
political religion; I have resisted the enticements
of a subtle religious philosophy, and victoriously
encountered it with God the almighty Creator of
all things; lastly, I have reared a great building, a
fortress with towers and bulwarks, where I guard
my treasure and protect the weak." This is the
answer which the Church might have given, and
truthfully given. But, some one may object,
it was no great achievement to wage war with
nature-worship and polytheism, and to beat them
back; they had already rotted and decayed, and
had little strength left. The objection does not
hold. Many of the forms in which that species
of religion had taken shape were, no doubt, antiquated and approaching extinction, but the religion
itself, *the religion of nature*, was a mighty foe. It
even still avails to beguile our souls and touch our
heart-strings with effect, when an inspired prophet
voices its message; how much more so then! The
hymn to the Sun, giving life to all that lives, produced a profound and lifelong religious impression
even upon a Goethe, and made him into a Sun-
worshipper. But how overpowering it was in the
days before science had banished the gods from
nature. Christianity exploded the religion of nature
—exploded it not for this or that individual;

that was already done—but exploded it in the sense
that there was now a large and compact community
refuting nature-worship and polytheism by its impressive doctrines, and affording the deeper religious
temper stay and support.   And then political religion !
Behind the imperial cult there was the whole
power of the state, and to come to terms with it
looked so safe and easy—yet the Church did not
yield a single inch ; it abolished the imperial system
of state-idols.   It was to place an irremovable land-
mark between religion and politics, between God
and Cæsar, that the martyrs shed their blood.
Lastly, in an age that was deeply moved by questions of religious philosophy, the Church maintained
a firm front against all the speculative ideas of
dualism ; and, although these ideas often seemed to
approximate closely to its own position, it passionately
met them with the monotheistic view.   The struggle
here, however, was rendered all the harder by the
fact that many Christians — and just the very
prominent and gifted ones too—made common cause
with the enemy, and themselves embraced the
dualistic theory.   The Church stood firm.   If we
recollect that, in spite of these counter-movements
against the Græco-Roman spirit, it also managed
to attach this very spirit to itself—otherwise than
Judaism, of whose dealings with the Greek world
the saying holds, "You had power to draw but
not to keep me"; if we recollect, further, that it
was in the second century that the foundations of

the whole of the ecclesiastical system prevailing up to the present day were laid, we can only be astonished at the greatness of the work which was then achieved.

We now return to the two questions which we raised : How was this great transformation accomplished ? and did the Gospel hold its own amid this change, or, if so, how ?

There were, if I am not mistaken, three leading forces engaged in bringing about this great revolution, and effecting the organisation of new forms. The first of these forces tallies with a universal law in the history of religion, for in every religious development we find it at work. When the second and third generations after the founding of a new religion have passed away ; when hundreds, nay thousands, have become its adherents no longer through conversion but by the influences of tradition and of birth—despite Tertullian's saying : *fiunt, non nascuntur Christiani* ; when those who have laid hold upon the faith as great spoil are joined by crowds of others who wrap it round them like an outer garment, a revolution always occurs. The religion of strong feeling and of the heart passes into the religion of custom and therefore of form and of law. A new religion may be instituted with the greatest vigour, the utmost enthusiasm, and a tremendous amount of inner emotion ; it may at the same time lay ever so much stress on spiritual freedom—where was all this

ever more powerfully expressed than in Paul's teaching?—and yet, even though believers be forced to
be celibates and only adults be received, the process
of solidifying and codifying the religion is bound to
follow. Its forms then at once stiffen; in the very
process of stiffening they receive for the first time a
real significance, and new forms are added. Not only
do they acquire the value of laws and regulations, but
they come to be insensibly regarded as though they
contained within them the very substance of religion;
nay, as though they were themselves that substance.
This is the way in which people who do not feel
religion to be a reality are compelled to regard it, for
otherwise they would have nothing at all; and this
is the way in which those who continue really to live
in it are compelled to handle it, or else they would
be unable to exercise any influence upon others.
The former are not by any means necessarily
hypocrites. Real religion, of course, is a closed
book to them; its most important element has
evaporated. But there are various points of view
from which a man may still be able to appreciate
religion without living in it. He may appreciate it
as discharging the functions of morality, or of
police; above all he may appreciate it on æsthetic
grounds. When the Romanticists re-introduced
Catholicism into Germany and France at the beginning of the nineteenth century, Chateaubriand, more
especially, was never tired of singing its praises and
fancied that he had all the feelings of a Catholic.

But an acute critic remarked that Monsieur Chateaubriand was mistaken in his feelings; he thought that he was a true Catholic, while as a matter of fact he was only standing before the ancient ruin of the Church and exclaiming: " How beautiful! " That is one of the ways in which a man can appreciate a religion without being an inward adherent of it; but there are many others, and, amongst them, some in which a nearer approach is made to its true substance. All of them, however, have this much in common, that any actual experience of religion is no longer felt, or felt only in an uncertain and intermittent way. Conversely, a high regard is paid to the outward shows and influences connected with it, and they are carefully maintained. Whatever finds expression in doctrines, regulations, ordinances and forms of public worship comes to be treated as the thing itself. This, then, is the first force at work in the transformation: *the original enthusiasm*, in the large sense of the word, *evaporates*, and the religion of law and form at once arises.

But not only did an original element evaporate in the course of the second century; another was introduced. Even had this youthful religion not severed the tie which bound it to Judaism, it would have been inevitably affected by the spirit and the civilisation of that Græco-Roman world on whose soil it was permanently settled. But to what a much greater extent was it exposed to the influence of this spirit after being sharply severed from the

Jewish religion and the Jewish nation. It hovered
bodiless over the earth like a being of the air;
bodiless and seeking a body. The spirit, no doubt,
makes to itself its own body, but it does so by
assimilating what is around it. The influx of
Hellenism, of the Greek spirit, and the union of
the Gospel with it, form the greatest fact in the
history of the Church in the second century, and
when the fact was once established as a foundation
it continued through the following centuries. In the
influence of Hellenism on the Christian religion three
stages may be distinguished, and a preliminary stage
as well. We have already mentioned the preliminary
stage in a previous lecture. It is to be found in the
circumstances in which the Gospel arose, and it
formed a very condition of its appearance. Not
until Alexander the Great had created an entirely
new position of affairs, and the barriers separating
the nations of the East from one another and from
Hellenism had been destroyed, could Judaism free
itself from its limitations and start upon its development into a religion for the world. The time was
ripe when a man in the East could also breathe the
air of Greece and see his spiritual horizon stretch
beyond the limits of his own nation. Yet we cannot
say that the earliest Christian writings, let alone the
Gospel, show, to any considerable extent, the presence
of a Greek element. If we are to look for it any-
where—apart from certain well-marked traces of it
in Paul, Luke, and John—it must be in the *possi-*

bility of the new religion appearing at all. We cannot enter further upon this question here. The first stage of any real influx of definitely Greek thought and Greek life is to be fixed at about the year 130. It was then that the religious philosophy of Greece began to effect an entrance, and it went straight to the centre of the new religion. It sought to get into inner touch with Christianity, and, conversely, Christianity itself held out a hand to this ally. We are speaking of Greek *philosophy* ; as yet, there is no trace of mythology, Greek worship, and so on ; all that was taken up into the Church, cautiously and under proper guarantees, was the great capital which philosophy had amassed since the days of Socrates. A century or so later, about the year 220 or 230, the second stage begins : Greek mysteries, and Greek civilisation in the whole range of its development, exercise their influence on the Church, but not mythology and polytheism ; these were still to come. Another century, however, had in its turn to elapse before Hellenism as a whole and in every phase of its development was established in the Church. Guarantees, of course, are not lacking here either, but for the most part they consist only in a change of label ; the thing itself is taken over without alteration, and in the worship of the saints we see a regular Christian religion of a lower order arising. We are here concerned, however, not with the second and third stage, but only with that influx of the Greek spirit which was marked by the absorption

of Greek philosophy and, particularly, of Platonism.
Who can deny that elements here came together
which stood in elective affinity? So much depth
and delicacy of feeling, so much earnestness and
dignity, and—above all—so strong a *monotheistic*
piety were displayed in the religious ethics of the
Greeks, acquired as it had been by hard toil on a
basis of inner experience and metaphysical speculation, that the Christian religion could not pass this
treasure by with indifference. There was much in
it, indeed, which was defective and repellent; there
was no personality visibly embodying its ethics as
a living power; it still kept up a strange connexion
with "demon-worship" and polytheism; but both
as a whole and in its individual parts it was felt
to contain a kindred element, and it was absorbed.

But besides the Greek ethics there was also a
cosmological conception which the Church took
over at this time, and which was destined in a
few decades to attain a commanding position in its
doctrinal system—*the Logos.* Starting from an examination of the world and the life within, Greek
thought had arrived at the conception of an *active
central idea*—by what stages we need not here
mention. This central idea represented the unity
of the supreme principle of the world, of thought,
and of ethics; but it also represented, at the same
time, the divinity itself as a creative and active as
distinguished from a quiescent power. The most
important step that was ever taken in the domain

of Christian doctrine was when the Christian apologists at the beginning of the second century drew the equation : the Logos = Jesus Christ. Ancient teachers before them had also called Christ " the Logos " among the many predicates which they ascribed to him ; nay, one of them, John, had already formulated the proposition : " The Logos is Jesus Christ." But with John this proposition had not become the basis of every speculative idea about Christ ; with him, too, " the Logos " was only a predicate. But now teachers came forward who previous to their conversion had been adherents of the platonico-stoical philosophy, and with whom the conception " Logos " formed an inalienable part of a general philosophy of the world. They proclaimed that Jesus Christ was the Logos incarnate, which had hitherto been revealed only in the great effects which it exercised. In the place of the entirely unintelligible conception " Messiah," an intelligible one was acquired at a stroke ; Christology, tottering under the exuberance of its own affirmations, received a stable basis ; Christ's significance for the world was established ; his mysterious relation to God was explained ; the cosmos, reason, and ethics, were comprehended as one. It was, indeed, a marvellous formula ; and was not the way prepared for it, nay hastened, by the speculative ideas about the Messiah propounded by Paul and other ancient teachers ? The knowledge that the divine in Christ must be conceived as the Logos opened up a number

of problems, and at the same time set them definite
limits and gave them definite directives. Christ's
unique character as opposed to all rivals appeared
to be established in the simplest fashion, and yet
the conception provided thought with so much
liberty and free play that Christ could be regarded,
as the need might arise, on the one side as operative
deity itself, and on the other as still the first
born among many brethren and as the first created
of God.

What a proof it is of the impression which Christ's
teaching created that Greek philosophers managed
to identify him with the Logos! For the assertion
that the incarnation of the Logos had taken place
in an historical personage there had been no pre-
paration. No philosophising Jew had ever thought
of identifying the Messiah with the Logos; no
Philo, for instance, ever entertained the idea of
such an equation! *It gave a metaphysical significance to an historical fact; it drew into the domain
of cosmology and religious philosophy a person
who had appeared in time and space;* but by so
distinguishing one person it raised all history to
the plane of the cosmical movement.

The identification of the Logos with Christ was the
determining factor in the fusion of Greek philosophy
with the apostolic inheritance and led the more
thoughtful Greeks to adopt the latter. Most of us
regard this identification as inadmissible, because the
way in which we conceive the world and ethics does

not point to the existence of any logos at all. But
a man must be blind not to see that for that age
the appropriate formula for uniting the Christian
religion with Greek thought was the Logos. Nor is
it difficult even to-day to attach a valid meaning to
the conception. An unmixed blessing it has not been.
To a much larger extent than the earlier speculative
ideas about Christ it absorbed men's interest;
it withdrew their minds from the simplicity of
the Gospel, and increasingly transformed it into
a philosophy of religion. The proposition that the
Logos had appeared among men had an intoxicating
effect, but the enthusiasm and transport which it
produced in the soul did not lead with any certainty
to the God whom Jesus Christ proclaimed.

The loss of an original element and the gain of
a fresh one, namely, the Greek, are insufficient to
explain the great change which the Christian religion
experienced in the second century. We must bear in
mind, thirdly, the great struggle which that religion
was then carrying on within its own domain.
Parallel with the slow influx of the element of
Greek philosophy experiments were being made all
along the line in the direction of what may be briefly
called "acute Hellenisation." While they offer us a
most magnificent historical spectacle, in the period
itself they were a terrible danger. More than any
before it, the second century is the century of religious fusion, of theocracy. The problem was to
bring Christianity into the realm of theocracy, as

one element among others, although the chief. The "Hellenism" which made this endeavour had already attracted to itself all the mysteries, all the philosophy of Eastern worship, elements the most sublime and the most absurd, and by the never failing aid of philosophical, that is to say, of allegorical interpretation, had spun them all into a glittering web. It now fell upon—I cannot help so expressing it—the Christian religion. It was impressed by the sublime character of this religion; it did reverence to Jesus Christ as the Saviour of the world; it offered to give up everything that it possessed—all the treasures of its civilisation and its wisdom—to this message, if only the message would suffer them to stand. As though endowed with the right to rule, the message was to make its entry into a ready-made theory of the world and religion, and into mysteries already prepared for it. What a proof of the impression which this message made, and what a temptation! This "Gnosticism"—such is the name which the movement has received—strong and active in the plenitude of its religious experiments, established itself under Christ's name, developed a vigorous and abiding feeling for many Christian ideas, sought to give shape to what was still shapeless, to settle accounts with what was externally incomplete, and to bring the whole stream of the Christian movement into its own channel. The majority of the faithful, led by their bishops, so far from yielding to these enticements, took up the struggle with them in the

conviction that they masked a demonic temptation.
But struggle in this case meant definition, that is
to say, drawing a sharp line of demarcation around
what was Christian and declaring everything heathen
that would not keep within it. *The struggle with
Gnosticism compelled the Church to put its teaching,
its worship, and its discipline, into fixed forms and
ordinances, and to exclude everyone who would not
yield them •obedience.* In the conviction that it was
everywhere only conserving and honouring what had
been handed down, it never for a moment doubted
that the obedience which it demanded was anything
more than subjection to the divine will itself, and
that in the doctrines with which it encountered the
enemy it was exhibiting *the impress of religion
itself.*

If by "Catholic" we mean the church of doctrine
and of law, then the Catholic church had its origin
in the struggle with Gnosticism. It had to pay a
heavy price for the victory which kept that tendency
at bay; we may almost say that the vanquished imposed their terms upon the victor : *Victi victoribus
legem dederunt.* It kept Dualism and the acute
phase of Hellenism at bay; but by becoming a
community with a fully worked out scheme of
doctrine, and a definite form of public worship, it
was of necessity compelled to take on forms
analogous to those which it combated in the
Gnostics. To encounter our enemy's theses by
setting up others one by one, is to change over

to his ground. How much of its original freedom
the Church sacrificed! It was now forced to say:
You are no Christian, you cannot come into any
relation with God at all, unless you have first of all
acknowledged these doctrines, yielded obedience to
these ordinances, and followed out definite forms of
mediation. Nor was anyone to think a religious
experience legitimate that had not been sanctioned
by sound doctrine and approved by the priests.
The Church found no other way and no other
means of maintaining itself against Gnosticism,
and what was set up as a protection against
enemies from without became the palladium, nay, the
very foundation, within. This entire development,
it is true, would probably have taken place apart
from the struggle in question—the two elements
which we first discussed would have produced it—
but that it took place so rapidly and assumed so
positive, nay, so Draconian, a shape, was due to the
fact that the struggle was one in which the very
existence of the traditional religion was at stake. The
superficial view that the personal ambition of certain
individuals was at the bottom of the whole system
of established ordinance and priesthood is absolutely
untenable. The loss of the original, living element
is by itself sufficient to explain the phenomena. *La
médiocrité fonde l'autorité.* It is the man who
knows religion only as usage and obedience that
creates the priest, for the purpose of ridding himself of an essential part of the obligations which

he feels by loading him with them. He also makes ordinances, for the semi-religious prefer an ordinance to a Gospel.

We have endeavoured to indicate the tendencies by which the great change was effected. It remains to answer the second question : Did the Gospel hold its own amid the change, and, if so, how ? That it entered upon an entirely new set of circumstances is already obvious ; but we shall have to study them more closely.

LECTURE XII.

No one can compare the internal state of Christendom at the beginning of the third century with the state in which it found itself a hundred and twenty years earlier without being moved by conflicting views and sentiments. Admiration for the vigorous achievement presented in the creation of the Catholic Church, and for the energy with which it extended its activity in all directions, is balanced by concern at the absence of those many elements of freedom and directness, united, however, by an inward bond, which the primitive age possessed. Although we are compelled gratefully to acknowledge that this Church repelled all attempts to let the Christian religion simply dissolve into contemporary thought, and protected itself against the acute phase of Hellenisation, still we cannot shut our eyes to the fact that it had to pay a high price for maintaining its position. Let us determine a little more precisely what the alteration was which was effected in it, and on which we have already touched.

The first and most prominent change is the way in which freedom and independence in matters of religion is endangered. No one is to feel and count himself a Christian, that is to say, a child of God, who has not previously subjected his religious knowledge and experience to the controlling influence of the Church's creed. The "Spirit" is confined within the narrowest limits, and forbidden to work where and as it will. Nay, more; not only is the individual, except in special cases, to begin by being a minor and by obeying the Church ; he is never to become of full age, that is to say, he is never to lose his dependence on doctrine, on the priest, on public worship, and on the "book." It was then that what we still specifically call the Catholic form of godliness, in contrast with Evangelicalism, originated. A blow was dealt to the direct and immediate element in religion ; and for any individual to restore it afresh for himself became a matter of extraordinary difficulty.

Secondly, although the acute phase of Hellenisation was avoided, Christendom became more and more penetrated by the Greek and philosophical idea that true religion is first and foremost "doctrine," and doctrine, too, that is coextensive with the whole range of knowledge. That this faith of "slaves and old women" attracted to itself the entire philosophy of God and the world which the Greeks had formed, and undertook to recast that philosophy as though teaching it were part of its own substance, and unite it with the teaching of Jesus Christ, was certainly a proof of the inner power of the Christian

religion ; but the process involved, as a necessary
consequence, a displacement of the fundamental
religious interest, and the addition of an enormous
burden. The question "What must I do to be
saved ?" which in Jesus Christ's and the Apostles'
day could still receive a very brief answer, now
evoked a most diffuse one ; and even though in view
of the laymen shorter replies might still be provided,
the laymen were in so far regarded as imperfect, and
expected to observe a submissive attitude towards the
learned. The Christian religion had already received
that tendency to Intellectualism which has clung
to it ever since. But when thus presented as a
huge and complex fabric, as a vast and difficult
system of doctrine, not only is it encumbered, but
its earnest character threatens to disappear. This
character depends upon the emotional and gladdening
element in it being kept directly accessible. The
Christian religion is assuredly informed with the desire
to come to terms with all knowledge and with intellectual life as a whole ; but when achievements in
this field—even presuming that they always accord
with truth and reality—are held to be equally binding
with the evangelical message, or even to be a necessary preliminary to it, mischief is done to the cause
of religion. This mischief is already unmistakeably
present at the beginning of the third century.

Thirdly, the church obtained a special, independent value as an *institution* ; it became a *religious
power*. Originally only a developed form of that

community of brothers which furnished place and manner for God's common worship and a mysterious shadow of the heavenly Church, it now became, *as an institution*, an indispensable factor in religion. People were taught that in this institution Christ's Spirit had deposited everything that the individual man can need ; that he is wholly bound to it, therefore, not only in love but also in faith ; that it is there only that the Spirit works, and therefore there only that all its gifts of grace are to be found. That the individual Christian who did not subordinate himself to the ecclesiastical institution relapsed, as a rule, into heathenism, and fell into false and evil doctrines or an immoral life, was, indeed, an actual fact. The effect of this, combined with the struggle against the Gnostics, was that the institution, together with all its forms and arrangements, became more and more identified with the "bride of Christ," "the true Jerusalem," and so on, and accordingly was even itself proclaimed as the inviolable creation of God, and the fixed and unalterable abode of the Holy Ghost. Consistently with this, it began to announce that all its ordinances were equally sacred. How greatly religious liberty was thus encumbered I need not show.

Fourthly and lastly, the Gospel was not proclaimed as the glad message with the same vigour in the second century as it had been in the first. The reasons for this are manifold : on the one hand personal experience of religion was not felt so

strongly as Paul, or as the author of the fourth
gospel, felt it; on the other, the prevalent eschatological expectations, which those teachers had re-
strained by their more profound teaching, remained
in full sway. *Fear* and *hope* are more prominent in
the Christianity of the second century than they are
with Paul, and it is only in appearance that the
former stands nearer to Jesus' sayings; for, as we
saw, God's Fatherhood is the main article in Jesus'
message. But, as Romans viii. proves, the knowledge of this truth is just what Paul embodied in
his preaching of the faith. While the element of
fear thus obtained a larger scope in the Christianity of the second century—this scope increased
in proportion as the original buoyancy died down
and conformity to the world extended—the ethical
element became less free and more a matter of law
and rigorism. In religion, rigorism always forms
the obverse side of secularity. But as it appeared
impossible to expect a rigoristic ethics of everyone, the distinction between a perfect and a sufficient morality already set in as an element in the
growth of Catholicism. That the roots of this
distinction go further back is a fact of which we
need not here take account; it was only towards
the end of the second century that the distinction became a fatal one. Born of necessity and
erected into a virtue, it soon grew so important
that the existence of Christianity as a Catholic
Church came to depend upon it. The uniformity of

the Christian ideal was thereby disturbed and a
quantitative view of moral achievement suggested
which is unknown to the Gospel. The Gospel does,
no doubt, make a distinction between a strong and
a weak faith, and greater and smaller moral achievements; but he that is least in the kingdom of God
may be perfect in his kind.

These various tendencies together denote the essential changes which the Christian religion experienced up to the beginning of the third century,
and by which it was modified. Did the Gospel
hold its own in spite of them, and how may that
be shown? Well, we can cite a whole series of
documents, which, so far as written words can
attest inner and genuinely Christian life, bear very
clear and impressive testimony that such life existed. Martyrdoms like those of Perpetua and
Felicitas, or letters passing between communities,
like those from Lyons to Asia Minor, exhibit the
Christian faith and the strength and delicacy of
moral sentiment with a splendour only paralleled
in the days when the faith was founded; while of
all that had been done in the external development
of the Church they make no mention whatever.
The way to God is found with certainty, and the
simplicity of the life within does not appear to be
disturbed or encumbered. Again, let us take a
writer like the Christian religious philosopher,
Clement of Alexandria, who flourished about the
year 200. We can still feel from his writings

that this scholar, although he was absolutely
steeped in speculative ideas, and as a thinker reduced the Christian religion to a boundless sea of
" doctrines "—a Greek in every fibre of his being
—won peace and joy from the Gospel, and he can
also express what he won and testify of the power
of the living God.   It is as a new man that he
appears, one who has pressed on through the whole
range of philosophy, through authority and speculation, through all the externals of religion, to the
glorious liberty of the children of God.   His faith
in Providence, his faith in Christ, his doctrine of
freedom, his ethics — everything is expressed in
language that betrays the Greek, and yet everything is new and genuinely Christian.   Further,
if we compare him with a Christian of quite another stamp, namely, his contemporary Tertullian,
it is easy to show that what they have in common
in religion is what they have learned from the
Gospel, nay, is the Gospel itself.   And in reading
Tertullian's exposition of the Lord's Prayer and
turning it over in our minds, we see that this hot-
blooded African, this stern foe of heretics, this
resolute champion of *auctoritas* and *ratio*, this
dogmatic advocate, this man, at once Churchman and enthusiast, nevertheless possessed a deep
feeling for the main substance of the Gospel and
a good knowledge of it as well.   In this Old-
Catholic Church the Gospel, truly, was not as yet
stifled !

Further, this Church still kept up the all-important idea that the Christian community must present itself as a society of brothers active in work, and it gave expression to this idea in a way that puts subsequent generations to shame.

Lastly, there can be no doubt—and while so truth-loving a man as Origen confirms the fact for us, heathen writers like Lucian also attest it— that the hope of an eternal life, the full confidence in Christ, a readiness to make sacrifices, and a purity of morals, were still, in spite of all frailties— here, too, not lacking—the *real* characteristics of this society.   Origen can challenge his heathen opponents to compare any community whatever with the Christian community, and to say where the greater moral excellence lies.   This religion had, no doubt, already developed a husk and integument, to penetrate through to it and grasp the kernel had become more difficult ; it had also lost much of its original life.   But the gifts and the tasks which the Gospel offered still remained in force, and the fabric which the Church had erected around them also served many a man as the means by which he attained to the thing itself.

We now pass to the consideration of

THE CHRISTIAN RELIGION IN GREEK CATHOLICISM.

I must invite you to descend several centuries with me and to look at *the Greek Church* as it is to-day, and as it has been preserved, essentially unaltered, for more than a thousand years. Between the third and the nineteenth century the history of the Church of the East nowhere presents any deep gulf. Hence we may take up our position in the present. Here, in turn, we ask the three following questions :—

What did this Greek Catholicism achieve ?

What are its characteristics ?

What modifications did the Gospel here undergo and how did it hold its own ?

What did this Greek Catholicism achieve ? Two facts may be cited on this point : firstly, in the great domain which it embraces, the countries of the eastern part of the Mediterranean and northwards to the Arctic Ocean, it made an end of heathenism and polytheism. The decisive victory was accomplished from the third to the sixth century, and so effectually accomplished that the gods of Greece really perished—perished unwept and unmourned. Not in any great battle did they die, but from sheer exhaustion, and without offering any resistance worth mention. I may just point out that before dying they transferred a considerable portion of their power to the Church's saints. But what is more important, with the death of the gods, Neoplatonism, the last great product of Greek philosophy, was also vanquished. The religious philosophy of the Church proved the stronger. The victory over Hellenism is an achievement of the

Eastern Church on which it still subsists. Secondly,
this Church managed to effect such a fusion with
the individual nations which it drew into its bosom
that religion and church became to them national
palladia, nay, palladia pure and simple. Go amongst
Greeks, Russians, Armenians, etc., and you will
everywhere find that religion and nationality are
inseparable, and the one element exists only in and
alongside of the other. Men of these nationalities
will, if need be, suffer themselves be cut in pieces
for their religion. This is no mere consequence of
the pressure exercised by the hostile power of
Mohammedanism; the Russians are not subject to
this pressure. Nor is it only — shall I say? —
in the Moscow press that we can see what a firm
and intimate connexion exists between Church and
nation in these peoples, in spite of " sects " which
are not wanting here either ; to convince ourselves of it we must read—to take an instance at
random—Tolstoi's *Village Tales*. They bring before
the reader a really touching picture of the deep
influence of the Church, with its message of the
Eternal, of self-sacrifice, of sympathy and fraternity,
on the national mind. That the clergy stand low
in the social scale, and frequently encounter contempt, must not delude us into supposing that
as the representatives of the Church they do not
occupy an incomparably high station. In Eastern
Europe the monastic ideal is deeply rooted in the
national soul.

But the mention of these two points includes everything that can be said about the achievements of this Church. To add that it has disseminated a certain amount of culture would involve pitching our standard of culture very low. In comparison with Islam, too, it is no longer so successful in doing what it has done in the past and still does in regard to polytheism. The missions of the Russian Church are still overthrowing polytheism even to-day; but large territories have been lost to Islam, and the Church has not recovered them. Islam has extended its victories as far as the Adriatic and in the direction of Bosnia. It has won over numerous Albanian and Slav tribes which were once Christian. It shows itself to be at least a match for the Church, although we must not forget that in the heart of its dominions there are Christian nations who have maintained their creed.

Our second question was, What are the characteristics of this Church? The answer is not easy; for as it presents itself to the spectator this Church is a highly complex structure. The feelings, the superstitions, the learning, and the devotional philosophy of hundreds, nay, of thousands of years, are built into it. But, further; no one can look at this Church from outside, with its forms of worship, its solemn ritual, the number of its ceremonies, its relics, pictures, priests, monks, and the philosophy of its mysteries, and then compare it on the one hand with the Church of the first

century, and on the other with the Hellenic cults in
the age of Neoplatonism, without arriving at the
conclusion that it belongs not to the former but to
the latter. *It takes the form, not of a Christian
product in Greek dress, but of a Greek product
in Christian dress.* It would have done battle
with the Christians of the first century just as it
did battle with the worship of Magna Mater and
Zeus Soter. There are innumerable features of this
Church which are counted as sacred as the Gospel,
and towards which not even a tendency existed
in primitive Christianity. Of the whole perform-
ance of the chief religious service, nay, even of
many of the dogmas, the same thing may, in the
last resort, be said : if certain words, like Christ,
etc., are omitted, there is nothing left to recall
the original element. In its external form as a
whole this Church is nothing more than a continuation of the history of Greek religion under the
alien influence of Christianity, parallel to the many
other alien influences which have affected it. We
might also describe it as the natural product of
the union between Hellenism, itself already in a
state of oriental decay, and Christian teaching ;
it is the transformation which history effects in
a religion by "natural" means, and, as was here
the case, was bound to effect between the third and
the sixth century. In this sense it is *a natural
religion.* The conception admits of a double meaning.   It is generally understood as an abstract

term covering all the elementary feelings and pro-
cesses traceable in every religion. Whether there are
any such elements, or, on the other hand, whether
they are sufficiently stable and articulate to be
followed as a whole, admits, however, of a doubt.
The conception "natural religion" may be better
applied to the growth which a religion produces when
the "natural" forces of history have ceased playing on
it. At bottom these forces are everywhere the same,
although differing in the way in which they are
mounted. They mould religion until it answers
their purpose; not by expelling what is sacred,
venerable, and so on, but by assigning it the
place and allowing it the scope which they consider
right. They immerse everything in a uniform
medium,—that medium which, like the air, is the
first condition of their "natural" existence. In
this sense, then, the Greek Church is a *natural*
religion; no prophet, no reformer, no genius, has
arisen in its history since the third century to
disturb the ordinary process by which a religion
becomes naturalised into common history. The
process attained its completion in the sixth century
and asserted itself victoriously against severe assaults
in the eighth and ninth. The Church has since been
at rest, and no further essential, nay, not even any
unessential, change has taken place in the condition
which it then reached. Since then, apparently, the
nations belonging to this Church have undergone
nothing to make it seem intolerable to them and

to call for any reform in it. They still continue, then, in this "natural" religion of the sixth century.

I have, however, advisedly spoken of the Church in its external form. Its complex character is partly due to the fact that we cannot arrive at its inner condition by simple deduction from its outer. It is not sufficient to observe, although the observation is correct, that this Church is part of the history of Greek religion. It exercises influences which from this point of view are not easily intelligible. We cannot form a correct estimate of it unless we dwell more closely on the factors which lend it its character.

The first factor which we encounter is *tradition*, and the observance of it. The sacred and the divine do not exist in free action—we shall see later to what reservations this statement is subject—but are put, as it were, into a storehouse, in the form of an immense capital. The capital is to provide for all demands, and to be coined in the precise way in which the Fathers coined it. Here, it is true, we have an idea which can be traced to something already existing in the primitive age. We read in the Acts of the Apostles that "They continued steadfastly in the apostles' doctrine." But what became of this practice and this obligation? Firstly, everything was designated "apostolic" which was deposited in this Church in the course of the succeeding centuries; or, rather, what the Church considered necessary to possess in order to suit the historical

position in which it was placed, it called apostolic,
because it fancied that otherwise it could not exist,
and what is necessary for the Church's existence
must be simply apostolic. Secondly, it has been
established as an irrefragable fact that the "continuing steadfastly in the apostles' doctrine" applies,
first and foremost, to the punctilious observance
of every direction as to ritual : the sacred element
is bound up with *text* and *form*. Both are conceived in a thoroughly antique way. That the
divine is, so to speak, stored up as though it were
an actual commodity, and that the supreme demand
which the Deity makes is the punctilious observance
of a ritual, were ideas that in antiquity were perfectly familiar and admitted of no doubt. Tradition and ceremony are the conditions under which
the Holy alone existed and was accessible. Obedience, respect, reverence, were the most important
religious feelings. Whilst they are doubtless inalienable features of religion, it is only as ac-
companiments of an active feeling quite different
in its character that they possess any value, and
that further presumes that the object to which
they are directed is a worthy one. Traditionalism
and the ritualism so closely connected with it are
prominent characteristics of the Greek Church, but
this is just what shows how far it has departed
from the Gospel.

The second point that fixes the character of this
Church is the value which it attaches to *orthodoxy*,

to sound doctrine. It has stated and re-stated its doctrines with the greatest precision and often enough made them a terror to men of different creed. No one, it claims, can be saved who does not possess the correct doctrine ; the man who does not possess it is to be expelled and must forfeit all his rights ; if he be a fellow-countryman, he must be treated as a leper and lose all connexion with his nation. This fanaticism, which still flares up here and there in the Greek Church even to-day and in principle has not been abandoned, is not Greek, although a certain inclination towards it was not lacking in the ancient Greeks ; still less did it originate in Roman law ; it is the result, rather, of an unfortunate combination of several factors. When the Roman empire became Christian, the hard fight for existence which the Church had waged with the Gnostics was not yet forgotten ; still less had the Church forgotten the last bloody persecutions which the State had inflicted upon it in a kind of despair. These two circumstances would in themselves be sufficient to explain how the Church came to feel that it had a right of reprisal, and was at the same time bound to suppress heretics. But, in addition, there had now appeared in the highest place, since the days of Diocletian and Constantine, the absolutist conception, derived from the East, of the unlimited right and the unlimited duty of the ruler in regard to his " subjects." The unfortunate factor in the

P

great change was that the Roman Emperor was
at once, and almost in the same moment, a Christian Emperor and an oriental despot. The more
conscientious he was, the more intolerant he was
bound to be ; for the deity had committed to his
care not only men's bodies but their souls as well.
Thus arose the aggressive and all-devouring orthodoxy of State and Church, or, rather, of the State-
Church. Examples which were to hand from the
Old Testament completed and sanctified the process.

Intolerance is a new growth in the land of the
Greeks and cannot be roundly laid to their charge ;
but the way in which doctrine developed, namely,
as a philosophy of God and the world, was due
to their influence ; and the fact that religion and
doctrine were directly identified is also a product
of the Greek spirit. No mere reference to the
significance which doctrine already possessed in
the apostolic age, and to the tendencies operating
in the direction of bringing it into a speculative
form, is sufficient to explain the change. These are
matters, as I hope that I have shown in the previous
lectures, which are rather to be understood in a
different sense. It is in the second century, and
with the apologists, that Intellectualism commences ;
and, supported by the struggle with the Gnostics
and by the Alexandrian school of religious philosophers in the Church, it manages to prevail.

But it is not enough to assess the teaching of

the Greek Church by its formal side alone, and ascertain in what way and to what extent it is exhibited, and what is the value to be placed upon it. We must also examine its substance; for it possesses two elements which are quite peculiar to it and separate it from the Greek philosophy of religion—*the idea of the creation*, and the doctrine of the *God-Man nature of the Saviour.* We shall treat of these two elements in our next lecture, and, further, of the two other elements which, side by side with tradition and doctrine, characterise the Greek Church; namely, the form of worship and the order of monkhood.

LECTURE XIII.

So far we have established the fact that Greek Catholicism is characterised as a religion by two elements: by *traditionalism* and by *intellectualism*. According to traditionalism, the reverent preservation of the received inheritance, and the defence of it against all innovation, is not only an important duty, but is itself the practical proof of religion. That is an idea quite in harmony with antiquity and foreign to the Gospel; for the Gospel knows absolutely nothing of intercourse with God being bound up with reverence for tradition itself. But the second element, intellectualism, is also of Greek origin. The elaboration of the Gospel into a vast philosophy of God and the world, in which every conceivable kind of material is handled; the conviction that because Christianity is the absolute religion it must give information on all questions of metaphysics, cosmology, and history; the view of revelation as a countless multitude of doctrines and explanations, all equally holy and important—this is Greek intellectualism. According to it, *Knowledge* is the highest good, and spirit is spirit only in so far as it knows; everything that is of an æsthetical, ethical, and religious character must be converted into some form of knowledge, which human will and life will then with certainty obey. The development of the Christian faith into an all-embracing theosophy, and the identification of faith with theological knowledge, are proofs that the Christian religion on Greek soil entered the proscribed circle of the native religious philosophy and has remained there.

But in this vast philosophy of God and the world, which possesses an absolute value as the "substance of what has been revealed" and as "orthodox doctrine," there are two elements which radically distinguish it from Greek religious philosophy and invest it with an entirely original character. I do not mean the appeal which it makes to revelation—for to that the Neoplatonists also appealed—but the *idea of creation* and the doctrine of *the God-Man nature of the Saviour.* They traverse the scheme of Greek religious philosophy at two critical points, and have therefore always been felt to be alien and intolerable by its genuine representatives.

The idea of creation we can deal with in a few words. It is undoubtedly an element which is as important as it is in thorough keeping with the Gospel. It abolishes all intertwining of God and world, and gives expression to the power and actuality of the living God. Attempts were not wanting, it is true, among Christian thinkers on Greek soil—just because they were Greeks—to conceive the Deity only as the uniform power operating in the fabric of the world, as the unity in diversity, and as its goal. Traces of this speculative idea are even still to be found in the Church doctrine; the idea of creation, however, triumphed, and therewith Christianity won a real victory.

The subject of the God-Man nature of the Saviour is one on which it is much more difficult to arrive at a correct opinion. It is indubitably the central point in the whole dogmatic system of the Greek Church. It supplied the doctrine of the Trinity. In the Greek view these two doctrines together make up Christian teaching *in nuce.* When a Father of the Greek Church once said, as he did say: "The idea of the God-Man nature, the idea of God becoming a man, is what is new in the new, nay, is the only new thing under the sun," not only did he correctly represent the opinion of all his fellow-believers, but he also at the same time strikingly expressed their view that, while sound intelligence and earnest reflection yield all the other points of doctrine of themselves, this one lies beyond them. The theologians of the Greek Church are convinced that the only real distinction between the Christian creed and natural philosophy is that the former embraces the doctrine of the God-Man nature, including the Trinity. Side by side with this, the only other doctrine that can at most come in question is that of the idea of creation.

If that be so, it is of radical importance to obtain a

correct view of the origin, meaning, and value of this doctrine. In its completed form it must look strange to anyone who comes to it straight from the evangelists. While no historical reflection can rid us of the impression that the whole fabric of ecclesiastical Christology is a thing absolutely outside the concrete personality of Jesus Christ, historical considerations nevertheless enable us not only to explain its origin but also even to justify, in a certain degree, the way in which it is formulated. Let us try to get a clear idea of the leading points.

We saw in a previous lecture how it came about that the Church teachers selected the conception of the Logos in order to define Christ's nature and majesty. They found the conception of the "Messiah" quite unintelligible; it conveyed no meaning to them. As conceptions cannot be improvised, they had to choose between representing Christ as a deified man, that is to say, as a hero, or conceiving his nature after the pattern of one of the Greek gods, or identifying it with the Logos. The first two possibilities had to be put aside, as they were "heathenish," or seemed to be so. There remained, therefore, the Logos. How well this formula served different purposes we have already pointed out. Did it not readily admit of being combined with the conception of the Sonship, without leading to any objectionable theogonies? It involved, too, no menace to monotheism. But the formula had a logic of its own, and this logic led to results which were not absolutely free from suspicion. The conception of the Logos was susceptible of very varied expression; in spite of its sublime meaning, it could be also so conceived as to permit of the bearer of the title not being by any means of a truly divine nature but possessing one that was only half divine.

The question as to the more exact definition of the nature of the Logos-Christ could not have attained the enormous significance which it received in the Church, and might have been stilled by various speculative answers, if it had not been accompanied by the triumph of a very precise idea of the nature of redemption, which acted as a peremptory challenge. Among all the possible ideas on the subject of redemption—forgiveness of sins, release from the power of the demons, and so on—that idea came victoriously to the front in the Church in the third century which conceived of it as *redemption from death and therewith as elevation to the divine life, that is to say, as deification.* It is true that this conception found a safe starting-point in the Gospel, and support in the Pauline theology; but in the form in which it was now developed it was foreign to both of them and conceived on Greek lines; *mortality is in itself reckoned as the greatest evil, and as the cause of all evil, while the greatest of blessings is to live for ever.* What a severely Greek idea this is we can see, in the first place, from the fact that redemption from death is presented, in a wholly realistic fashion, as a *pharmacological* process

—the divine nature has to flow in and transform the mortal nature—and, in the second, from the way in which eternal life and deification were identified. But if actual interference in the constitution of human nature and its deification are involved, then *the redeemer must himself be God and must become man.* It is only on this condition that so marvellous a process can be imagined as actually taking place. Word, doctrine, individual deeds, are here of no avail —how can life be given to a stone, or a mortal made immortal, by preaching at them? Only when the divine itself bodily enters into mortality can mortality be transformed. It is not, however, the hero, but God Himself alone, who possesses the divine, that is to say, eternal life, and so possesses it as to permit of His *giving it to others.* The Logos, then, must be God Himself, and He must have actually become man. With the satisfying of these two conditions, real, natural redemption, that is to say, the deification of humanity, is actually effected. These considerations enable us to understand the prodigious disputes over the nature of the Logos-Christ which filled several centuries. They explain why Athanasius strove for the formula that the Logos-Christ was of the same nature as the Father, as though the existence or non-existence of the Christian religion were at stake. They show clearly how it was that other teachers in the Greek Church regarded any menace to the complete *unity* of the divine and the human in the Redeemer, any notion of a merely moral connexion, as a death-blow to Christianity. These teachers secured their formulas, which for them were anything but scholastic conceptions; rather, they were the statement and establishment of a matter of fact, in the absence of which the Christian religion was as unsatisfactory as any other. The doctrines of the identical nature of the three persons of the Trinity—how the doctrine of the Holy Ghost came about, I need not mention—and of the God-Man nature of the Redeemer are in strict accordance with the distinguishing notion of the redemption as a deification of man's nature by making him immortal. Without the help of the notion those formulas would never have been attained; but they also stand and fall with it. They prevailed, however, not because they were akin to the ideas of Greek philosophy, but because they were contrasted with them. Greek philosophy never ventured, and never aspired, to meet, in any similar way by "history" and specu- lative ideas, that wish for immortality which it so vividly entertained. To attribute any such interfer- ence with the Cosmos to an *historical* personality and the manner in which it appeared, and to ascribe to that personality a transformation in what, given once for all, was in a state of eternal flux, must necessarily have seemed, to Greek philosophy, pure mythology and superstition. The "only new thing under the sun" must necessarily have appeared to it, and did appear, to be the worst kind of fable.

The Greek Church still entertains the conviction
to-day that in these doctrines it possesses the essence
of Christianity, regarded at once as a mystery and
as a mystery that has been revealed. Criticism of
this contention is not difficult. We must acknowledge that those doctrines powerfully contributed
to keeping the Christian religion from dissolving
into Greek religious philosophy; further, that they
profoundly impress us with the absolute character
of this religion; again, that they are in actual
accordance with the Greek notion of redemption;
lastly, that this very notion has *one* of its roots
in the Gospel. But beyond this we can acknowledge
nothing; nay, it is to be observed (i.) that the
notion of the redemption as a deification of mortal
nature is subchristian, because the moral element
involved can at best be only tacked on to it; (ii.)
that the whole doctrine is inadmissible, because it
has scarcely any connexion with the Jesus Christ
of the Gospel, and its formulas do not fit him; it
is, therefore, not founded in truth; and (iii.) that
as it is connected with the real Christ only by uncertain threads, it leads us away from him; it does
not keep his image alive, but, on the contrary,
demands that this image should be apprehended
solely in the light of alleged hypotheses about him
expressed in theoretical propositions. That this
substitution produces no very serious or destructive
effects is principally owing to the fact that in spite of
them the Church has not suppressed the Gospels, and

that their own innate power makes itself felt. It may also be conceded that the notion of God having become man does not everywhere produce the effect only of a bewildering mystery, but, on the contrary, is capable of leading to the pure and definite conviction that God was in Christ. We may admit, lastly, that the egoistic desire for immortal existence will, within the Christian sphere, experience a moral purification through the longing *to live with and in God*, and to remain inseparably bound to His love. But all these admissions cannot do away with the palpable fact that in Greek dogma we have a fatal connexion established between the desire of the ancients for immortal life and the Christian message. Nor can anyone deny that this connexion, implanted in Greek religious philosophy and the intellectualism which characterised it, has led to formulas which are incorrect, introduce a supposititious Christ in the place of the real one, and, besides, encourage the delusion that, if only a man possesses the right formula, he has the thing itself. Even though the Christological formula were the theologically right one—what a departure from the Gospel is involved in maintaining that a man can have no relation with Jesus Christ, nay, that he is sinning against him and will be cast out, unless he first of all acknowledges that Christ was *one* person with two natures and two powers of will, one of them divine and one human. Such is the demand into which intellectualism has developed. Can such a system still find a place for the Gospel story of the Syro-phœnician woman or the centurion at Capernaum ?

But with traditionalism and intellectualism a further element is associated, namely, ritualism. If religion is presented as a complex system of traditional doctrine, to which the few alone have any real access, the majority of believers cannot practise it at all except as ritual. Doctrine comes to be administered in stereotyped formulas accompanied by symbolic acts. Although no inner understanding of it is thus possible, it produces the feeling of something mysterious. The very deification which the future is expected to bring, and which in itself is something that can neither be described nor conceived, is now administered as though it were an earnest of what is to come, by means of ritual acts. An imaginative mood is excited, and disposes to its reception ; and this excitement, when enhanced, is its seal.

Such are the feelings which move the members of the Greek Catholic Church. Intercourse with God is achieved through the cult of a mystery, and by means of hundreds of efficacious formulas small and great, signs, pictures, and consecrated acts, which, if punctiliously and submissively observed, communicate divine grace and prepare the Christian for eternal life. Doctrine as such is for the most part something unknown ; if it appears at all, it is only in the form of liturgical aphorisms. For ninety-nine per cent. of these Christians, religion exists only as a ceremonious ritual, in which it is externalised. But even for Christians of advanced intelligence all these ritual acts are absolutely necessary, for it is only in them that doctrine receives its correct application and obtains its due result.

There is no sadder spectacle than this transformation of the Christian religion from a worship of God in spirit and in truth into a worship of God in signs, formulas, and idols. To feel the whole pity of this development, we need not descend to such adherents of this form of Christendom as are religiously and intellectually in a state of complete abandonment, like the Copts and Abyssinians; the Syrians, Greeks, and Russians are, taken as a whole, only a little better. Where, however, can we find in Jesus' message even a trace of any injunction that a man is to submit to solemn ceremonies as though they were mysterious ministrations, to be punctilious in observing a ritual, to put up pictures, and to mumble maxims and formulas in a prescribed fashion? *It was to destroy this sort of religion that Jesus Christ suffered himself to be nailed to the cross*, and now we find it re-established under his name and authority! Not only has "mystagogy" stepped into a position side by side with the "mathesis," that is to say, the doctrine, which called it forth; but the truth is that "doctrine"— be its constitution what it may, it is still a spiritual principle—has disappeared, and ceremony dominates everything. This is what marks the relapse into the ancient form of the lowest class of religion. Over the vast area of Greek and Oriental Christendom religion has been almost stifled by ritualism. It is not that religion has sacrificed one of its essential elements. No! it has entered an entirely different plane; it has descended to the level where religion may be described as a cult and nothing but a cult.

Nevertheless, Greek and Oriental Christianity contains within itself an element which for centuries has been capable of offering, and still offers here and there to-day, a certain resistance to the combined forces of traditionalism, intellectualism, and ritualism—I mean monasticism. To the question, Who is in the highest sense of the word a Christian? the Greek Christian replies: the monk. The man who practises silence and purity, who shuns not only the world but also the Church of the world, who avoids not only false doctrine but any statement about the true, who fasts, gives himself up to contemplation, and steadily waits for God's glorious light to dawn upon his gaze, who attaches no value to anything but tranquillity and meditation on the Eternal, who asks nothing of life but death, and who from such utter unselfishness and purity makes mercy arise—this is the Christian. To him not even the Church and the consecration which it bestows is an absolute necessity. For such a man the whole system of sanctified secularity has vanished. Over

and over again in ascetics of this kind the Church
has seen in its ranks figures of such strength and
delicacy of religious feeling, so filled with the divine,
so inwardly active in forming themselves after certain
features of Christ's image, that we may, indeed,
say : here there is a living religion, not unworthy
of Christ's name. We Protestants must not take
direct offence at the form of monasticism. The
conditions under which our Churches arose have
made a harsh and one-sided opinion of it a kind
of duty. And although for the present, and in
view of the problems which press on us, we may
be justified in retaining this opinion, we must not
summarily apply it to other circumstances. Nothing
but monasticism could provide a leaven and a coun-
terpoise in that traditionalistic and ritualistic secular
Church, such as the Greek Church was and still is.
Here there was freedom, independence, and vivid
experience ; here the truth that it is only what is
experienced and comes from within that has any
value in religion carried the day.

And yet, the invaluable tension which in this part of
Christendom existed between the secular Church and
monasticism has unhappily almost disappeared, and
of the blessing which it established there is scarcely
a trace left. Not only has monasticism become
subject to the Church and is everywhere bent
under its yoke, but the secular spirit has in a
special degree invaded the monasteries. Greek
and oriental monks are now, as a rule, the

instruments of the lowest and worst functions of the Church, of the worship of pictures and relics, of the crassest superstition and the most imbecile sorcery. Exceptions are not wanting, and it is still to the monks that we must pin our hopes of a better future ; but it is not easy to see how a Church is to be reformed which, teach what it will, is content with its adherents finding the Christian *faith* in the observance of certain ceremonies, and Christian *morality* in keeping fast-days correctly.

As to our last question : What modifications did the Gospel undergo in this Church and how did it hold its own ? Well, in the first place, I do not expect to be contradicted if I answer that this official ecclesiasticism with its priests and its cult, with all its vessels, saints, vestments, pictures and amulets, with its ordinances of fasting and its festivals, has absolutely nothing to do with the religion of Christ. It is the religion of the ancient world, tacked on to certain conceptions in the Gospel ; or, rather, it is the ancient religion with the Gospel absorbed into it. The religious moods which are here produced, or which turn towards this kind of religion are, in so far as they can still be called religious at all, of a class lower than Christian. But neither have its traditionalism and its "orthodoxy" much in common with the Gospel ; they, too, were not derived from it and cannot be traced back to it. Correct doctrine, reverence,

Q

obedience, the shudderings of awe, may be valuable
and edifying things; they may avail to bind and
restrain the individual, especially when they draw
him into the community of a stable society; but
they have nothing to do with the Gospel, as long
as they fail to touch the individual at the point
where freedom lies, and inner decision for or against
God. In contrast with this, monasticism, in its
resolve to serve God by an ascetic and contemplative
life, contains an incomparably more valuable element,
because sayings of Christ, even though applied in
a one-sided and limited way, are nevertheless taken
as a standard, and the possibility of an independent
inner life being kindled is not so far removed.

Not so far removed—entirely lacking, thank God,
it is not, even in the waste shrines of this
ecclesiasticism, and Christ's sayings sound in the
ear of any who visit its churches. On the Church
as a Church, apparatus and all, there is nothing
more favourable to be said than has been said
already; the best thing about it is that it keeps
up, although to a modest extent, the knowledge
of the Gospel. Jesus' words, even though only
mumbled by the priests, take the first place in
this Church, too, and the quiet mission which
they pursue is not suppressed. Side by side with
the magical apparatus and the transports of feeling,
of which the ceremony is only the *caput mortuum*,
stand Jesus' sayings; they are read in private and
in public, and no superstition avails to destroy

their power. Nor can its fruits be mistaken by anyone who will look below the surface. Among these Christians, too, priests and laity, there are men who have come to know God as the Father of mercy and the leader of their lives, and who love Jesus Christ, not because they know him as the person with two natures, but because a ray of his being has shone from the Gospel into their hearts, and this ray has become light and warmth to their own lives. And although the idea of the fatherly providence of God more readily assumes an almost fatalistic form in the East, and produces too much quietism, it is certain that here, too, it endows men with strength and energy, unselfishness and love. I need only refer again to Tolstoi's *Village Tales*, which I have already quoted. The picture which they present is not artificial. But from much also that I have myself seen and experienced I can testify how even with the Russian peasant or the humbler priests, in spite of all the Saint- and picture-worship, a power of simple trust in God is to be found, a delicacy of moral feeling, and an active brotherly love, which does not disclaim its origin in the Gospel. Where they exist, however, the entire ceremonial service of religion is capable of undergoing a spiritualisation, not by any "symbolical re-interpretation"—that is much too artificial a process—but because, if only the soul is touched by the living God at all, thought can rise to him even by the help of an idol.

But it is truly no accidental circumstance that, in so far as any independent religious life is to be found among the members of this Church, it at once takes shape in trust in God, in humility, in unselfishness and mercy, and that Jesus Christ is at the same time laid hold of with reverence; for these are just the indications which show us that the Gospel is not as yet stifled, and that it is in these religious virtues that it has its real substance.

As a whole and in its structure the system of the oriental Churches is foreign to the Gospel; it means at once a veritable transformation of the Christian faith and the depression of religion to a much lower level, namely, that of the ancient world. But in its monasticism, in so far as this is not entirely subject to the secular Church and itself secularised, there is an element which reduces the whole ecclesiastical apparatus to a secondary position, and which opens up the possibility of attaining a state of Christian independence. Above all, however, by not having suppressed the Gospel, but by having kept it accessible, even though in a meagre fashion, the Church still possesses the corrective in its midst. Side by side with the Church the Gospel exercises its own influence on individuals. This influence, however, takes shape in a type of religion exhibiting the very characteristics which we have shown to be most distinctive of Jesus' message. Thus on the ground occupied by this

Church the Gospel has not completely perished. Here, too, human souls find a dependence on God and a freedom in Him, and when they have found these, they speak the language which every Christian understands, and which goes to every Christian's heart.

LECTURE XIV.

THE CHRISTIAN RELIGION IN ROMAN CATHOLICISM.

THE Roman Church is the most comprehensive and the vastest, the most complicated and yet at the same time the most uniform structure which, as far as we know, history has produced. All the powers of the human mind and soul, and all the elemental forces at mankind's disposal, have had a hand in creating it. In its many-sided character and severe cohesion Roman Catholicism is far in advance of Greek. We ask, in turn :—

What did the Roman Catholic Church achieve?

What are its characteristics?

What modifications has the Gospel suffered in this Church, and how much of it has remained?

What did the Roman Catholic Church achieve? Well, in the first place, it educated the Romano-Germanic nations, and educated them in a sense other than that in which the Eastern Church educated the Greeks, Slavs, and Orientals. However much their original nature, or primitive and historical circumstances, may have favoured those

nations and helped to promote their rise, the value
of the services which the Church rendered is not
thereby diminished. It brought Christian civilisation to young nations, and brought it, not once
only, so as to keep them at its first stage—no! it
gave them something which was capable of exercising
a progressive educational influence, and for a period
of almost a thousand years it itself led the advance.
Up to the fourteenth century it was a leader and a
mother; it supplied the ideas, set the aims, and disengaged the forces. Up to the fourteenth century—
thenceforward, as we may see, those whom it educated
became independent, and struck out paths which it
did not indicate, and on which it is neither willing
nor able to follow them. But even so, however,
during the period covered by the last six hundred
years, it has not fallen so far behind as the Greek
Church. With comparatively brief interruptions it
has proved itself fully a match for the whole movement of politics—we in Germany know that well
enough!—and even in the movement of thought it
still has an important share. The time, of course, is
long past since it was a leader; on the contrary, it
is now a drag; but, in view of the mistaken and
precipitate elements in modern progress, the drag
which it supplies is not always the reverse of a
blessing.

In the second place, however, this Church upheld
the idea of religious and ecclesiastical independence
in Western Europe in the face of the tendencies,

not lacking here either, towards State-omnipotence in the spiritual domain. In the Greek Church, as we saw, religion has become so intimately allied with nationality and the State that, public worship and monasticism apart, it has no room left for independent action. On Western ground it is otherwise ; the religious element and the moral element bound up with it occupy an independent sphere and jealously guard it. This we owe in the main to the Roman Church.

These two facts embrace the most important piece of work which this Church achieved and in part still achieves. We have already indicated the bounds which must be set to the first. To the second also a sensible limitation attaches, and we shall see what it is as we proceed.

What are the characteristics of the Roman Church ? This was our second question. Unless I am mistaken, the Church, complicated as it is, may be resolved into three chief elements. The first, *Catholicism*, it shares with the Greek Church. The second is the *Latin spirit* and the *Roman World-Empire* continuing in the Roman Church. The third is the spirit and religious fervour of *St. Augustine*. So far as the inner life of this Church is religious life and religious thought, it follows the standard which St. Augustine authoritatively fixed. Not only has he arisen again and again in his many successors, but he has awakened and kindled numbers of men

ROMAN CATHOLICISM 249

who, coming forward with independent religious
and theological fervour, are nevertheless spirit of
his spirit.

These three elements, the Catholic, the Latin in
the sense of the Roman World-Empire, and the
Augustinian, constitute the peculiar character of the
Roman Church.

So far as the first is concerned, you may recognise
its importance by the fact that the Roman Church
to-day receives every Greek Christian, nay, at once
effects a "union" with every Greek ecclesiastical
community, without more ado, as soon as the Pope
is acknowledged and submission is made to his
apostolic supremacy. Any other condition that
may be exacted from the Greek Christians is of
absolutely no moment; they are even allowed to
retain divine worship in their mother tongue, and
married priests. If we consider what a "purification" Protestants have to undergo before they can
be received into the bosom of the Roman Church,
the difference is obvious. Now a Church cannot
make so great a mistake about itself as to omit
any essential condition in taking up new members,
especially if they come from another confession.
The element which the Roman Church shares with
the Greek must, then, be of significant and critical
importance, when it is sufficient to make union
possible on the condition that the papal supremacy
is recognised. As a matter of fact, the main points
characteristic of Greek Catholicism are all to be

found in Roman as well, and are, on occasion, just
as energetically maintained here as they are there.
Traditionalism, orthodoxy, and ritualism play just
the same part here as they do there, so far as
"higher considerations" do not step in ; and the
same is true of monasticism also.

So far as "higher considerations" do not step in—
here we have already passed to the examination of the
second element, namely, the Latin Spirit in the sense
of the Roman World-dominion.   In the Western half
of Christendom the Latin spirit, the spirit of Rome,
very soon effected certain distinct modifications in the
general Catholic idea.   As early as the beginning of
the third century we see the thought emerging in the
Latin Fathers that salvation, however effected and
whatever its nature, is bestowed in the form of a
contract under definite conditions, and only to the
extent to which they are observed; it is *salus
legitima* ; in fixing these conditions the Deity
manifested its mercy and indulgence, but it guards
their observance all the more jealously.   Further,
the whole contents of revelation are *lex*, the Bible
as well as tradition.   Again, this tradition is attached
to a class of officials and to their correct succession.
The "mysteries," however, are "sacraments"; that
is to say, on the one hand, they are binding acts;
on the other, they contain definite gifts of grace
in a carefully limited form and with a specific
application.   Again, the discipline of penance is a
procedure laid down by law and akin to the process

adopted in a civil action or a suit in defence of honour. Lastly, the Church is a *legal institution*; and it is so, not side by side with its function of preserving and distributing salvation, but it is a legal institution for the sake of this very function.

But it is in its constitution as a Church that it is a legal establishment. We must briefly see how things stand in regard to this constitution, as its foundations are common to the Eastern and the Western Church. When the monarchical episcopate had developed, the Church began to approximate its constitution to State government. The system of uniting sees under a metropolitan who was, as a rule, the bishop of the provincial capital, corresponded with the distribution of the Empire into provinces. Above and beyond this, the ecclesiastical constitution in the East was developed a step further when it adapted itself to the division of the Empire introduced by Diocletian, by which large groups of provinces were united. Thus arose the constitution of the patriarchate, which was not, however, strictly enforced, and was in part counteracted by other considerations.

In the West no division into patriarchates came about; but on the other hand something else happened : in the fifth century the Western Roman Empire perished of internal weakness and through the inroads of the barbarians. What was left of what was Roman took refuge in the Roman Church —civilisation, law, and orthodox faith as opposed to the Arian. The barbarian chiefs, however, did not venture to set themselves up as Roman Emperors, and enter the vacant shrine of the *imperium*; they founded empires of their own in the provinces. In these circumstances the Bishop of Rome appeared as the guardian of the past and the shield of the future. All over the provinces occupied by the barbarians, even in those which had previously maintained a defiant independence in the face of Rome, bishops and laity looked to him. Whatever Roman elements the barbarians and Arians left standing in the provinces —and they were not few—were ecclesiasticised and at the same time put under the protection of the Bishop of Rome, who was the chief person there after the Emperor's disappearance. But in Rome the episcopal throne was occupied in the fifth century by men who understood the signs of the times and utilised them to the full. *The Roman Church in this way privily pushed itself into the place of the Roman World-Empire, of which it is the actual continuation;* the empire has not perished, but has only undergone a transformation. If we assert, and mean the assertion to hold good even of the present time, that the Roman Church is the old Roman Empire consecrated by the Gospel, that is no mere " clever remark," but the recognition of the true state of the matter historically, and the most appropriate and fruitful way of describing the character of this Church. It still governs the nations; its Popes rule like Trajan and Marcus Aurelius; Peter and

Paul have taken the place of Romulus and Remus; the bishops and archbishops, of the proconsuls; the troops of priests and monks correspond to the legions; the Jesuits, to the imperial body-guard. The continued influence of the old Empire and its institutions may be traced in detail, down to individual legal ordinances, nay, even in the very clothes. That is no Church like the evangelical communities, or the national Churches of the East; it is a political creation, and as imposing as a World-Empire, because the continuation of the Roman Empire. The Pope, who calls himself "King" and "Pontifex Maximus," is Cæsar's successor. The Church, which as early as the third and fourth century was entirely filled with the Roman spirit, has re-established in itself the Roman Empire. Nor have patriotic Catholics in Rome and Italy in every century from the seventh and eighth onwards understood the matter otherwise. When Gregory VII. entered upon the struggle with the imperial power, this is the way in which an Italian prelate fired his ardour:

> *Seize the first Apostle's sword,*
> *Peter's glowing sword, and smite!*
> *Scatter far the savage horde;*
> *Break their wild, impetuous might!*
> *Let them feel the yoke of yore,*
> *Let them bear it evermore!*
>
> *What with blood in Marius' day,*
> *Marius and his soldiers brave,*

Or by Julius' mighty sway,
 Romans did their land to save;
Thou canst do by simple word.
Great the Church's holy sword!

Rome made great again by thee
 Offers all thy meed of praise;
Not for Scipio's victory
 Did it louder pœans raise,
Nor entwine the laurel crown
For a deed of more renown.

Who is it that is thus addressed, a bishop or a
Cæsar? A Cæsar, I imagine; it was felt to be so
then, and it is still felt to be so to-day. It is an
Empire that this priestly Cæsar rules, and to attack
it with the armament of dogmatic polemics alone is
to beat the air.

I cannot here show what immense results follow
from the fact that the Catholic Church is the Roman
Empire. Let me mention only a few conclusions
which the Church itself draws. It is just as essential
to this Church to exercise governmental power as
to proclaim the Gospel. The phrase " Christus
vincit, Christus regnat, Christus triumphat," must
be understood in a political sense. He rules on
earth by the fact that his Rome-directed Church
rules, and rules, too, by law and by force; that is to
say, it employs all the means of which States avail
themselves. Accordingly it recognises no form of religious fervour which does not first of all submit to
this papal Church, is approved by it, and remains in

constant dependence upon it. This Church, then,
teaches its "subjects" to say : "Though I understand all mysteries, and though I have all faith, and
though I bestow all my goods to feed the poor, and
though I give my body to be burned, and have not
unity in love which alone floweth from unconditional
obedience to the Church, it profiteth me nothing."
Outside the pale of the Church, all faith, all love, all
the virtues, even martyrdoms, are of no value whatever. Naturally ; for even an earthly State appre-
ciates only those services which a man has rendered
for its sake. But here the State identifies itself with
the kingdom of Heaven, in other respects proceeding just like other States. From this fact you can
yourselves deduce all the Church's claims ; they
follow without difficulty. Even the most exorbitant
demand appears quite natural as soon as you only
admit the truth of the two leading propositions :
"The Roman Church is the kingdom of God," and
"The Church must govern like an earthly State."
It is not to be denied that Christian motives have
also had a hand in this development—the desire
to bring the Christian religion into a real connexion
with life, and to make its influence felt in every
situation that may arise, as well as anxiety for
the salvation of individuals and of nations. How
many earnest Catholic Christians there have been
who had no other real desire than to establish
Christ's rule on earth and build up his kingdom !
But while there can be no doubt that their in-

tention, and the energy with which they put their hands to the work, made them superior to the Greeks, there can be as little that it is a serious misunderstanding of Christ's and the apostles' injunctions to aim at establishing and building up the kingdom of God by political means. The only forces which this kingdom knows are religious and moral forces, and it rests on a basis of freedom. But when a Church comes forward with the claims of an earthly State, it is bound to make use of all the means at the disposal of that State, including, therefore, crafty diplomacy and force; for the earthly State, even a State governed by law, must on occasion become a State that acts contrary to law. The course of development which this Church has followed as an earthly State was, then, bound to lead logically to the absolute monarchy of the Pope and his infallibility; for in an earthly theocracy infallibility means, at bottom, nothing more than full sovereignty means in a secular State. That the Church has not shrunk from drawing this last conclusion is a proof of the extent to which the sacred element in it has become secularised.

That this second element was bound to produce a radical change in the characteristic features of Catholicism in Western Europe, in its traditionalism, its orthodoxy, its ritualism, and its monasticism, is obvious. Traditionalism holds the same position after the change as it did before; but when any

element in it has become inconvenient, it is dropped
and its place taken by the papal will.   " La tradition,
c'est moi," as Pius IX. is reported to have said.
Further, " sound doctrine " is still a leading principle,
but, as a matter of fact, it can be altered by the
ecclesiastical policy of the Pope ; subtle distinctions
have given many a dogma a new meaning.   New
dogmas, too, are promulgated.   In many respects
doctrine has become more arbitrary, and a rigid
formula in a matter of dogma may be set aside by
a contrary injunction in a matter of ethics and in
the confessional.   The hard and fast lines of the past
can be everywhere relaxed in favour of the needs of
the present.   The same holds good of ritualism, as
also of monasticism.   The extent to which the old
monasticism has been altered, by no means always to
its disadvantage alone, and has even in some important aspects been transformed into its flat opposite,
I cannot here show.   In its organisation this Church
possesses a faculty of adapting itself to the course
of history such as no other Church possesses ; it
always remains the same old Church, or seems to do
so, and is always becoming a new one.

The third element determining the character of
the spirit prevalent in the Church is opposed to
that which we have just discussed, and yet has held
its own side by side with the second : it goes by the
names of Augustine and Augustinianism.   In the
fifth century, at the very time when the Church

R

was setting itself to acquire the inheritance of the Roman Empire, it came into possession of a religious genius of extraordinary depth and power, accepted his ideas and feelings, and up to the present day has been unable to get rid of them. That the Church became at one and the same time Cæsarian and Augustinian is the most important and marvellous fact in its history. What kind of a spirit, however, and what kind of a tendency, did it receive from Augustine?

Well, in the first place, Augustine's theology and his religious fervour denote a special resuscitation of the Pauline experience and doctrine of sin and grace, of guilt and justification, of divine predestination and human servitude. In the centuries that had elapsed since the apostle's day this experience and the doctrine embodying it had been lost, but Augustine went through the same inner experiences as Paul, gave them the same sort of expression, and clothed them in definite conceptions. There was no question here of mere imitation; the individual differences between the two cases are of the utmost importance, especially in the way in which the doctrine of justification is conceived. With Augustine, it was represented as a constant process, continuing until love and all the virtues completely filled the heart; but, as with Paul, it is all a matter of individual experience and inner life. If you read Augustine's *Confessions* you will acknowledge that in spite of all the rhetoric—and rhetoric there is—it is the work of a genius who has felt God, the God of the Spirit,

to be the be-all and the end-all of his life ; who thirsts
after Him and desires nothing beside Him. Further,
all the sad and terrible experiences which he had had
in his own person, all the rupture with himself, all
the service of transient things, the "crumbling away
into the world bit by bit," and the egoism for which
he had to pay in loss of strength and freedom, he
reduces to the one root, *sin* ; that is to say, lack of
communion with God, godlessness. Again, what re-
leased him from the entanglements of the world,
from selfishness and inner decay, and gave him
strength, freedom, and a consciousness of the Eternal,
he calls, with Paul, *grace*. With him he feels, too,
that grace is wholly the work of God, but that it
is obtained through and by Christ, and possessed as
forgiveness of sins and as the spirit of love. He is
much less free and more beset with scruples in his
view of sin than the great apostle ; and it is this
which gives his religious language and everything
that proceeded from him quite a peculiar colour.
"Forgetting those things which are behind, and
reaching forth unto those things which are before"—
the apostolic maxim is not Augustine's. *Consolation
for the misery of sin*—this is the complexion of his
entire Christianity. Only rarely was he capable of
soaring to the sense of the glorious liberty of the
children of God ; and, where he was so capable, he
could not testify to it in the same way as Paul. But
he could express the sense of consolation for the
misery of sin with a strength of feeling and in words

of an overwhelming force such as no one before him
ever displayed; nay, more : he has managed by what
he has written to go so straight to the souls of
millions, to describe so precisely their inner condition,
and so impressively and overpoweringly to put the
consolation before them, that what he felt has been
felt again and again for fifteen hundred years.   Up
to the day in which we live, so far as Catholic
Christians are concerned, inward and vivid religious
fervour, and the expression which it takes, are in their
whole character Augustinian.   It is by what he felt
that they are kindled, and it is his thoughts that they
think.   Nor is it otherwise with many Protestants, and
those not of the worst kind.   This juxtaposition of sin
and grace, this interconnexion of feeling and doctrine,
seems to possess an indestructible power which no lapse
of time is able to touch ; this feeling of mixed pain
and bliss is an unforgettable possession with those who
have once experienced it ; and even though they may
have subsequently emancipated themselves from religion it remains for them a sacred memory.

   The Western Church opened, and was compelled to
open, its doors to this Augustine at the very moment
when it was preparing to enter upon its dominion.
It was defenceless in face of him ; it had so little
of any real value to offer from its immediate
past that it weakly capitulated.   Thus arose the
astonishing "complexio oppositorum" which we see
in Western Catholicism : the Church of rites, of law, of
politics, of world-dominion, and the Church in which

a highly individual, delicate, sublimated sense and
doctrine of sin and grace is brought into play. The
external and the internal elements are supposed to
unite ! To speak frankly, this has been impossible
from the beginning ; internal tension and conflict
were bound to arise at once ; the history of Western
Catholicism is full of it. Up to a certain point,
however, these antitheses admit of being reconciled ;
they admit of it at least so far as the same men are
concerned.   That is proved by no less a person
than Augustine himself, who, in addition to his other
characteristics, was also a staunch Churchman ; nay,
who in such matters as power and prestige pro-
moted the external interests of the Church, and its
equipment as a whole, with the greatest energy.
I cannot here explain how he managed to accomplish
this work, but that there could be no lack of internal
contradictions in it is obvious.   Only let us be clear
about two facts : firstly, that the outward Church is
more and more forcing the inward Augustinianism
into the background, and transforming and modify-
ing it, without, however, being able wholly to destroy it ; secondly, that all the great personalities
who have continued to kindle religious fervour afresh
in the Western Church, and to purify and deepen it,
have directly or indirectly proceeded from Augustine
and formed themselves on him.   The long chain of
Catholic reformers, from Agobard and Claudius of
Turin in the ninth century down to the Jansenists
in the seventeenth and eighteenth, and beyond them,

is Augustinian.   And if the Council of Trent may be in many respects rightly called a Council of Reform ; if the doctrine of penance and grace was formulated then with much more depth and inwardness than could be expected from the state of Catholic theology in the fourteenth and fifteenth centuries, that is only owing to the continued influence of Augustine. With the doctrine of grace taken from Augustine, the Church has, indeed, associated a practice of the confessional which threatens to make that doctrine absolutely ineffective.   But, however far it may stretch its bounds so as to keep all those within its pale who do not revolt against its authority, it after all not only tolerates such as take the same view of sin and grace as Augustine, but it also desires that, wherever possible, everyone may feel as strongly as he the gravity of sin and the blessedness of belonging to God.

Such are the essential elements of Roman Catholicism.   There is much else that might be mentioned, but what has been said denotes the leading points.

We pass to the last question : What modifications has the Gospel here undergone, and how much of it is left ?   Well—this is not a matter that needs many words—the whole outward and visible institution of a Church claiming divine dignity has no foundation whatever in the Gospel.   It is a case, not of distortion, but of total perversion.   Religion has here strayed away in a direction that is not its own.

As Eastern Catholicism may in many respects be more appropriately regarded as part of the history of Greek religion than of the history of the Gospel, so Roman Catholicism must be regarded as part of the history of the Roman World-Empire. To contend, as it does, that Christ founded a kingdom; that this kingdom is the Roman Church; that he equipped it with a sword, nay, with two swords, a spiritual and a temporal, is to secularise the Gospel; nor can this contention be sustained by appealing to the idea that Christ's spirit ought certainly to bear rule amongst mankind. The Gospel says, "Christ's kingdom is not of this world," but the Church has set up an earthly kingdom; Christ demands that his ministers shall not rule but serve, but here the priests govern the world; Christ leads his disciples away from political and ceremonious religion and places every man face to face with God —God and the soul, the soul and its God, but here, on the contrary, man is bound to an earthly institution with chains that cannot be broken, and he must obey; it is only when he obeys that he approaches God. There was a time when Roman Christians shed their blood because they refused to do worship to Cæsar, and rejected religion of the political kind; to-day they do not, indeed, actually pray to an earthly ruler, but they have subjected their souls to the despotic orders of the Roman papal King.

LECTURE XV.

THE point to which we referred at the close of the last lecture was that, as an outward and visible Church and a State founded on law and on force, Roman Catholicism has nothing to do with the Gospel, nay, is in fundamental contradiction with it. That this State has borrowed a divine lustre from the Gospel, and finds this lustre extraordinarily advantageous, cannot avail to upset the verdict. To mix the divine with the secular, and what is innermost in a man with a political element, is to work the greatest of mischiefs, because the conscience is thereby enslaved and religion robbed of its solemn character. It is inevitable that this character should be lost when every possible measure which serves to maintain the *earthly* empire of the Church—for example, the sovereignty of the Pope—is proclaimed as the divine will. We are reminded, however, that it is just this independent action on the part of the Church which saves religion in Western Europe from entirely degenerating into nationality, or the State, or police. The Church, it is urged, has maintained intact the high idea

of the complete self-subsistence of religion and
its independence of the State. We may admit
the claim, but the price which Western Europe
has had to pay for this service, and still pays, is
much too great; by having to pay so heavy a
tribute, the nations are threatened with bankruptcy
within; and, as for the Church, the capital which
it has amassed is truly a capital that consumes.
With all the apparent increase in its power, a
pauperising process is slowly being accomplished
in the Church; slowly but surely. Let me here
digress from our subject for a moment.

No one who looks at the present political situation
can have any ground for asserting that the power
of the Roman Church is on the wane. What a
growth it has experienced in the nineteenth century!
And yet—any one with a keen eye sees that the
Church is far from possessing now such a plenitude
of power as it enjoyed in the twelfth and thirteenth
centuries, when all the material and spiritual forces
available were at its disposal. Since that epoch its
power has, in point of intensity, suffered an enormous decline, arrested by a few brief outbursts of
enthusiasm between 1540 and 1620, and in the nineteenth century. Earnest Catholics, concerned at this
fact, make no secret of it; they know and admit
that an important portion of the spiritual possessions
necessary to the dominion of the Church has been
lost to it. And again; what is the position of the
Latin nations which, when all is said, form the

proper province of the Roman Church's rule? There
is only one of them which can really be called a
great Power, and what sort of spectacle will it
present in another generation? As a State this
Church lives to-day, to a not inconsiderable extent,
on its history, its old Roman and mediæval history;
and it lives as the Roman Empire of the Romans.
But empires do not live for ever. Will the Church
be capable of maintaining itself in the great changes
to come? Will it bear the increasing tension between it and the intellectual life of the people?
Will it survive the decline of the Latin nations?

But let us leave this question to answer itself.
Let us recollect, rather, that this Church, thanks
above all to its Augustinianism, possesses in its
orders of monkhood and its religious societies a
deep element of life in its midst. In all ages it
has produced saints, so far as men can be so called,
and it still produces them to-day. Trust in God,
unaffected humility, the assurance of redemption,
the devotion of one's life to the service of one's
brethren, are to be found in it; many brethren
take up the cross of Christ and exercise at one
and the same time that self-judgment and that
joy in God which Paul and Augustine achieved.
The *Imitatio Christi* kindles independent religious
life, and a fire which burns with a flame of its
own. Ecclesiasticism has not availed to suppress
the power of the Gospel, which, in spite of the
frightful weight that it has to carry, makes its

way again and again. It still works like leaven,
nor can we fail to see that this Church, side by
side with a lax morality for which it has often
enough been to blame, has, by the mouth of its
great mediæval theologians, fruitfully applied the
Gospel to many circumstances of life and created
a Christian ethics. Here and elsewhere it has
proved that it not only carries, as it were, the
thoughts of the Gospel with it, as a river carries
grains of gold, but that they are bound up with
it and have been further developed in it. The
infallible Pope, the "Apostolico-Roman polytheism,"
the veneration of the Saints, blind obedience, and
apathetic devotion — these things seem to have
stifled all inwardness, and yet there are Christians
still to be found in this Church, too, of the kind
which the Gospel has awakened, earnest and loving,
filled with joy and peace in God. Lastly, the mischief is not that the Gospel has been bound up with
political forms at all—Melanchthon was no traitor
when he expressed his willingness to acknowledge the
Pope if he would permit the Gospel to be preached
in its purity—but it lies in the *sanctification* of
the political element, and in the inability of this
Church to get rid of what was once of service in
particular historical circumstances, but has now become an obstruction and a clog.

We now pass to the last section in the exposition
of our subject.

The Christian Religion in Protestantism.

Anyone who looks at the external condition of Protestantism, especially in Germany, may, at first sight, well exclaim : "What a miserable spectacle !" But no one can survey the history of Europe from the second century to the present time without being forced to the conclusion that in the whole course of this history the greatest movement and the one most pregnant with good was the Reformation in the sixteenth century ; even the great change which took place at the transition to the nineteenth is inferior to it in importance. What do all our discoveries and inventions and our advances in outward civilisation signify in comparison with the fact that to-day there are thirty millions of Germans, and many more millions of Christians outside Germany, who possess a religion without priests, without sacrifices, without 'fragments' of grace, without ceremonies—a spiritual religion !

Protestantism must be understood, first and foremost, by the contrast which it offers to Catholicism, and here there is a double direction which any estimate of it must take, first as *Reformation* and secondly as *Revolution*. It was a reformation in regard to the doctrine of salvation ; a revolution in regard to the Church, its authority, and its apparatus. Hence Protestantism is no spontaneous phenomenon, created as it were by a " generatio

equivoca"; but, as its very name implies, it was
called into being by the misdeeds of the Roman
Church having become intolerable. It was the
close of a long series of cognate but ineffectual
attempts at reform in the Middle Ages. If the
position which it thus holds in history proves its
continuity with the past, the fact is still more
strongly in evidence in its own and not inappro-
priate contention that it was not an innovation in
regard to religion, but a restoration and renewal
of it. But from the point of view of the Church
and its authority Protestantism was undoubtedly
a revolutionary phenomenon. We must, then, take
account of it in both these relations.

Protestantism was a *Reformation*, that is to say,
a renewal, as regards the core of the matter, as
regards religion, and consequently as regards the
doctrine of salvation. That may be shown in the
main in three points.

In the first place, religion was here brought back
again to itself, in so far as the Gospel and the
corresponding religious experience were put into
the foreground and freed of all alien accretions.
Religion was taken out of the vast and monstrous
fabric which had been previously called by its
name—a fabric embracing the Gospel and holy
water, the priesthood of all believers and the
Pope on his throne, Christ the Redeemer and St.
Anne—and was *reduced* to its essential factors, to
the Word of God and to faith. This truth was

imposed as a *criterion* on everything that also claimed to be "religion" and to unite on terms of equality with those great factors.   In the history of religions every really important reformation is always, first and foremost, *a critical reduction* to principles ; for in the course of its historical development, religion, by adapting itself to circumstances, attracts to itself much alien matter, and produces, in conjunction with this, a number of hybrid and apocryphal elements, which it is necessarily compelled to place under the protection of what is sacred.   If it is not to run wild from exuberance, or be choked by its own dry leaves, the reformer must come who purifies it and brings it back to itself.   This critical reduction to principles Luther accomplished in the sixteenth century, by victoriously declaring that the Christian religion was given only in the Word of God and in the inward experience which accords with this Word.

In the *second* place, there was the definite way in which the "Word of God" and the "experience" of it were grasped.   For Luther the "Word" did not mean Church doctrine ; it did not even mean the Bible ; it meant the message of the free grace of God in Christ which makes guilty and despairing men happy and blessed ; and the "experience" was just the certainty of this grace.   In the sense in which Luther took them, both can be embraced in one phrase : *the confident belief in a God of grace.*   They put an end—such was his own experience, and such was what he taught—to all inner discord in a man; they overcome the burden of every ill; they destroy the sense of guilt; and, despite the imperfection of a man's own acts, they give him the certainty of being inseparably united with the holy God:

> *Now I know and believe*
> *And give praise without end*
> *That God the Almighty*
> *Is Father and Friend,*
> *And that in all troubles,*
> *Whatever betide,*
> *He hushes the tempest*
> *And stands at my side.*

Nothing, he taught, is to be preached but the God of Grace, with whom we are reconciled through Christ. Conversely, it is not a question of ecstasies and visions; no transports of feeling are necessary; it is *faith* that is to be aroused. Faith is to be the beginning, middle, and end of all religious fervour. In the correspondence of Word and faith " justification " is experienced, and hence justification holds the chief place in the Reformers' message; it means nothing less than the attainment of peace and freedom in God through Christ, dominion over the world, and an eternity within.

Lastly, the third feature of this renewal was the great transformation which *God's worship* now inevitably underwent, God's worship by the individual and by the community. Such worship—

this was obvious—can and ought to be nothing
but putting *faith* to practical proof. As Luther
declared over and over again, " all that God asks
of us is faith, and it is through faith alone that
He is willing to treat with us." To let God be
God, and to pay Him honour by acknowledging
and invoking Him as Father — it is thus alone
that a man can serve Him. Every other path on
which a man tries to approach Him and honour
Him leads astray, and vain is the attempt to
establish any other relation with Him. What an
enormous mass of anxious, hopeful, and hopeless
effort was now done away with, and what a revolution in worship was effected! But all that is
true of God's worship by the individual is true in
exactly the same way of public worship. Here, too,
it is only the Word of God and prayer which have
any place. All else is to be banished; the community assembled for God's worship is to proclaim
the message of God with praise and thanksgiving,
and call upon His name. Anything that goes beyond this is not worship at all.

These three points embrace the chief elements in the
Reformation. What they involved was a *renewal* of
religion; for not only do they denote, albeit in a
fashion of their own, a return to Christianity as it
originally was, but they also existed themselves in
Western Catholicism, although buried in a heap of
rubbish.

But, before we go further, permit me two brief

digressions. We were just saying that the community assembled for God's worship must not solemnise its worship in any other way than by proclaiming the Word and by prayer. To this, however, we must add, according to the Reformers' injunctions, that all that is to stamp this community as a Church is its existence as a community of the faith in which God's Word is preached aright. Here we may leave the sacraments out of account, as, according to Luther, they, too, derive their entire importance from the Word. But if Word and faith are the only characteristics of worship, it looks as if those who contend that the Reformation did away with the visible Church and put an invisible one in its place were right. But the contention does not tally with the facts. The distinction between a visible and an invisible Church dates back as far as the Middle Ages, or even, from one point of view, as far as Augustine. Those who defined the true Church as " the number of the predestined " were obliged to maintain that it was wholly invisible. But the German Reformers did not so define it. In declaring the Church to be a community of the faith in which God's Word is preached aright, they rejected all the coarser characteristics of a Church, and certainly excluded the visibility that appeals to the senses ; but—to take an illustration—who would say that an intellectual community, for example, a band of young

S

men all alike eagerly devoted to knowledge or the interests of their country, was "invisible," because it possesses no external characteristics, and cannot be counted on one's fingers? Just as little is the evangelical Church an "invisible" community. It is a community of the spirit, and therefore its "visibility" takes different phases and different degrees of strength. There are phases of it where it is absolutely unrecognisable, and others, again, where it stands forth with the energy of a power that appeals to the senses. It can never, indeed, take the sharp contours of a State like the Venetian republic or the kingdom of France—such was the comparison which a great exponent of Catholic dogmatics declared to be applicable to his Church —but as Protestants we ought to know that we belong, not to an "invisible" Church, but to a spiritual community which disposes of the forces pertaining to spiritual communities; a spiritual community resting on earth, but reaching to the Eternal.

And now as to the other point : Protestantism maintains that, objectively, the Christian community is based upon the Gospel alone, but that the Gospel is contained in Holy Scripture. From the very beginning it has encountered the objection that, if that be so, and at the same time there be no recognised authority to decide what the purport and meaning of the Gospel is and how it is to be ascertained from the Scriptures, general confusion will

be the result; that of this confusion the history of
Protestantism affords ample testimony; that if every
man has a warrant to decide what the "true understanding" of the Gospel is, and in this respect is
bound to no tradition, no council, and no pope, but
exercises the free right of research, any unity, community, or Church is absolutely impossible; that the
State, therefore, must interfere, or some arbitrary
limit be fixed. That no Church possessing the Sacred
Office of the Inquisition can arise in this way is
certainly true; further, that to impose any *external*
limits on a community *from the inside* is a simple
impossibility. What has been done by the State or
under pressure of historical necessities does not affect
the question at all; the structures which have arisen
in the way are, in the evangelical sense, only figura-
tively called "Churches." *Protestantism reckons—*
this is the solution—*upon the Gospel being something
so simple, so divine, and therefore so truly human,
as to be most certain of being understood when it is
left entirely free, and also as to produce essentially
the same experiences and convictions in individual
souls.* In this it may often enough make mistakes;
differences of individuality and education may issue
in very heterogeneous results; but still, in this its
attitude, it has not up to now been put to shame. A
real, spiritual community of evangelical Christians; a
common conviction as to what is most important
and as to its application to life in all its forms, has
arisen and is in full force and vigour. This com-

munity embraces Protestants in and outside Germany,
Lutherans, Calvinists, and adherents of other de-
nominations. In all of them, so far as they are
earnest Christians, there lives a common element,
and this element is of infinitely greater importance
and value than all their differences. It keeps us
to the Gospel and it protects us from modern
heathenism and from relapse into Catholicism. More
than this we do not need; nay, any other fetter we
reject. This, however, is no fetter, but the condition
of our freedom. And when we are reproached with
our divisions and told that Protestantism has as many
doctrines as heads, we reply, "So it has, but we do
not wish it otherwise; on the contrary, we want
still more freedom, still greater individuality in utterance and in doctrine; the historical circumstances
necessitating the formation of national and free
churches have imposed only too many rules and
limitations upon us, even though they be not proclaimed as divine ordinances; we want still more
confidence in the inner strength and unifying power
of the Gospel, which is more certain to prevail in free
conflict than under guardianship; we want to be a
spiritual realm and we have no desire to return to
the fleshpots of Egypt; we are well aware that in the
interests of order and instruction outward and visible communities must arise; we are ready to foster
their growth, so far as they fulfil these aims and
deserve to be fostered; but we do not hang our hearts
upon them, for they may exist to-day and to-morrow

give place, under other political or social conditions, to new organisations; let anyone who has such a Church have it as though he had it not; our Church is not the particular Church in which we are placed, but the 'societas fidei' which has its members everywhere, even among Greeks and Romans." That is the evangelical answer to the reproach that we are " divided," and that is the language which the liberty that has been given to us employs. Let us now return from these digressions to the exposition of the essential features of Protestantism.

Protestantism was not only a Reformation but also a *Revolution*. From the legal point of view the whole Church system against which Luther revolted could lay claim to full obedience. It had just as much legal validity in Western Europe as the laws of the State themselves. When Luther burnt the papal bull he undoubtedly performed a revolutionary act—revolutionary, not in the bad sense of a revolt against legal ordinance which is also moral ordinance as well, but certainly in the sense of a violent breach with a given legal condition. It was against this state of things that the new movement was directed, and it was to the following chief points that its protest in word and deed extended. Firstly: It protested against the entire hierarchical and priestly system in the Church, demanded that it should be abolished, and abolished it in favour of a common priesthood and an established order formed on the basis of the congregation. What a range this demand had, and

to what an extent it interfered with the previously
existing state of things, cannot be told in a few
sentences. To explain it all would take hours.
Nor can we here show how the various arrangements
actually took shape in the evangelical churches.
That is not a matter of fundamental importance, but
what is of fundamental importance is that the
"divine" rights of the Church were abolished.

Secondly : It protested against all formal, external
authority in religion ; against the authority, therefore,
of councils, priests, and the whole tradition of the
Church. That alone is to be authority which shows
itself to be such within and effects a deliverance ; the
thing itself, therefore, the Gospel. Thus Luther
also protested against the authority of the letter
of the Bible ; but we shall see that this was a point
on which neither he nor the rest of the Reformers
were quite clear, and where they failed to draw the
conclusions which their insight into fundamentals
demanded.

Thirdly : It protested against all the traditional
arrangements for public worship, all ritualism, and
every sort of "holy work." As it neither knows nor
tolerates, as we have seen, any specific form of worship,
any material sacrifice and service to God, any mass and
any works done for God and with a view to salvation,
the whole traditional system of public worship, with
its pomp, its holy and semi-holy articles, its gestures
and processions, came to the ground. How much could
be retained in the way of form for *æsthetic* or *educa-*

tional reasons was, in comparison with this, a question of entirely secondary importance.

Fourthly : It protested against Sacramentalism. Baptism and the Lord's Supper it left standing, as institutions of the primitive Church, or, as it might be, of the Lord himself ; but it desired that they should be regarded either as symbols and marks by which the Christian is known, or as acts deriving their value exclusively from that message of the forgiveness of sins which is bound up with them. All other sacraments it abolished, and with them the whole notion of God's grace and help being accessible in bits, and fused in some mysterious way with definite corporeal things. To sacramentalism it opposed the *Word*, and to the notion that grace was given by bits, the conviction that there is only one grace, namely, to possess *God himself* as the source of grace. It was not because Luther was so very enlightened that in his tract " On the Babylonian Captivity " he rejected the whole system of Sacramentalism— he had enough superstition left in him to enable him to advance some very shocking contentions— but because he had had inner experience of the fact that where " grace " does not endow the soul with the living God Himself it is an illusion. Hence for him the whole doctrine of sacramentalism was an infringement of God's majesty and an enslavement of the soul.

Fifthly : It protested against the double form of morality, and accordingly against the higher form ;

against the contention that it is particularly well-pleasing to God to make no use of the powers and gifts which are part of creation. The Reformers had a strong sense of the fact that the world passes away with the lusts thereof; we must certainly not represent Luther as the modern man cheerfully standing with his feet firmly planted on the earth; on the contrary, like the men of the Middle Ages he had a strong yearning to be rid of this world and to depart from the "vale of tears." But because he was convinced that we neither can nor ought to offer God anything but trust in Him, he arrived, in regard to the Christian's position in the world, at quite different theses from those which were advanced by the grave monks of previous centuries. As fastings and ascetic practices had no value before God, and were of no advantage to one's fellowmen, and as God is the Creator of all things, the most useful thing that a man can do is to remain in the position in which God has placed him. This conviction gave Luther a cheerful and confident view of earthly ordinances, which contrasts with and actually got the upperhand of his inclination to turn his back upon the world.

He advanced the definite thesis that all positions in life—constituted authority, the married state, and so on, down to domestic service—existed by the will of God, and were therefore genuinely spiritual positions in which we are to serve God; a faithful maidservant stands higher, with him, than a contemplative monk. Christians are not to be always devising how they may find some new paths of their own, but to show patience and love of neighbour within the sphere of their given vocation. Out of this there grew up in his mind the notion that all worldly laws and spheres of activity have an independent title. It is not that they are to be merely tolerated, and have no right to exist until they receive it from the Church. No! they have rights of their own, and they form the vast domain in which the Christian is to give proof of his faith and love; nay, they are even to be respected in places which are as yet ignorant of God's revelation in the Gospel.

It was thus that the same man who asked nothing of the world, so far as his own personal feelings were concerned, and whose soul was troubled only by thought for the Eternal, delivered mankind from the ban of asceticism. He was thereby really and truly the life and origin of a new epoch, and he gave it back a simple and unconstrained attitude towards the world, and a good conscience in all earthly labour. This fruitful work fell to his share, not because he secularised religion, but because he took it so seriously and so profoundly that, while in his view it was to pervade all things, it was itself to be freed from everything external to it.

LECTURE XVI.

THE question has often been raised whether, and to what extent, the Reformation was a work of the *German* spirit. I cannot here go into this complicated problem. But this much seems to me to be certain, that while we cannot, indeed, connect Luther's momentous religious experiences with his nationality, the results positive as well as negative with which he invested them display the German; the German man and German history. From the time that the Germans endeavoured to make themselves really at home in the religion handed down to them—this did not take place until the thirteenth century onwards—they were preparing the way for the Reformation. And just as Eastern Christianity is rightly called Greek, and the Christianity of the Middle Ages and of Western Europe is rightly called Roman, so the Christianity of the Reformation may be described as German, in spite of Calvin. For Calvin was Luther's pupil, and he made his influence most lastingly felt, not among the Latin nations but among the English, the Scotch, and the Dutch. Through the Reformation the Germans mark a stage in the history of the Universal Church.   No similar statement can be made of the Slavs.

The recoil from asceticism, which as an ideal never penetrated the Germans to the same extent as other nations, and the protest against religion as external authority, are to be set down as well to the Pauline Gospel as to the German spirit.   Luther's warmth and heartiness in preaching, and his frankness in polemical utterance, were felt by the German nation to be an opening out of its own soul.

In the previous lecture we touched upon the chief provinces in which Luther raised an emphatic and still effective protest.   There is much upon which I could also dwell : for example, upon the opposition which, especially at the commencement of his reforming activity, he offered to the whole terminology of dogmatics, its formulæ and doctrinal utterances.   To sum up : he protested, because his aim was to restore the Christian religion in its purity, without priests and sacrifices, without external authorities and ordinances, without solemn ceremonies, without all the chains with which the Beyond was to be bound to the Here.   In its revising ardour the Reformation went back not only earlier than the eleventh century, not only earlier than the fourth or the second, but to the very beginnings of religion. Nay, without being aware of it, the Reformation even modified or entirely put aside forms which existed even in the apostolic age : thus in matters

of discipline it abolished fasting; in matters of
constitution it abolished bishops and deacons; in
matters of doctrine it abolished, among other things,
Chiliasm.

But with the change effected by Reformation and
Revolution, how does the new creation stand *as a
whole* in regard to the Gospel? We may say that
in the four leading points which we emphasised in
the previous lecture—inwardness and spirituality,
the fundamental thought of the God of grace, His
worship in spirit and in truth, and the idea of the
Church as a community of faith—the Gospel was in
reality re-won. Need I prove this in detail, or are
we to be shaken in our conviction because, as is
surely the case, a Christian in the sixteenth and in
the nineteenth century presents an appearance different from that which a Christian presented in
the first? That the inwardness and individualism
which the Reformation disengaged accord with the
character of the Gospel is certain. Further, Luther's
pronouncement on justification not only reflects in the
main, and in spite of certain irreducible differences,
Paul's train of thought, but is also in point of
aim in exact correspondence with Jesus' teaching.
To know God as one's Father, to possess a God of
grace, to find comfort in His grace and providence,
to believe in the forgiveness of sins—in both cases
that is the point on which everything turns. And
in the troubled times of Lutheran orthodoxy a Paul

Gerhardt succeeded in giving such grand expression to this fundamental conviction of the Gospel in his hymns, " Is God for me, then let all," and " Commit thy ways," as to convince us how truly Protestantism was penetrated with it. Again, that the right worship of God ought to be nothing but the acknowledgment of God in praise and prayer, but that the love of neighbour is also worship, is taken direct from the Gospel and Paul's corresponding injunctions. Lastly, that the true Church is held together by the Holy Ghost and by faith ; that it is a spiritual community of brothers and sisters, is a conviction which is in line with the Gospel, and was most clearly expressed by Paul. In so far as the Reformation restored all this, and also recognised Christ as the only Redeemer, it may in the strictest sense of the word be called *evangelical* ; and in so far as these convictions, crippled and burdened though they may be, retain their ascendency in the Protestant Churches, they have every warrant for being so described.

But what was here achieved had its dark side as well. If we ask what the Reformation cost us, and to what extent it made its principles prevail, we shall see this dark side very clearly.

We get nothing from history without paying for it, and for a violent movement we have to pay double. What did the Reformation cost us ? I will not speak of the fact that the unity of Western civilisation was destroyed, since it was after all only over a part of Western Europe that the Reformation prevailed, for the freedom and many-sided character of the resulting development brought us a greater gain. But the necessity of establishing the new Churches as *State-Churches* was attended by serious disadvantages. The system of an ecclesiastical State is, of course, worse, and its adherents have truly no cause to praise it in contrast with the State-Churches. But still the latter—which are not solely the outcome of the breach with ecclesiastical authority, but were already prepared for in the fifteenth century—have been the cause of much stunted growth. They have weakened the feeling of responsibility, and diminished the activity, of the evangelical communities ; and, in addition, they have aroused the not unfounded suspicion that the Church is an institution set up by the State, and accordingly to be adjusted to the State. Much has happened, indeed, in the last few decades to check that suspicion by the greater independence which the Churches have obtained ; but further progress in this direction is necessary, especially in regard to the freedom of individual communities. The connexion with the State must not be violently severed, for the Churches have derived much advantage from it ; but steps must be taken to further the development upon which we have entered. If this results in multifarious organisations in the Church, it will do no harm ; on the contrary, it will remind us, in a forcible way, that these forms are all arbitrary.

Further, Protestantism was forced by its opposition to Catholicism to lay exclusive emphasis on the inward character of religion, and upon " faith alone " ; but to formulate one doctrine in sharp opposition to another is always a dangerous process. The man in the street is not sorry to hear that " good works " are unnecessary, nay, that they constitute a danger to the soul. Although Luther is not responsible for the convenient misunderstanding that ensued, the inevitable result was that in the reformed Churches in Germany from the very start there were accusations of moral laxity and a want of serious purpose in the sanctification of life. The saying " If ye love me, keep my commandments " was unwarrantably thrust into the background. Not until the Pietistic movement arose was its central importance once more recognised. Up till then the pendulum of the conduct of life took a suspicious swing in the contrary direction, out of opposition to the Catholic "justification by works." But religion is not only a state of the heart ; it is a deed as well ; it is faith active in love and in the sanctification of life. This is a truth with which evangelical Christians must become much better acquainted, if they are not to be put to shame.

There is another point closely connected with what I have just mentioned. The Reformation abolished monasticism, and was bound to abolish it. It rightly affirmed that to take a vow of lifelong asceticism was a piece of presumption ; and it rightly considered that any worldly vocation, conscientiously followed in the sight of God, was equal to, nay, was better than, being a monk. But something now happened which Luther neither foresaw nor desired : "monasticism," of the kind that is conceivable and necessary in the evangelical sense of the word, disappeared altogether. But every community stands in need of personalities living *exclusively* for its ends. The Church, for instance, needs volunteers who will abandon every other pursuit, renounce "the world," and devote themselves entirely to the service of their neighbour; not because such a vocation is "a higher one," but because it is a necessary one, and because no Church can live without also giving rise to this desire. But in the evangelical Churches the desire has been checked by the decided attitude which they have been compelled to adopt towards Catholicism. It is a high price that we have paid; nor can the price be reduced by considering, on the other hand, how much simple and unaffected religious fervour has been kindled in home and family life. We may rejoice, however, that in the past century a beginning has been made in the direction of recouping this loss. In the institution of deaconesses and many cognate phenomena the evangelical Churches are getting back what they once ejected through their inability to recognise it in the form which it then took. But it must undergo a much ampler and more varied development.

Not only had the Reformation to pay a high price ;

it was also incapable of perceiving all the conclusions
to which its new ideas led, and of giving them pure
effect. It is not that the work which it did was not
absolutely valid and permanent in every particular—
how could that be, and who could desire it to have
been so? No! it remained stationary in its development even at the point at which, to judge by the
earnest foundation that was laid at the start, higher
things might have been expected. Various causes
combined to produce this result. From the year
1526 onwards national Churches had to be founded
at headlong speed on evangelical lines; they were
forced to be "rounded and complete" at a time
when much was still in a state of flux. Then again,
a mistrust of the left wing, of the "enthusiasts,"
induced the Churches to offer an energetic resistance
to tendencies which they could have accompanied for
a good bit of their way. Luther's unwillingness to
have anything to do with them, nay, the manner in
which he became suspicious of his own ideas when
they coincided with those of the "enthusiasts," was
bitterly avenged and came home to the evangelical
Churches in the Age of Enlightenment. Even at the
risk of being reckoned among Luther's detractors, we
must go further. This genius had a faith as robust
as Paul's, and thereby an immense power over the
minds and hearts of men; but he was not abreast
of the knowledge accessible even in his own time.
The *naïve* age had gone by; it was an age of deep
feeling, of progress, an age in which religion could

not avoid contact with all the powers of mind. In this age it was his destiny to be forced to be not only a reformer but also an intellectual and spiritual leader and teacher. The way of looking at the world and at history he had to plan afresh for generations; for there was no one there to help him, and to no one else would people listen. But he had not all the resources of clear knowledge at his command. Lastly, he was always anxious to go back to the original, to the Gospel itself, and, so far as it was possible to do it by intuition and inward experience, he did it; moreover, he made some admirable studies in history, and in many places broke victoriously through the serried lines of the traditional dogmas. But any trustworthy knowledge of the history of those dogmas was as yet an impossibility, and still less was any historical acquaintance with the New Testament and primitive Christianity attainable. It is marvellous how in spite of all this Luther possessed so much power of penetration and sound judgment. We have only to look at his introductions to the books of the New Testament, or at his treatise on " Churches and Councils." But there were countless problems of which he did not even know, to say nothing of being able to solve them; and so it was that he had no means of distinguishing between kernel and husk, between what was original and what was of alien growth. How can we be surprised, then, if in its doctrine, and in the view which it took of history, the Reformation was far from being a finished product;

and that, where it perceived no problems, confusion in its own ideas was inevitable? It could not, like Pallas Athene, spring complete from Jupiter's head; as doctrine it could do no more than mark a *beginning*, and it had to reckon on future development. But by being rapidly formed into national Churches it came near to itself cutting short its further development for all time.

As regards the confusion and the checks which it brought upon itself, we must content ourselves with referring to a few leading points. Firstly, Luther would admit nothing but the Gospel, nothing but what frees and binds the consciences of men, what everyone, down to the man-servant and the maid-servant, can understand. But then he not only took the old dogmas of the Trinity and the two natures as part of the Gospel—he was not in a position to examine them historically—and even framed new ones, but he was absolutely incapable of making any sound distinction between "doctrine" and Gospel; in this respect falling far behind Paul. The necessary result was that intellectualism was still in the ascendant; that a scholastic doctrine was again set up as necessary to salvation; and that two classes of Christians once more arose: those who understand the doctrine, and the minors who are dependent on the others' understanding of it.

Secondly, Luther was convinced that that alone is the "Word of God" whereby a man is inwardly born anew—the message of the free grace of God in

Christ. At the highest levels to which he attained in his life he was free from every sort of bondage to the letter. What a capacity he had for distinguishing between law and Gospel, between Old and New Testament, nay, for distinguishing in the New Testament itself! All that he would recognise was the kernel of the matter, clearly revealed as it is in these books, and proving its power by its effect on the soul. But he did not make a clean sweep. In cases where he had found the letter important, he demanded submission to the "it is written"; and he demanded it peremptorily, without recollecting that, where other sayings of the Scriptures were concerned, he himself had declared the "it is written" to be of no binding force.

Thirdly, grace is the forgiveness of sins, and therefore the assurance of possessing a God of grace, and life, and salvation. How often Luther repeated this, always with the addition that what was efficacious here was the *Word*—that union of the soul with God in the trust and childlike reverence which God's Word inspires; it was a personal relation which was here involved. But the same man allowed himself to be inveigled into the most painful controversies about the means of grace, about communion and infant baptism. These were struggles in which he ran the risk of again exchanging his high conception of grace for the Catholic conception, as well as of sacrificing the fundamental idea that it is a purely spiritual possession that is in question, and that,

compared with Word and faith, all else is of no
importance.   What he here bequeathed to his Church
has become a legacy of woe.

Fourthly, the counter-Church which, as was inevitable, rapidly arose in opposition to the Roman
Church, and under the pressure which that Church
exercised, perceived, not without reason, that its
truth and its title lay in the re-establishment of
the Gospel.   But whilst the counter-Church privily
identified the sum and substance of its doctrine
with the Gospel, the thought also stole in surrepti-
tiously : *We*, that is to say, the particular Churches
which had now sprung up, *are the true Church*.
Luther, of course, was never able to forget that the
true Church was the sacred community of the faithful ; but still he had no clear ideas as to the relation
between it and the visible new Church which had
now arisen, and subsequent generations settled down
more and more into the sad misunderstanding :
We are the true Church *because we have the right
"doctrine."* This misunderstanding, besides giving
rise to evil results in self-infatuation and intolerance,
still further strengthened that mischievous distinction between theologians and clergy on the one side,
and the laity on the other, on which we have already
dwelt.   Not, perhaps, in theory, but certainly in
practice, a double form of Christianity arose, just
as in Catholicism ; and in spite of the efforts of the
Pietistic movement, it still remains with us to-day.
The theologian and the clergyman must defend the

whole doctrine, and be orthodox; for the layman it suffices if he adheres to certain leading points and refrains from attacking the orthodox creed. A very well-known man, as I have been lately told, expressed the wish that a certain inconvenient theologian would go over to the philosophical faculty; "for then," he said, "instead of an unbelieving theologian we should have a believing philosopher." Here we have the logical outcome of the contention that in the evangelical Churches, too, doctrine is something laid down for all time, and that in spite of being generally binding it is a matter of so much difficulty that the laity need not be expected to defend it. But if we persist on this path, and other confusions become worse confounded and take firmer root, there is a risk of Protestantism becoming a sorry double of Catholicism. I say a sorry double, because there are two things which Protestantism will never obtain, namely, a pope and monastic priests. Neither the letter of the Bible nor any belief embodied in creeds can ever produce the unconditional authority which Catholics possess in the pope; and Protestantism cannot now return to the monastic priest. It retains its national Churches and its married clergy, neither of which looks very stately by the side of Catholicism, if competition with Catholicism is what the evangelical Churches desire.

Gentlemen, Protestantism is not yet, thank God, in such a bad way that the imperfections and con-

fusions in which it began have got the upperhand
and entirely stunted or stifled its true character.
Even those among us who are convinced that the
Reformation in the sixteenth century is something
that is over and done with are by no means ready
to abandon the momentous ideas on which it was
based, and there is a large field in which all earnest
evangelical Christians are in complete unanimity.
But if those who think that the Reformation is
done with cannot see that its continuance in the
sense of a pure understanding of God's Word is a
question of life and death for Protestantism—its
continuance has already borne abundant fruit in
associations like the *Evangelical Union*—let them
at least promote the liberty for which Luther fought
in his best days: " Let the minds of men rush
one against another and strike ; if some are mean-
while led astray—well ! that is what we must expect
in war ; where there is battle and slaughter, some
must fall and be wounded, but whoso fights honestly
will receive the crown."

The reason why the catholicising of the Protestant
Churches—I do not mean that they are becoming
papal ; I mean that they are becoming Churches of
ordinance, doctrine, and ceremony—is so burning
a question is that three powerful forces are working together to further this development. First
there is the indifference of the masses. The
tendency of all indifference is to put religion on
the same plane with authority and tradition, but

also with priests, hierarchies, and the cult of ceremonies. It puts religion there, and then goes on
to complain of the external character and stationary
condition of religion, and of the "pretensions" of the
clergy ; nay, it is capable, apparently, at one and the
same moment, of mingling those complaints with
abuse, of contemptuously jeering at every active expression of religious feeling, and doing homage to
every kind of ceremony. This kind of indifference
has no understanding whatever for evangelical Christianity, instinctively tries to suppress it, and praises
Catholicism at its expense. The second of the
forces to be taken into consideration is what I
may call "natural religion." Those who live by
fear and hope ; whose chief endeavour is to find
some authority in matters of religion ; who are
eager to be rid of their own responsibility and
want to be reassured ; who are looking for some
"adjunct" to life, whether in its solemn hours or
in its worst distress, some æsthetic transfiguration,
or some violent form of assistance till time itself
assists—all these people are also, without being
aware of it, putting religion on the Catholic plane ;
they want "something that they can lean upon,"
and a good deal else, too—all kinds of things to
stir them up and help them ; but they do not
want the Christianity of the Gospel. But the
Christianity of the Gospel in yielding to such
demands becomes Catholic Christianity. The third
force I mention unwillingly, and yet I cannot pass

it over in silence; it is the *State*. We must not
blame the State for setting chief store by the conservative influence which religion and the Churches
exercise, and the subsidiary effects which they produce in respect of reverence, obedience, and public
order.   But this is just the reason why the State
exercises pressure in this direction, protects all the
elements of stability in the Churches, and seeks to
keep them from every inner movement that would call
their unity and their " public utility " in question ;
nay, it has tried often enough to approximate the
Church to the police, and employ it as a means
of maintaining order in the State.   We can pardon
this—let the State take the means of power where-
ever it can find them ; but the Church must not
allow itself to be made into a pliant instrument ;
for, side by side with all the desolating consequences
to its vocation and prestige, it would thereby become
an outward institution in which public order is of
greater consequence than the spirit, form more
important than matter, and obedience of higher
value than truth.

In the face of these three so different forces, what
we have to do is to maintain Christian earnestness
and liberty as presented in the Gospel.   Theology
alone is unavailing ; what is wanted is firmness of
Christian character.   The evangelical Churches will
be pushed into the background if they do not make
a stand.   It was out of such free creations as the
Pauline communities were that the Catholic Church

once arose.   Who can guarantee that those Churches,
too, will not become "Catholic" which had their
origin in "the liberty of a Christian man"?

That, however, would not involve the destruction
of the Gospel : so much, at least, history proves. It
would be still traceable like a red thread in the
centre of the web, and somewhere or other it
would emerge afresh, and free itself from its entangling connexions.   Even in the outwardly decor-
ated but inwardly decayed temples of the Greek
and Roman Church it has not been effaced.
"Venture onwards! deep down in a vault you will
still find the altar and its sacred, ever-burning
lamp!"   This Gospel, associated as it was with
the speculative ideas and the mystery-worship of
the Greeks, yet did not perish in them; united
with the Roman Empire, it held its own even in
this fusion, nay, out of it gave birth to the Reformation.   Its dogmatic doctrines, its ordinances
of public worship, have changed; nay, what is
much more, it has been embraced by the simplest
and purest minds and by the greatest thinkers; it
endeared itself to a St. Francis and to a Newton.
It has outlived all the changing philosophies of the
world; it has cast off like a garment forms and
ideas which were once sacred; it has participated
in the entire progress of civilisation; it has become
spiritualised, and in the course of history it has
learnt how to make a surer application of its ethical
principles.   In its original earnestness and in the

consolation which it offers, it has come home to thousands in all ages; and in all ages, too, it has thrown off all its encumbrances, and broken down all barriers. If we were right in saying that the Gospel is the knowledge and recognition of God as the Father, the certainty of redemption, humility and joy in God, energy and brotherly love; if it is essential to this religion that the founder must not be forgotten over his message, nor the message over the founder, history shows us that the Gospel has, in point of fact, remained in force, struggling again and again to the surface.

You will perhaps have felt that I have not entered into present questions, the relation, namely, of the Gospel to our present intellectual condition, our whole knowledge of the world, and our task therein. But to do this with any success in regard to the actual situation of affairs would require longer than a few fleeting hours. As regards the kernel of the matter, however, I have said all that is needful, for no new phase in the history of the Christian Religion has occurred since the Reformation. Our knowledge of the world has undergone enormous changes—every century since the Reformation marks an advance, the most important being those in the last two; but, looked at from a religious and ethical point of view, the forces and principles of the Reformation have not been outrun or rendered obsolete. We need only grasp them in their purity and courageously apply them, and modern ideas will not put any *new* difficulties in their way. The real difficulties in the way of the religion of the Gospel remain the old ones. In face of them we can "prove" nothing, for our proofs are only variations of our convictions. But the course which history has taken has surely opened up a wide province, in which the Christian sense of brotherhood must give practical proof of itself quite otherwise than it knew how, or was able, to do in the early centuries—I mean the social province. Here a tremendous task confronts us, and in the measure in which we accomplish it shall we be able to answer with a better heart the deepest of all questions—*the question of the meaning of life.*

Gentlemen, it is religion, the love of God and neighbour, which gives life a meaning; knowledge cannot do it. Let me, if you please, speak of my own experience, as one who for thirty years has taken an earnest interest in these things. Pure knowledge is a glorious thing, and woe to the man who holds it light or blunts his sense for it. But to the question, Whence, whither, and to what purpose, it gives an answer to-day as little as it did two or three thousand years ago. It does, indeed, instruct us in facts; it detects inconsistencies; it links phenomena; it corrects the deceptions of sense and idea. But where and how the curve of the world and the curve of our own life begin—that curve of which it shows us only a section—and whither this curve leads, knowledge does not tell us. But if with a steady will we affirm the forces and the standards which on the summits of our inner life shine out as our highest good, nay, as our real self; if we are earnest and courageous enough to accept them as the great Reality and direct our lives by them ; and if we then look at the course of mankind's history, follow its upward development, and search, in strenuous and patient service, for the communion of minds in it, we shall not faint in weariness and despair, but become certain of God, of the God whom Jesus Christ called his Father, and who is also our Father.

THE END.

PRINTED BY
NEILL AND COMPANY LIMITED
EDINBURGH

THE
THEOLOGICAL TRANSLATION LIBRARY.

𝔑ew 𝔖eries.

A Series of Translations by which the best results of recent Theological investigations on the Continent, conducted without reference to doctrinal considerations, and with the sole purpose of arriving at truth, will be placed within reach of English Readers.

SUBSCRIPTION IN ADVANCE—

For a Year's issue of Three Volumes, 21s. net; 22s. 6d. Post Free.
Single Volumes, Cloth, 10s. 6d. ; Half-leather, 12s. 6d.

Just published. FIFTH YEAR. VOL. I.

AN INTRODUCTION TO THE TEXTUAL CRITICISM OF THE GREEK NEW TESTAMENT.

By Prof. EBERHARD NESTLE of Maulbronn. Translated by WM. EDIE, B.D., and Edited by Prof. ALLAN MENZIES, D.D., of St. Andrews.

With Eleven Reproductions of Texts.

Prof. Eberhard Nestle, now of Maulbronn, has done much to facilitate the study of the text of the New Testament. His "Novum Testamentum Graece" is highly valued by all who know it as giving in the smallest bulk, and at a very low price, the text now approved by critics and his contributions to theological magazines in this country, mostly on textual questions, have made his name familiar. His "Einführung in das Griechische Neue Testament" has had a great success in Germany, and has specially recommended itself to students. It is believed that the translation of this book will be welcomed by theological teachers and students in this country also. Written by one whose life has been spent in teaching, it gives in a clear and lively way what the student requires to know of the complex subject of Textual Criticism. A much smaller book than Scrivener's "Introduction," which few can afford to buy, it is fuller than the small handbooks of Haumard, Schaff, and Kenyon, and shows criticism in actual operation at the hands of a competent scholar.

In Half-leather, 12s. 6d.

FIFTH YEAR. VOL. II.

WHAT IS CHRISTIANITY?

BY

ADOLPH HARNACK,

Rector and Ordinary Professor of Church History in the University, and Fellow of the Royal Academy of Science, Berlin.

Translated by T. BAILEY SAUNDERS, with a Special Preface to the English Edition by the Author.

A CATALOGUE

OF SOME OF

WILLIAMS & NORGATE'S

THEOLOGICAL AND PHILOSOPHICAL WORKS.

◆

ALVIELLA (Count Goblet d') The Contemporary Evolution of Religious Thought in England, America, and India. Translated from the French, by the Rev. J. Moden. 8vo, cloth. 10s. 6d.

—— **Evolution of the Idea of God,** according to Anthropology and History. Translated by the Rev. P. H. Wicksteed. (Hibbert Lectures, 1891.) Cloth. 10s. 6d. (Cheap Ed., 3s. 6d.)

BARNABAS' Epistle, in Greek, from the Sinaitic Manuscript of the Bible, with a Translation by S. Sharpe, Crown 8vo, cloth. 2s. 6d.

BARROW (E. P., M. A.) Regni Evangelium. A Survey of the Teaching of Jesus Christ. Crown 8vo, cloth. 6s.

BAUR (F. C.) Church History of the First Three Centuries. Translated from the Third German Edition. Edited by Rev. Allan Menzies. 2 vols. 8vo, cloth. (*Vide* Theological Translation Fund.) 12s.

—— **Paul,** the Apostle of Jesus Christ, his Life and Work, his Epistles and Doctrine. A Contribution to a Critical History of Primitive Christianity. By Rev. Allan Menzies. 2nd Edition. 2 vols. 8vo,

cloth. (*Vide* Theological Translation Fund.) 12s.

BAYNES (H.) The Idea of God and the Moral Sense in the light of Language ; being a philological Enquiry into the rise and growth of Spiritual and Moral Concepts. 8vo, cloth. 10s. 6d.

BEARD (Rev. Dr. C.) The Uni- versal Christ, and other Sermons. Crown 8vo, cloth. 7s. 6d.

—— **Lectures** on the Reformation of the Sixteenth Century in its relation to Modern Thought and Knowledge. (Hibbert Lectures, 1883.) 8vo, cloth. 10s. 6d. (Cheap Edition, 3rd Edition, 3s. 6d.)

BEARD (Rev. Dr. John R.) The Autobiography of Satan. Crown 8vo, cloth. 7s. 6d.

Bible, translated by Samuel Sharpe, being a Revision of the Authorized English Version. 6th Edition of the Old, 10th Edition of the New Testament. 8vo, roan. 5s.

—— *vide also* Testament.

Biblia Hebraica ad optimos editiones, imprimis. E. van der Hooght recensa et expressa. Chr. C. G. G. Theile, Lips., 1889. 7s.

14, *Henrietta Street, Covent Garden, London ;* 20, *South Frederick Street, Edinburgh ;* and 7, *Broad Street, Oxford.*

BLEEK (F.) Lectures on the Apocalypse. Translated. Edited by the Rev. Dr. S. Davidson. 8vo, cloth. (*Vide* Theological Translation Fund.) 6*s.*

CAMPBELL (Rev. Colin, D.D.) The First Three Gospels in Greek. Arranged in Parallel Columns. Demy 8vo. Second Edition, Revised and Improved. Cloth. 5*s.* nett.

CHANNING'S Complete Works, including "The Perfect Life," and containing a copious general Index and a Table of Scripture References. Tenth Thousand. 658 pp. Demy 4to, cloth. 7*s.* 6*d.*

CLARK (Archd. Jas.) De Successione Apostolica nec non Missione et Jurisdictione Hierarchiae Anglicanae et Catholicae. 8vo. (*Georgetown, Guiana.*) Cloth. 21*s.*

—— **Seven Ages of the Church;** or Exposition of the Apocalypse. Sewed. 1*s.*

COLLINS (F. H.) An Epitome of the Synthetic Philosophy. By F. Howard Collins. With a Preface by Herbert Spencer. 4th Edition. The Synthetic Philosophy Completed. 8vo, cloth. 21*s.*

Common Prayer for Christian Worship : in Ten Services for Morning and Evening. 32mo, cloth. 1*s.* 6*d.* Also in 8vo, cloth, 3*s.*

CONWAY (Moncure D.) Centenary History of the South Place Ethical Society. With numerous Portraits, a facsimile of the original MS. of the hymn, "Nearer, my God, to Thee," and Appendices. Crown 8vo, half-vellum, paper sides. 5*s.*

Critical Review (The) of Theological and Philosophical Literature. Edited by Principal S. D. F. Salmond, D.D., F.E.I.S. Bi-monthly parts, 1*s.* 6*d.* nett; yearly subscriptions 8*s.* 6*d.* post free.

CURETON (Dr. W.) History of the Martyrs in Palestine, by Eusebius, in Syriac. Edited and translated. Royal 8vo, cloth. 10*s.* 6*d.*

CURTIN (Jeremiah) Creation Myths of Primitive America in relation to the Religious History and Mental Development of Mankind. Author of "Myths and Folk-Tales of Ireland," etc. It contains Twenty Long Myths taken down word for word by Mr. Curtin from Indians who knew no religion or language but their own, and many of whom had not seen a white man until they had attained years of maturity. With an elaborate Introduction and Notes. Demy 8vo, cloth. 10*s.* 6*d.* nett.

"There can be no doubt that Mr. Curtin has collected a number of traditions that will be of great interest to students of the beliefs of savage and undeveloped races."—*Nature.*

"Mr. Curtin is to be congratulated on having produced a book on an abstruse subject, which can be read by the student with profit, and by the amateur not without pleasure."—*Critic.*

"Mr. Curtin's book is most welcome. . . . . A delightful collection of primitive creation myths, which will help the student to understand the problem of man's early conceptions of the universe."—*Athenæum.*

"This is a specially valuable contribution to folk-lore. The American myths have a place of their own in the science, and the analogies and differences which we can discern between them and those of the Old World are instructive in no common degree."—*Spectator.*

"Of great scientific value." — *Expository Times.*

"Deserves the attention of every student of folk-lore."—*Manchester Guardian.*

DAVIDS (T. W. Rhys) Lectures on some Points in the History of Indian Buddhism. (Hibbert Lectures, 1881.) 2nd Edition. 8vo, cloth. 10*s.* 6*d.* (Cheap Edition, 3*s.* 6*d.*)

DELITZSCH (Prof. F.) Assyrian Grammar, with Paradigms, Exercises, Glossary, and Bibliography, Translated by the Rev. Prof. A. R. S. Kennedy. Crown 8vo, cloth. 15*s.*

—— **The Hebrew Language** viewed in the light of Assyrian Research. Demy 8vo, cloth. 4*s.*

Die Massorah der Östlichen und Westlichen Syrer in Ihren Angaben zum Propheten Jesaia, Nach fünf Handschriften des British Museum in Verbindung mit zwei Tractaten über Accente herausgegeben und bearbeitet von Gustav Diettrich, Pfarrer der Deutschen Evangelischen Gemeinde zu Sydenham. Cr. 8vo, sewed, 8s. 6d. nett.

DRUMMOND (Dr.) Philo Judæus; or, the Jewish Alexandrian Philosophy in its Development and Completion. By James Drummond, LL.D., Principal of Manchester New College, Oxford. 2 vols. 8vo, cloth. 21s.

"This treatise of Dr. Drummond's fills a place of its own in the English language, and may be put beside, or even above, the best German books on the subject."—*Athenæum.*

—— **Via, Veritas, Vita. Lectures** on Christianity in its most Simple and Intelligible Form. (The Hibbert Lectures, 1894.) 10s. 6d. (Cheap Edition, 3s. 6d.)

Echoes of Holy Thoughts: Arranged as Private Meditations before a First Communion. 2nd Edition, with a Preface by Rev. J. Hamilton Thom. Printed with red lines. Fcap. 8vo, cloth. 1s.

EWALD'S (Dr. H.) Commentary on the Prophets of the Old Testament. Translated by the Rev. J. F. Smith. [Vol. I. General Introduction, Yoel, Amos, Hosea, and Zakharya 9—11. Vol. II. Yesaya, Obadya, and Mikah. Vol. III. Nahûm, Ssephanya, Habaqqûq, Zachârya, Yéremya. Vol. IV. Hezekiel, Yesaya xl.—lxvi. Vol. V. Haggai, Zakharya, Malaki, Jona, Baruc, Daniel, Appendix and Index.] 5 vols. 8vo. (*Vide* Theological Translation Fund.) Cloth. Each 6s.

—— **Commentary on the Psalms.** Translated by the Rev. E. Johnson, M.A. 2 vols. (*Vide* Theological Translation Fund.) 8vo, cloth. Each 6s.

—— **Commentary on the Book of** Job, with Translation. Translated from the German by the Rev. J. Frederick Smith. (*Vide* Theological Translation Fund.) 8vo, cloth. 6s.

FIGG (E. G.) Analysis of Theology, Natural and Revealed. Crown 8vo, cloth. 6s.

Four Gospels (The) as Historical Records. (Anonymous.) Demy 8vo, 15s.

"The conclusions here reached are justified and upheld, directly or by legitimate inference, by the series of judgments which have been delivered by the Sovereign in Council as the final interpreter of the standards and formularies of the Church of England." — *Extract from Preface.*

"The facts to which he addresses himself are those relating to the Four Gospels. He comes to very different conclusions from those that are generally accepted in the Church to which he belongs—the Church of England. But he claims that though this is the case his position is entirely tenable according to the terms of the constitution of that Church. . . . . The great ability and abundant learning which it everywhere displays."—*Scotsman.*

"The anonymous author of this volume is a keen and uncompromising critic of the Gospel narratives. Undeterred by the fact that the questions raised by him concerning the origin of the Gospels and their historical credibility have been raised over and over again, and, to say the least, have not been decided in the negative sense, he discusses them afresh with an undisguised negative bias. The controversy thus raised afresh is of a vast and momentous character. His Christian belief—for he writes as a Christian and even as a Churchman—appears to be founded on a mystical or spiritual interpretation of the Nicene creed."—*Times.*

"This anonymous treatise is admirably printed and got up, and written in a fine, jaunty style. The object of this is to demolish and lay flat the Acts and the Four Gospels by one cannonade."—*Sat. Review.*

Free Inquiry (A) into the Origin of the Fourth Gospel. (Written anonymously.) 456 pp. Demy 8vo, cloth. 7s. 6d.

FUERST (Dr. Jul.) Hebrew and Chaldee Lexicon to the Old Testament. 5th Edition, improved and enlarged. Translated by Rev. Dr. Samuel Davidson. Royal 8vo, cl. 21s.

GILL (C.) The Evolution of Christianity. By Charles Gill. 2nd Edition. With Dissertations in Answer to Criticism. 8vo, cloth. 12s.

—— **The Book of Enoch the** Prophet. Translated from an Ethiopic M.S. in the Bodleian Library, by the late Richard Laurence, LL.D.,

Archbishop of Cashel. The Text corrected from his latest Notes by Charles Gill. Re-issue, 8vo, cloth. 5s.

Gospel Catechism. An Unsectarian Christian Primer. For use in Families and Schools. By the author of "King and Kingdom," Discipleship, etc. Medium 8vo, in stiff paper wrapper. 1s.

GOULD (Rev. S. Baring) Lost and Hostile Gospels. An Account of the Toledoth Jesher, two Hebrew Gospels circulating in the Middle Ages, and Extant Fragments of the Gospels of the first Three Centuries of Petrine and Pauline Origin. Crown 8vo, cloth. 7s. 6d.

GWYNN (The Very Rev. John, D.D.) On a Syriac MS. of the New Testament belonging to the Earl of Crawford and Balcarres, and on an inedited version of the Apocalypse therein contained. Trans. R. I. A. XXX. 10. Plate 21. 4to, sewed. 3s. 6d.

HARDY (R. Spence) Manual of Buddhism in its Modern Development. Translated from Singhalese MSS. 2nd Edition, with a complete Index and Glossary. 8vo, cloth. 21s.

HARNACK (Dr. Adolph, Ordinary Professor of Church History in the University, and Fellow of the Royal Academy of Science, Berlin) History of Dogma. Translated from the Third German Edition. Edited by Rev. Prof. A. B. Bruce, D.D. Vols. I.—VI. (*Vide* Theological Translation Library, New Series.) Demy 8vo.

"This valuable work, the translation of which may be justly regarded as one of the most important events that has happened of recent times to our theological literature. We earnestly hope that many of our readers will find it possible to procure this and the other works of the Theological Translation Library."—*Primitive Methodist Quarterly.*

"The translation is good . . . . creditably free from the barbarisms so common in translations, and can be read with pleasure."—Principal RAINY in *The Critical Review.*

"No work on Church History in recent times has had the influence of Professor Harnack's *History of Dogma*."—*The Times.*

"The third volume of Harnack's *History of Dogma* needs but the announcement of its issue. The work is known ; the translator now is known also. One wondered if ever we were to see *The History of Dogma* in English ; no one hoped to see it in better English than this."—*Expository Times.*

". . . . A book which is admitted to be one of the most important theological works of the time."—*Daily News.*

"It is needless to expatiate on the value of Harnack's works , . . . for thorough study no history of Dogma is so full and suggestive as this. Greater praise cannot be given to the translation than to say that it is worthy of the original, and that must in justice be said."—*Literature.*

HATCH (Rev. Dr.) Lectures on the Influence of Greek Ideas and Usages upon the Christian Church. Edited by Dr. Fairbairn. (Hibbert Lectures, 1888.) 3rd Edition. 8vo, cloth. 10s. 6d. (Cheap Edition, 3s. 6d.)

HAUSRATH (Prof. A.) History of the New Testament Times. The Time of Jesus. Translated by the Revds. C. T. Poynting and P. Quenzer. 2 vols. 8vo, cloth. (*Vide* Theological Translation Fund.) 12s.

—— **History of the New Testa**ment Times. The Time of the Apostles. Translated by Leonard Huxley. With a Preface by Mrs. Humphry Ward. 4 vols. 8vo, cloth. 42s.

From the two latest Reviews:

"He is something of a German Renan. He has won his spurs in the field of Historical Research. He has a brilliant and fascinating style, and works for the public as well as for the scholar. Christian students of every school may profit by his fine historical sense and descriptive power."—*Christian World.*

"For insight and graphic portraiture the work is sure to take high place among translated theology of the most attractive sort. As Mrs. Ward says, Hausrath's is a brilliant picture of the first Christian times, and Mr. Huxley has not blurred it."—*Literary World.*

Hebrew Texts, in large type for Classes :

Genesis. 2nd Ed. 16mo, cloth. 1s. 6d.
Psalms. 16mo, cloth. 1s.
Isaiah. 16mo, cloth. 1s.
Job. 16mo, cloth. 1s.

HEMANS (Chas. I.) Historic and Monumental Rome. A Handbook for the Students of Classical and Christian Antiquities in the Italian Capital. Crown 8vo, cloth. 10s. 6d.

HERRMANN (W.) The Communion of the Christian with God : a Discussion in agreement with the View of Luther. By W. Herrmann, Dr. Theol., Professor of Dogmatic Theology in the University of Marburg.

Translated from the Second thoroughly revised Edition, with special Annotations by the Author, by J. Sandys Stanyon, M.A. 1 vol. Demy 8vo.

"It will be seen from what has been said that this book is a very important one. . . . . The translation is also exceedingly well done."— *Critical Review.*

"We trust the book will be widely read, and should advise those who read it to do so twice." —*Primitive Methodist Quarterly.*

"Instinct with genuine religious feeling . . . . exceedingly interesting and suggestive."—*Glasgow Herald.*

HIBBERT LECTURES (THE).

Systematically arranged. Library Edition, demy 8vo, 10s. 6d. per volume. Cheap Popular Edition, 3s. 6d. per volume.

COMPARATIVE RELIGIONS.

MONTEFIORE (C. G.) On the Origin and Growth of Religion as illustrated by the Religion of the Ancient Hebrews. 2nd Edition.

RENOUF (P. Le Page) On the Religion of Ancient Egypt. 2nd Edition.

RÉVILLE (Prof. A.) On the Ancient Religions of Mexico and Peru. 3rd Edition.

RHYS (Prof. J.) On the Origin and Growth of Religion as illustrated by Celtic Heathendom. 3rd Edition.

RHYS DAVIDS (Prof. T. W.) On the Origin and Growth of Religion as illustrated by some Points in the History of Indian Buddhism. 2nd Edition.

SAYCE (Prof. A. H.) On the Religion of Ancient Assyria and Babylonia. 5th Edition.

PHILOSOPHY OF RELIGIONS.

D'ALVIELLA (Count G.) On the Evolution of the Idea of God. Translated by Rev. P. H. Wicksteed. 2nd Edition.

KUENEN (Prof. A.) On National Re- ligions and Universal Religions.

HISTORY OF RELIGIONS.

BEARD (Rev. C.) On the Reformation of the Sixteenth Century in its Relation to Modern Thought and Knowledge. 3rd Edition.

HATCH (Rev. Dr.) On the Influence of Greek Ideas and Usages upon the Christian Church. Edited by Dr. Fairbairn. 7th Edition.

PFLEIDERER (Prof.) On the Influ- ence of the Apostle Paul on the Development of Christianity. Translated by the Rev. J. Frederick Smith. 2nd Edition.

RENAN (M. E.) On the Influence of the Institutions, Thought, and Culture of Rome on Christianity, and the Development of the Catholic Church. Translated by the Rev. Charles Beard. 4th Edition.

CHRISTIANITY & PRESENT-DAY PROBLEMS.

DRUMMOND (Rev. Principal) Via, Veritas, Vita. Lectures on Christianity in its most Simple and intelligible form.

UPTON (Rev. C.B., B.A.) On the Bases of Religious Belief. 2nd Edition.

HOERNING (Dr. R.) The Karaite MSS., British Museum. The Karaite Exodus (i. to viii. 5) in 42 Autotype Facsimiles, with a Transcription in ordinary Arabic type. Together with Descriptions and Collation of that and five other MSS. of Portions of the Hebrew Bible in Arabic Characters in the same Collection. Royal 4to, cloth, gilt top. £2, 12s. 6d.

HOPPS (Rev. J. Page) Pilgrim Songs. With 2 Portraits. 3s.

—— **Sermons of Sympathy.** Cr. 8vo, cloth. 2s. 6d.

—— **Twenty Sermons for our** Day. 8vo, cloth. 2s.

—— **The Bible for Beginners.** Vol. I. The Old Testament. Crown 8vo, cloth. 2s.

—— **Bible Readings for Public** Worship and the Home (106). 1s. 6d.

—— **Pessimism, Science, and God.** Crown 8vo, cloth. 1s. nett.

—— **Death a Delusion:** with an Account of some Personal Experiences on the Border-land between Sense and Soul. Crown 8vo, cloth. 1s. nett.

—— **Verses by the Way.** 1s.

—— **Twelve Sunday Morning** Prayers: for the Twelve Months of the Year. 1s.

—— **Personal Prayers.** (20 in number, bound in grey and gold.) 1s.

—— **The Life of Jesus.** Re-written for Young Disciples. 5th Edition. Richly bound as a gift-book. 1s.

—— **Spirit-Life in God the Spirit:** a Meditation on God and Immortality. 1s.

—— **First Principles of Religion** and Morality. 20 Lectures, mainly for the Young. 1s.

—— **The Little Wicket Gate to** Life. Guiding Thoughts for the Young. 1s.

HOPPS (Rev. J. Page) Who was Jehovah? 1s.

—— **Scientific Basis of Belief in** a Future Life. 6d.

—— **Common Prayer.** 1s.

—— **Coming Day.** Pub. monthly, 3d.

JONES (Rev. R. Crompton) Hymns of Duty and Faith, selected and arranged. 247 pp. Foolscap 8vo, cloth. 2nd Edition. 3s. 6d.

—— **Chants, Psalms, and Can**ticles, selected and pointed for Chanting. 18mo, cloth. 1s. 6d.

—— **Anthems,** with Indexes and References to the Music. 18mo, cloth. 1s. 3d.

—— **The Chants and Anthems,** together in 1 vol. Cloth. 2s.

—— **A Book of Prayer,** in Thirty Orders of Worship, with Additional Prayers and Thanksgivings. 18mo, cloth. 2s. 6d.

—— The same, with Chants, in 1 vol. 18mo, cloth. 3s.

KAUTZSCH (E., Professor of Theology at the University of Halle) An Outline of the History of the Literature of the Old Testament. With Chronological Tables for the History of the Israelites, and other Aids to the Explanation of the Old Testament. Reprinted from the "Supplement to the Translation of the Old Testament." Edited by the Author. Translated by John Taylor, D.Lit., M.A., etc. Demy 8vo, cloth. 6s. 6d.

"There is no one who with open mind will read the book and not be better for it."—*Scotsman.*

"Nothing could be more admirable than the arrangement of the Outline." — *Leamington Chronicle.*

"As to matter, it is the work of a scholar who is not afraid of results suggested by fair research, but who never grasps at novelties merely for the sake of originality. In style and language, the book reads more like an original than a translation; an original, too, which in its terseness of expression has escaped the prolix obscurity so commonly complained of in the writings of the author's country."—*Church Gazette.*

" . . . . It is obviously a boon to have at convenient service the latest German analysis, and this *Literature of the Old Testament* supplies it."—*Literary World.*

"Of course, this work is only an outline, and therefore cannot find room for such fulness of detail as Dr. Driver gives us. Yet there are some points on which the student will find more information in the book before us. The author writes from the critical standpoint. . . . . We have read the book with great interest, and have pleasure in recommending it to our readers."—*Primitive Methodist Quarterly Review.*

"The work is exceedingly helpful, especially the Chronological Tables."—*Christian World.*

KEIM'S History of Jesus of Nazara.
Considered in its connection with the National Life of Israel, and related in detail. Translated from the German by Arthur Ransom and the Rev. E. M. Geldart. [Vol. I. Second Edition. Introduction, Survey of Sources, Sacred and Political Groundwork, Religious Groundwork. Vol. II. The Sacred Youth. Self-recognition, Decision. Vol. III. The First Preaching, the Works of Jesus, the Disciples, and Apostolic Mission. Vol. IV. Conflicts and Disillusions, Strengthened Self-confidence, Last Efforts in Galilee, Signs of the Approaching Fall, Recognition of the Messiah. Vol. V. The Messianic Progress to Jerusalem, the Entry into Jerusalem, the Decisive Struggle, the Farewell, the Last Supper. Vol. VI. The Messianic Death at Jerusalem. Arrest and Pseudo-Trial, the Death on the Cross, Burial and Resurrection, the Messiah's Place in History, Indices.] Complete in 6 vols. 8vo. (*Vide* Theological Translation Fund.) Each 6s. (Vol. I. only to be had when a complete set of the Work is ordered.)

KENNEDY (Rev. Jas.) Introduction
to Biblical Hebrew, presenting Graduated Instruction in the Language of the Old Testament. By James Kennedy, B.D., Acting Librarian in the New College, and one of the additional Examiners in Divinity at the University, Edinburgh. 8vo, cloth. 12s.

KENNEDY (Rev. Jas.) Studies in
Hebrew Synonyms. Demy 8vo, cloth. 5s.

King and the Kingdom (The): A
Study of the Four Gospels. Three Series, each complete in itself; with copious Indexes. Medium 8vo, cloth. 3s. 6d. each.

KITTEL (R.) A History of the
Hebrews. By R. Kittel, Ordinary Professor of Theology in the University of Breslau. In 2 vols. Vol. I. Sources of Information and History of the Period up to the death of Joshua. Translated by John Taylor, D.Lit., M.A. Vol. II. Sources of Information and History of the Period down to the Babylonian Exile. Translated by Hope W. Hogg, B.D., and E. B. Speirs, D.D. (*vide* Theological Translation Library, New Series). Demy 8vo, cloth. 21s.

"It is a sober and earnest reconstruction, for which every earnest student of the Old Testament should be grateful."—*Christian World.*

"It is a work which cannot fail to attract the attention of thoughtful people in this country."—*Pall Mall Gazette.*

"Dr. Taylor's translation is very readable."—*Manchester Guardian.*

"There are few works on this subject so luminous and so instructive."—*Glasgow Herald.*

"It will be a happy day for pulpit and pew when a well-thumbed copy of the *History of the Hebrews* is to be found in every manse and parsonage."—*Literary World.*

KUENEN (Dr. A.) The Religion of
Israel to the Fall of the Jewish State. By Dr. A. Kuenen, Professor of Theology at the University, Leyden. Translated from the Dutch by A. H. May. 3 vols. 8vo, cloth. (*Vide* Theological Translation Fund.) 18s.

—— **Lectures** on National Religions and Universal Religions. (The Hibbert Lectures, 1882.) 8vo, cloth. 10s. 6d. (Cheap Edition, 3s. 6d.)

LAURIE (Professor Simon) Ethica:
or the Ethics of Reason. By Scotus Novanticus. 2nd Edition. 8vo, cloth, 6s.

—— **Metaphysica Nova et Vetusta**: a Return to Dualism. 2nd Edition. Crown 8vo, cloth. 6s.

LLOYD (Walter) The Galilean : A Portrait of Jesus of Nazareth. Cr. 8vo, cloth. 2s. 6d.

MALAN (Rev. Dr. S. C.) The Book of Adam and Eve, also called the Conflict of Adam and Eve with Satan. A Book of the early Eastern Church. Translated from the Ethiopic, with Notes from the Kufale, Talmud, Midrashim, and other Eastern Works. 8vo, cloth. 7s. 6d.

—— **Original Notes on the Book** of Proverbs. According to the Authorized Version. Vol. I. Chap. i. to x. 8vo, cloth. 12s.

—— Vol. II. Chap. xi. to xx. 8vo, cloth. 12s.

—— Vol. III. Chap. xxi. to xxxi. 8vo, cloth. 12s.

MARCHANT (James) Theories of the Resurrection of Jesus Christ. By James Marchant, sometime Evidential Lecturer to the Barking Rural Deaneries and the Christian Evidence Society. Contents :—The Theory of the Evangelists. The Swoon Theory. The Theory of Conspiracy. The Vision Theory. The Apparition Theory. Answers to Objections. With facsimile of Unpublished Letter from the late Cardinal Manning, and from Prof. Sir G. G. Stokes, Bart. Crown 8vo, cloth, 3s. ; paper boards, 2s. nett.

" A well-arranged little book treating of the critical and always urgent question on which the validity of Christian belief in the last resort depends. . . . . A bright, readable, and effective demolition of current errors."—*Saturday Review.*
" Mr. Marchant here critically examines the main theories advanced by sceptics to account for the belief in a risen Christ. He does a real service to the Christian faith in issuing thus cheaply a popularly written work, that so effectively exposes the hollowness of plausible speculations which bar many a man's progress along the road leading to life eternal. Mr. Marchant's reading is well abreast of the times." —*Christian Age.*

MARGOLIOUTH (Rev. G., M.A.) The Original Hebrew of Ecclesiasticus xxxi. 12–31, and xxxvi. 22–xxxvii. 26. Now for the first time edited, translated, and annotated, with a vocabulary at end.

MARTINEAU (Rev. Dr. James) The Relation between Ethics and Religion. An Address. 8vo, sewed. 1s.

—— **Modern Materialism :** its Attitude towards Theology. A Critique and Defence. 8vo, sewed. 2s. 6d.

MARTINEAU (Prof. Russell) The Roots of Christianity in Mosaism. 8vo, sewed. 1s.

MARTYN (Rev. H. J.) For Christ and the Truth. 5s. A New and Cheap Edition now ready, 234 pp., 2s. 6d.
" Full of thoughts of considerable apologetic value, on various topics of Theology, Christology, and Ecclesiastical matters in the Apostolic Times."—*The Guardian.*
" A series of excellent papers, treating of a number of well-worn subjects in an original way. . . . . The section treating of belief in a future life is most comprehensive and convincing. . . . A book that is full of power."—*The Church Gazette.*
" As a rule concise and reasonable, and his choice of subjects indicates a thoughtful and active mind, e.g., 'Is Christ a Historic Person ?' ' Was Christ Sinless ?' ' The Formation of the Gospels.' "—*The Christian World.*
" Certainly somewhat out of the ordinary course, and if it were within the capacity of the congregation for whom the discourses were originally intended, it ought to have been helpful in removing difficulties."—*The Church Times.*

Mind, A Quarterly Review of Psychology and Philosophy. Nos. 1—64. 1876–90. 8vo, each 3s. Vols. II.—XVI. in cloth, each 13s. Annual Subscription, post free, 12s.

—— New Series, Nos. 1—21, each 3s. Vols. I. II. III. IV. V. VI. and VII., each 13s.

MONTEFIORE (C. G.) Origin and Growth of Religion as illustrated by the Religion of the Ancient Hebrews. (The Hibbert Lectures, 1892.) 2nd Edition. 8vo, cloth. 10s. 6d. Cheap Edition, 3s. 6d.

14, *Henrietta Street, Covent Garden, London ;* 20, *South Frederick Street, Edinburgh ; and* 7, *Broad Street, Oxford.*

Mosheh Ben Shesheth's Com-mentary on Jeremiah and Ezekiel. Edited from a Bodleian M.S., with a Translation and Notes, by S. R. Driver. 8vo, sewed. 3s.

OLDENBERG (Prof. H.) Buddha; his Life, his Doctrine, his Order. By Dr. Hermann Oldenberg, Professor at the University of Berlin. Translated by W. Hoey, M.A. 8vo, cloth gilt. 18s.

PERRIN (R. S.) Religion of Philo-sophy (The), or the Unification of Knowledge : a Comparison of the chief Philosophical and Religious Systems of the World. 8vo, cloth. 16s.

PFLEIDERER (O.) Paulinism : a Contribution to the History of Primitive Christian Theology. Translated by E. Peters. 2nd Edition. 2 vols. 8vo, cloth. 12s.

—— **Philosophy of Religion on** the Basis of its History. (Vols. I. II. History of the Philosophy of Religion from Spinoza to the Present Day ; Vols. III. IV. Genetic-Speculative Philosophy of Religion.) Translated by Professor Alan Menzies and the Rev. Alex. Stewart. Complete in 4 vols. 8vo, cloth. Each 6s.

—— **Lectures on the Influence of** the Apostle Paul on the Development of Christianity. Translated by the Rev. J. Frederick Smith. (Hibbert Lectures, 1885.) 2nd Edition. 8vo, cloth. 10s. 6d. (Cheap Edition, 3s. 6d.)

—— *vide also* Protestant Commentary.

PIKLER (Jul.) The Psychology of the Belief in Objective Existence. Part I. 8vo, cloth. 4s. 6d.

POOLE (Reg. Lane) Illustrations of the History of Mediæval Thought in the Departments of Theology and Ecclesiastical Politics. 8vo, cloth. 10s. 6d.

PRINCE (J. D., Ph.D., Professor of Semitic Languages in the New York University) A Critical Commentary on the Book of Daniel. Designed especially for Students of the English Bible. Demy 8vo, cloth. 9s. nett.

Protestant Commentary on the New Testament ; with general and special Introductions. Edited by Professors P. W. Schmidt and F. von Holzendorff. Translated from the third German Edition by the Rev. F. H. Jones, B.A. 3 vols. 8vo, cloth. (*Vide* Theological Translation Fund.) Each 6s.

Psalterium Tetraglottum, Græce, Syriace, Chaldaice, Latine ex Cod. Vat. et Siniat. Græcis, Ambrosiano, Syriaco, Amiat. Latino, et Lagard. Targum curavit Dr. E. Nestle. 360 pages. 4to, cloth. 18s.

QUARRY (Rev. J.) Genesis and its Authorship. Two Dissertations. 2nd Edition, with notice of Animadversions of the Bishop of Natal. 8vo, cloth. 12s.

RENAN (E.) On the Influence of the Institutions, Thought, and Culture of Rome on Christianity and the Development of the Catholic Church. Translated by the Rev. Charles Beard. (Hibbert Lectures, 1880.) 8vo, cloth. 10s. 6d. (Cheap Edition, 3rd Edition, 3s. 6d.)

—— *vide also* Spinoza, Essays.

RENOUF (P. le Page) On the Religion of Ancient Egypt. (Hibbert Lectures, 1879.) 3rd Edition. 8vo, cloth. 10s. 6d. (Cheap Edition, 3s. 6d.)

REVILLE (Dr. A.) Prolegomena of the History of Religions. With an Introduction by Professor F. Max Müller. 8vo, cloth. (*Vide* Theological Translation Fund.) 6s.

10 *Williams and Norgate's*

REVILLE (Dr. A.) On the Native
Religions of Mexico and Peru. Translated by the Rev. P. H. Wicksteed.
(Hibbert Lectures, 1884.) 8vo, cloth.
10s. 6d. (Cheap Edition, 3s. 6d.)

—— The Devil: his Origin, Greatness, and Decadence. Translated from
the French. 2nd Edition. Crown
8vo, cloth. 2s.

—— The Song of Songs, commonly
called the Song of Solomon, or the
Canticle. Translated from the
French. Crown 8vo, cloth. 1s. 6d.

RHYS (Prof. J.) On the Origin
and Growth of Religion as illustrated
by Celtic Heathendom. (Hibbert
Lectures, 1886.) 8vo, cloth. 10s. 6d.
(Cheap Edition, 3s. 6d.)

ROBINSON (Alex., B.D., formerly
Minister of the Parish of Kilmun,
Argyleshire) A Study of the Saviour
in the Newer Light, or, A Present-
day Study of Jesus Christ. 2nd
Edition. Revised form. Demy 8vo,
cloth. 7s. 6d.

"It is a life of the Founder of Christianity,
with the miraculous part omitted, or rational-
istically explained away very much in the manner
of Renan. Mr. Robinson seems to have been
led to his present views largely by an examination
of the discrepancies between the Fourth Gospel
and the Synoptics, and he presents them in a
clear, temperate, and reverend tone."—*Academy*.

"As to the book itself, it is eminently readable, displaying command of language without
floweriness, and insight into character that avoids
metaphysical hair-splitting."—*Church Gazette*.

"The point of view throughout is very much
that of Prof. Pfleiderer and Dr. Martineau.....
It is an honest attempt founded on independent
thought and study to see the human life of Jesus
as it was."—*Inquirer*.

"Here is a book written in the most reverend
spirit, which, to a Southron, seems to do a good
deal to restore the human interest in Jesus
Christ that has, to a large extent, been evaporated
from the story by pressure of dogma and theological refining; and what we learn from the
Preface, is that Mr Robinson, called to account
by the General Assembly, declined to disavow
his ideas or his method, and was cast out of the
Church of Scotland."—*London Review*.

"The book is a genuinely honest production,
the work of a man supremely desirous of getting
at the truth, and fully resolved at all costs to
cleave loyally to it..... There is throughout it
a fine devotional spirit and it lifts into prominence
the high moral ideas of Christianity."—*Bradford
Observer*.

SADLER (Rev. Dr.) Prayers for
Christian Worship. Crown 8vo, cloth.
3s. 6d.

—— Closet Prayers, Original and
Compiled. 18mo, cloth. 1s. 6d.

SCHRADER (Prof. E.) The Cunei-
form Inscriptions and the Old Testament. Translated from the 2nd
Enlarged Edition, with Additions by
the Author, and an Introduction by
the Rev. Owen C. Whitehouse, M.A.
2 vols. (Vol. I. only sold with complete Sets of the Theological Translation Fund.) With a Map. 8vo,
cloth. Each 6s. (*Vide* Theological
Translation Fund.)

SCHURMAN (J. Gould) Kantian
Ethics and the Ethics of Evolution.
1882. 8vo, cloth. 5s.

—— The Ethical Import of Dar-
winism. Crown 8vo, cloth. 5s.

SHARPE (Samuel) History of the
Hebrew Nation and its Literature.
With an Appendix on the Hebrew
Chronology. 5th Edition. Crown
8vo, cloth. 4s. 6d.

—— Critical Notes on the Authorized English Version of the New
Testament. 2nd Edition. 12mo,
cloth. 1s. 6d.

—— Short Notes to accompany a
Revised Translation of the Hebrew
Scriptures. 12mo, cloth. 1s. 6d.

—— *vide* Barnabas, Bible, Testament.

SMITH (H. W.) Selected and compiled by :—

Modern Thoughts on Life and Conduct. A Collection of above
400 Extracts, designed to bring
into prominence the permanent
elements which go to make and
improve our social life. Crown
8vo, cloth gilt. 6s.

—— An Edition, extra gilt, printed
on antique paper. 7s. 6d.

SMITH (H. W.)—*continued.*

Modern Thoughts on Religion and Culture. A Collection of the Recorded Beliefs and Aspirations of Leaders of Thought in the Nineteenth Century, especially Illustrating the Transforming Influence of Science on Religion and Morals. 340 pages. Crown 8vo, cloth gilt. 6s.

SPEIRS (Rev. E. B.), *vide* Kittel, History of the Hebrews, Vol. II.

SPENCER (Herbert) First Principles. 10th Thousand, with an Appendix. 8vo, cloth. 16s.

—— **The Principles of Biology.** 2 vols. 6th Thousand. 8vo, cloth. Vol. I. Revised and greatly enlarged. 18s. Vol. II. 18s.

—— **The Principles of Psychology.** 5th Thousand. 2 vols. 8vo, cloth. 36s.

—— **The Principles of Sociology.** Vol. I. Part 1, The Data of Sociology, Part 2, The Inductions of Sociology; Part 3, Domestic Institutions. 4th Thousand, revised and enlarged. 8vo, cloth. 21s.

—— The same. Vol. II. Part 4, Ceremonial Institutions; Part 5, Political Institutions. 3rd Thousand. 8vo, cloth. 18s.

—— **The Principles of Sociology.** Vol. III. Part 6, Ecclesiastical Institutions; Part 7, Professional Institutions; Part 8, Domestic Institutions. 2nd Thousand. 8vo, cloth. 16s.

—— **The Principles of Ethics.** Vol. I. Part 1, The Data of Ethics; Part 2, The Inductions of Ethics; Part 3, The Ethics of Individual Life. 2nd Thousand. 8vo, cloth. 15s.

—— **The Principles of Ethics.** Vol. II. Part 4, Justice; Part 5, Negative Beneficence; Part 6, Positive Beneficence; Appendices. Demy 8vo, cloth. 12s. 6d.

Also to be had separately:

SPENCER Herbert) Ecclesiastical Institutions. Being Part 6 of the Principles of Sociology. 2nd Thousand. 8vo, cloth. 5s.

—— **Ethics.** Parts 2 and 3. 8vo, cloth. 7s.

—— **Justice.** Being Part 4 of the Principles of Ethics. 2nd Thousand. 8vo, cloth. 8s.

—— **Various Fragments.** Uniform in library binding. Demy 8vo, cloth. 4s.

—— **The Study of Sociology.** Library Edition (21st Thousand), with a Postscript. 8vo, cloth. 10s. 6d.

—— **Education.** Intellectual, Moral, and Physical. 7th Thousand. 8vo, cloth. 6s.

—— The same, cheaper Edition. 39th Thousand. 12mo, cloth. 2s. 6d.

—— **Essays :** Scientific, Political, and Speculative. A new Edition, rearranged with additional Essays. 3 vols. 8vo, cloth. (Each 10s.) 30s.

—— **Social Statics.** Abridged and revised, together with The Man *v.* The State. 8vo, cloth. 10s.

Also separately:

—— **The Man *versus* The State.** 13th Thousand. Sewed. 1s.

—— **A Rejoinder to Professor** Weismann. Sewed. 1s.

—— **Reasons for Dissenting from** the Philosophy of M. Comte. Sewed. 6d.

—— **The Inadequacy of Natural** Selection. Sewed. 1s.

—— **Descriptive Sociology,** or Groups of Sociological Facts. Compiled and abstracted by Professor D. Duncan, of Madras, Dr. Richard Scheppig, and James Collier. Folio, boards. No. 1. English. 18s.

SPENCER (Herbert) Descriptive Sociology. No. 2. Ancient American Races. 16s.

—— —— No. 3. Lowest Races, Negritto Races, Polynesians. 18s.

—— —— No. 4. African Races. 16s.

—— —— No. 5. Asiatic Races. 18s.

—— —— No. 6. American Races. 18s.

—— —— No. 7. Hebrews and Phœnicians. 21s.

—— —— No. 8. The French Civilization. 30s.

—— Collins (F. H.) An Epitome of the Synthetic Philosophy. By F. Howard Collins. Being a Digest of Mr. Herbert Spencer's Works. 4th Edition, the Synthetic Philosophy completed. With a Preface by Herbert Spencer. 8vo, cloth. 21s.

—— Drey (S.) Herbert Spencer's Theory of Religion and Morality. By Sylvan Drey. 8vo, sewed. 1s.

—— —— A Theory of Life deduced from the Evolution Philosophy. Demy 8vo, sewed. 1s.

—— Thompson (D. G.) Herbert Spencer: his Life, Writings, and Philosophy. By Daniel Greenleaf Thompson, Author of "A System of Psychology," "The Problem of Evil," "The Religious Sentiments of the Human Mind," etc. 1s.

SPINOZA. Four Essays by Professors Land, Van Vloten, and Kuno Fischer, and by E. Renan. Edited by Professor Knight, of St. Andrews. Crown 8vo, cloth. 5s.

STEPHENS (George) Professor Bugge's Studies on Northern Mythology examined. Illustrations. 8vo, cloth. 8s.

—— The Runes, Whence came they? 4to, sewed. 6s.

STOKES (G. J.) The Objectivity of Truth. 8vo, cloth. 5s.

STOKES (Whitley) Old Irish Glossaries. Cormac's Glossary. O'Davoran's Glossary. A Glossary to the Calendar of Oingus the Culdee. Edited, with an Introduction and Index. 8vo, cloth. 10s. 6d.

—— Middle-Breton Hours. Edited, with a Translation and Glossary. 8vo, boards. 6s.

—— The Creation of the World. A Mystery in Ancient Cornish. Edited, with Translations and Notes. 8vo, cloth. 6s.

STRACK (H. L.) Hebrew Grammar. Paradigms, Literature, Chrestomathy, and Glossary. Crown 8vo, cloth. 4s. 6d.

STRAUSS (Dr. D. F.) Life of Jesus; for the People. The Authorized English Edition. 2 vols. 8vo, cloth. Reduced to 10s. 6d. per set.

STUART (Jas.) Principles of Christianity: being an Essay towards a more correct Apprehension of Christian Doctrine, mainly Soteriological. 636 pp. 8vo, cloth. (Published at 12s. 6d.) 7s. 6d.

SUFFIELD, Life of the Rev. Robert Rudolph, Author of "The Crown of Jesus." Photogravure Portrait. Cr. 8vo, cloth. 4s. 6d.

Talmud of Jerusalem. Translated for the first time into English by Dr. Moses Schwab, of the Bibliothèque Nationale, Paris. Vol. I. The Treatise of Berakhoth (Blessings). Foolscap 4to, sewed. 9s.

TAUCHNITZ'S English New Testament. Authorized Version; with Introduction, and various Readings from the Three most celebrated Manuscripts of the Original Greek Text. By C. Tischendorf. 12mo, sewed 1s. 6d.; cloth, 2s.

14, *Henrietta Street, Covent Garden, London* ; 20, *South Frederick Street, Edinburgh* ; *and* 7, *Broad Street, Oxford.*

TAYLER (Rev. John James) An Attempt to ascertain the Character of the Fourth Gospel, especially in its relation to the first Three. 2nd Edition. 8vo, cloth. 5s.

TAYLOR (Rev. C.) The Dirge of Coheleth in Eccles. xii. discussed and literally interpreted. 8vo, cloth. 3s.

TAYLOR (Rev. Dr. J.) The Mas- soretic Text and the Ancient Versions of the Book of Micah. Crown 8vo, cloth. 5s.

Ten Services of Public Prayer, taken in Substance from the Common Prayer for Christian Worship, with a few additional Prayers for particular Days. 8vo, cloth, 2s. 6d. ; or 32mo, cloth, 1s.

Ten Services of Public Prayer, with Special Collects. 8vo, cloth, 3s. ; or 32mo, cloth, 1s. 6d.

—— **Psalms and Canticles.** 8vo, cloth. 1s. 6d.

—— the same, with Anthems. 8vo, cloth. 2s.

Testament (The New). Translated from Griesbach's Text by S. Sharpe, Author of "The History of Egypt." 14th Thousand. Fcap. 8vo, cloth. 1s. 6d.

THEOLOGICAL TRANSLATION FUND LIBRARY.

A Series of Translations by which the best results of recent Theological investigations on the Continent, conducted without reference to doctrinal considerations, and with the sole purpose of arriving at truth, are placed within reach of English Readers.

These Volumes are now reduced to 6s. per Volume.

BAUR (F. C.) Church History of the First Three Centuries. Translated from the Third German Edition. Edited by the Rev. Allan Menzies. 2 vols. 8vo. 12s.

—— **Paul, the Apostle of Jesus** Christ, his Life and Work, his Epistles and Doctrine. A Contribution to a Critical History of Primitive Christianity. 2nd Edition. By the Rev. Allan Menzies. 2 vols. 12s.

BLEEK'S Lectures on the Apoca- lypse. Edited by the Rev. Dr. S. Davidson. 6s.

EWALD (H.) Commentary on the Prophets of the Old Testament. Translated by the Rev. J. Frederick Smith. 5 vols. 8vo. Each 6s.

—— **Commentary on the Psalms.** Translated by the Rev. E. Johnson, M.A. 2 vols. 8vo. Each 6s.

EWALD (H.) Commentary on the Book of Job, with Translation by Professor H. Ewald. Translated from the German by the Rev. J. Frederick Smith. 8vo. 6s.

HAUSRATH (Professor A.) History of the New Testament Times. The Time of Jesus. By Dr. A. Hausrath, Professor of Theology, Heidelberg. Translated, with the Author's sanction, from the Second German Edition, by the Revs. C. T. Poynting and P. Quenzer. 2 vols. 8vo. 12s.

—— *vide end of List of this Series.*

KEIM (Th.) History of Jesus of Nazara. Considered in its connection with the National Life of Israel, and related in detail. Translated by Arthur Ransom and the Rev. E. M. Geldart. 6 vols. 8vo. Each 6s. (Vol. I. is not sold sepa-

14, *Henrietta Street, Covent Garden, London; 20, South Frederick Street, Edinburgh; and 7, Broad Street, Oxford.*

THEOLOGICAL TRANSLATION FUND LIBRARY—*continued.*

rately, and can only be had when a complete Set of the Work is ordered.)

KUENEN (A.) The Religion of Israel to the fall of the Jewish State. Translated by A. H. May. 2nd Edition. 3 vols. 8vo. 18s.

PFLEIDERER (Professor O.) The Philosophy of Religion on the Basis of its History. Translated by the Rev. Allan Menzies, and the Rev. Alex. Stewart, of Dundee. 4 vols. 8vo, cloth. Each 6s.

—— **Paulinism;** a contribution to the History of Primitive Christian Theology. Translated by E. Peters. 2nd Edition. 2 vols. 8vo. 12s.

Protestant Commentary on the New Testament; with General and Special Introductions to the Books, by Lipsius, Holsten, Lang, Pfleiderer, Holtzman, Hilgenfeld, and others. Translated by the Rev. F. H. Jones. 3 vols. 8vo. Each 6s.

REVILLE (Rev. Dr.) Prolegomena of the History of Religion. With Introduction by Professor Max Müller. 8vo. 6s.

SCHRADER (Professor E.) The Cuneiform Inscriptions and the Old Testament. Translated by the Rev. Owen C. Whitehouse, M.A. 2 vols. 8vo, Map. Each 6s. (Vol. I. is not supplied separately.)

ZELLER (E.) The Acts of the Apostles Critically Examined. To which is prefixed Overbeck's Introduction from de Wette's Handbook. Translated by Joseph Dare. 2 vols. 8vo. 12s.

Uniform with the above Series:

HAUSRATH (A.) History of the New Testament Times. The Time of the Apostles. Translated by Leonard Huxley; with an Introduction by Mrs. Humphry Ward. 4 vols 42s.

THEOLOGICAL TRANSLATION LIBRARY.

New Series. Edited by the Rev. T. K. Cheyne, M.A., D.D., Oriel Professor of Interpretation in the University of Oxford, and Canon of Rochester; and the late Rev. Prof. A. B. Bruce, D.D., Professor of Apologetics, Free Church College, Glasgow. Uniform price, 10s. 6d. per vol.

"We once more call the attention of our readers to this admirable series."—*Quarterly Review.*

Vol. *First Year's Issue.*

1. **WEIZSÄCKER. Apostolic Age, I.**
2. **HARNACK. History of Dogma, I.**
3. **KITTEL.** History of the Hebrews, I.

Second Year's Issue.

4. **HERRMANN. The Communion** of the Christian with God.
5. **WEIZSÄCKER. Apostolic Age,** II.
6. **KITTEL.** History of the Hebrews, II.

Vol. *Third Year's Issue. First Vol.*

7. **HARNACK.** History of Dogma, II.
8. —— —— III.
9. —— —— IV.

Fourth Year's Issue. First Vol.

10. —— —— V.
11. —— —— VI.
12. —— —— VII.

—— —— *Vide* under separate titles.

TISCHENDORF (C.) Novum Testa-mentum Græce. 3 vols. 8vo. 70*s.* nett.

TURPIE (Dr. D. McC.) The Old Testament in the New. The Quotations from the Old Testament in the New classified according to their Agreement with or Variation from the Original: the various Readings and Versions of the Passages, Critical Notes. Royal 8vo, cloth. 12*s.*

—— **Manual** of the Chaldee Language: containing Grammar of the Biblical Chaldee and of the Targums, and a Chrestomathy, with a Vocabulary. Square 8vo, cloth. 7*s.*

UPTON (Rev. C. B.) On the Bases of Religious Belief. (Hibbert Lectures, 1893.) Demy 8vo, cloth. 10*s. 6d.* (Cheap Edition, 3*s. 6d.*)

VICKERS (J.) History of Herod; or Another Look at a Man emerging from Twenty Centuries of Calumny. Crown 8vo, cloth. 6*s.*

—— **The Real Jesus:** a Review of his Life, Character, and Death, from a Jewish Standpoint. Crown 8vo. 6*s.*

—— **The Crucifixion Mystery.** Crown 8vo, cloth. 3*s. 6d.*

—— **The Book of Bander.** A Scripture-form Story of Past and Present Times. Crown 8vo, cloth. 3*s. 6d.*

"There are good things in it." — *Literary World.*

"'The Book of Bander' is a marvellously vivid narrative in Scriptural form of the historical progress of the human race . . . . it deserves much praise . . . . it has a distinct ethical value."—*Westminster Review.*

Vinaya Pitakam : one of the principal Buddhist Holy Scriptures. Edited in Pali by Dr. H. Oldenberg, 5 vols. 8vo, cloth. Each 21*s.*

VIZARD (P. E.) Prayers, New and Old. New Edition. Printed at the Chiswick Press. Crown 8vo, buckram. 1*s.* nett.

VOYSEY (Rev. C.) The Testimony of the Four Gospels concerning Jesus Christ. Crown 8vo, cloth. 3*s. 6d.*

—— **The Sling and the Stone.** Vol. VII. On Prophecy. 8vo, cloth. 5*s.*

—— Vol. VIII. On the Lord's Prayer. 8vo, cloth. 3*s. 6d.*

—— Vol. IX. The Fatherhood of God, Sermon on the Mount, etc. 8vo, cloth. 7*s. 6d.*

—— Vol. X. Revelation tested on Moral Grounds, etc. 8vo, cloth. 10*s. 6d.*

—— **Theism ;** or, The Religion of Common Sense. 8vo, cloth. 2*s. 6d.*

—— **Theism as a Science of** Natural Theology and Natural Religion. 8vo, cloth. 2*s. 6d.*

—— **Family Prayers.** 8vo, cloth. 1*s.*

—— **Theistic Prayer Book.** 3rd Edition. 12mo, cloth. 3*s. 6d.*

—— **Lectures on the Theistic** Faith and its Foundations, and on the Bible. 8vo, sewed. 1*s.*

—— **Prayers and Meditations,** for Family and Private Use. 3rd Edition. Fcap. 8vo, cloth. 6*d.*

—— **The Bible and Modern Criticism.** Three Sermons. 8vo, sewed. 4*d.*

WEIR (T. H., B.D.) A Short History of the Hebrew Text of the Old Testament. By Thomas H. Weir, B.D., Assistant to the Professor of Oriental Languages in the University of Glasgow. Illustrated with Facsimiles. Crown 8vo, sewed, 5*s.* ; cloth, 6*s.*

"This excellent book should be welcomed by all Hebrew tutors in theological colleges, and read with their senior classes."—*Manchester Guardian.* "The remarkably well-informed outline that is here presented appeals at once to the cultivated Hebraist, to the general reader, and perhaps, above all, to the divinity student."—*Glasgow Herald.*

"In the great range of the ancillary literature of the Bible, there is no one book that sticks so closely to the same subject; and its substantial learning and good exposition will, no doubt, recommend it to many readers."—*Scotsman.*

"We cannot close our review of the book without recognising the author's accurate scholarship and the clear and concise style in which he puts the results of his studies before his readers. It is a book which every student of divinity and every minister should possess. We know of no other book which contains so much valuable information on the Hebrew text in such a brief compass."—*St. Andrew.*

WEIZSÄCKER (Prof. Carl von) The Apostolic Age. Translated by James Millar, B.D. 2 vols. Demy 8vo, cloth. 21s.

"Weizsäcker is an authority of the very first rank, the present work marks an epoch in New Testament criticism. The English reader is fortunate in having a masterpiece of this kind rendered accessible to him."—*Expository Times.*

". . . . No student of theology or of the early history of Christianity can afford to leave Weizsäcker's great book unread."—*Manchester Guardian.*

"In every direction in this work we find the mark of the independent thinker and investigator . . . . this remarkable volume . . . . this able and learned work."—*Christian World.*

"This book itself . . . . is of great interest, and the work of the translation has been done in a most satisfactory way."—*Critical Review.*

"One thing that must strike every reader is that the volume is very readable and very interesting."—*Scotsman.*

"We part from the book with warm admiration for the qualities displayed by the author, tempered with regret that his undue scepticism as to the Acts has imparted a defective quality to a work which, apart from this, would have been as nearly perfect as we could have expected. We must add a tribute to the general excellence of the translation, which reads like an English book as a rule."—*Primitive Methodist Quarterly.*

WICKSTEED (Rev. P. H.) The Ecclesiastical Institutions of Holland, treated with Special Reference to the Position and Prospects of the Modern School of Theology. A Report presented to the Hibbert Trustees, and published by their direction. 8vo, sewed. 1s.

WRIGHT (Rev. C. H. H.) Book of Genesis in Hebrew Text. With a critically revised Text, various Readings, and Grammatical and Critical Notes. Demy 8vo. Reduced to 3s. 6d.

WRIGHT (Rev. C. H. H.) Book of Ruth in Hebrew Text. With a critically revised Text, various Readings, including a new Collation of Twenty-eight Hebrew MSS., and a Grammatical and Critical Commentary; to which is appended, The Chaldee Targum. Demy 8vo. 7s. 6d.

WRIGHT (G. H. Bateson) The Book of Job. A new critically revised Translation, with Essays on Scansion, Date, etc. 8vo, cloth. 6s.

—— **Was Israel ever in Egypt?** or, a Lost Tradition. By G. H. Bateson Wright, D.D., Queen's College, Oxford; Head-master Queen's College, Hong-Kong; Author of "A Critical Revised Translation of the Book of Job." 8vo, art-linen. 7s. 6d.

"The book displays not only sound learning and critical insight, but a freedom from theological bias which is almost unique amongst doctors of divinity. We give it a most cordial welcome."—*Westminster Review.*

"It is a carefully reasoned and acute book, which will add to the author's already high reputation as a critic of the Scriptures."—*Scotsman.*

"The book is written in a fresh, vigorous style, and is reverent in spirit, while thoroughgoing in its critical method."—*Boston Christian Register.*

WRIGHT (Rev. J.) Grounds and Principles of Religion. Crown 8vo, cloth. 3s.

ZELLER (Dr. E.) The Contents and origin of the Acts of the Apostles critically investigated. Preceded by Dr. Fr. Overbeck's Introduction to the Acts of the Apostles from De Wette's Handbook. Translated by Joseph Dare. 2 vols. 8vo, cloth. (*Vide* Theological Translation Fund.) 12s.

ZIEGLER (Th.) Social Ethics. Outlines of a Doctrine of Morals. Translated from the German. Crown 8vo, cloth. 3s.

ZOMPOLIDES (Dr. D.) A Course of Modern Greek, or the Greek Language of the Present Day. I. The Elementary Method. Crown 8vo, cloth. 5s.

Page 148.
— 152.
185
238